My View from the Blackened Rocks

A Woman's Battle for Equality and Respect in Canada's Mining Industry.

Cathy Mulroy

My View from the Blackened Rocks
Copyright © 2019 by Cathy Mulroy

No part of this publication may be reproduced, distributed, or transmitted in any form or by any means, including photocopying, recording, or other electronic or mechanical methods, without the prior written permission of the author, except in the case of brief quotations embodied in critical reviews and certain other non-commercial uses permitted by copyright law.

To learn more about the author, please visit www.mulroysview.com

tellwell

Tellwell Talent
www.tellwell.ca

ISBN
978-0-2288-1203-6 (Hardcover)
978-0-2288-1202-9 (Paperback)
978-0-2288-1204-3 (eBook)

Table of Contents

Acknowledgements 15
Prologue..17
Chapter 1 19
   In the Beginning... 19
Chapter 2 21
   Kindergarten
   1959 21
Chapter 3 23
   Oratory Speeches
   1963/'64 23
Chapter 4 25
   The Plague Motorcycle Gang
   1969 25
Chapter 5 29
   My First Protest
   1970 29
Chapter 6 31
   Draft Dodgers, Summer
   1970 31
Chapter 7 35
   Getting Married
   1970 35
Chapter 8 39
   Our First Apartment
   1970 39
Chapter 9 41
   Having My Baby
   1971 41
Chapter 10 43
   Not the Real Meaning of Christmas
   1972 43
Chapter 11 45
   Peppy Gets the London Flu
   1973 45

Chapter 12 .... **47**
    Getting Hired at Inco
    1974 47

Chapter 13 .... **53**
    Working for the French Diefenbaker
    19v74 53

Chapter 14 .... **57**
    The Anode Process 57

Chapter 15 .... **61**
    Poling Stage 61

Chapter 16 .... **65**
    My Accident on August 9: Meeting the Union and the Company
    1974 65

Chapter 17 .... **69**
    Having Melanie
    1975 69

Chapter 18 .... **73**
    Rebuilding a Furnace
    1976 73

Chapter 19 .... **79**
    My Gallbladder 79

Chapter 20 .... **81**
    The Rifle 81

Chapter 21 .... **83**
    The Hot Car 83

Chapter 22 .... **87**
    My First Car
    1976 87

Chapter 23 .... **89**
    Innocence Lost
    1976 89

Chapter 24 .... **95**
    Fine Casting
    1977 95

Chapter 25 .... **103**
    Coveralls 103

Chapter 26 .... **107**

    Hamilton McMaster University *107*

Chapter 27 .... **111**
    Cassi Summer and History Layoffs
    1977 .... *111*

Chapter 28 .... **117**
    The Bombing
    December 1977... *117*

Chapter 29 .... **119**
    Layoffs
    January 1978.. *119*

Chapter 30 .... **121**
    Bill 70 (139): The Right to Refuse Unsafe Work *121*

Chapter 31 .... **127**
    The Strike Vote
    September 1978... *127*

Chapter 32 .... **131**
    Getting Involved
    1978 .... *131*

Chapter 33 .... **137**
    Queen's Park
    1978 .... *137*

Chapter 34 .... **141**
    Steelworkers Benefit in Toronto
    December 8, 1978... *141*

Chapter 35 .... **147**
    Christmas 1978
    Spotting the Split.. *147*

Chapter 36 .... **151**
    The Real Meaning of Christmas.................................... *151*

Chapter 37 .... **155**
    Miguel Angel Albizures... *155*

Chapter 38 .... **159**
    The Bus Trip
    January 1979.. *159*

Chapter 39 .... **163**
    Negotiation Talks Break Down Again.............................. *163*

Chapter 40 .... **165**

Cambrian College Strike and the Popcorn 165

Chapter 41 . . . . **167**
Meeting the Wives:
the Story of the Women of 1958 167

Chapter 42 . . . . **171**
Wives Organize Festivities 171

Chapter 43 . . . . **173**
The Filmmakers of The Wives' Tale. 173

Chapter 44 . . . . **177**
The Burning of the Effigy 177

Chapter 45 . . . . **181**
The Mock Trial 181

Chapter 46 . . . . **183**
Too Much Fighting. 183

Chapter 47 . . . . **185**
The Smoke Detectors
May 8, 1979. 185

Chapter 48 . . . . **189**
The Contract is Turned Down
Wives Get a Blast. 189

Chapter 49 . . . . **209**
Back to Work After the Strike
June 3, 1979 209

Chapter 50 . . . . **215**
Applying to be a Steward 215

Chapter 51 . . . . **217**
Back in the Anode
Summer 1979 217

Chapter 52 . . . . **223**
The Current
1979 223

Chapter 53 . . . . **231**
Dating Ray
August 1979 231

Chapter 54 . . . . **235**
Sally's Death. 235

Chapter 55 . . . . **241**

The Artist Comes to the Anode 241

Chapter 56 . . . . **243**
Norm Takes a Puck in the Face for Me
January 1981. 243

Chapter 57 . . . . **245**
First Aid Competitions
1981 245

Chapter 58 . . . . **249**
Insubordination
April 1981 249

Chapter 59 . . . . **253**
Patterson's Campaign
May 1981 253

Chapter 60 . . . . **257**
Goodbye Little Person
June 1981 257

Chapter 61 . . . . **261**
Jennifer Penny is Writing a Book: Hard Earned Wages
October 1981. 261

Chapter 62 . . . . **263**
Susan and Christmas
1981 263

Chapter 63 . . . . **265**
The Spirits of Christmas
1981 265

Chapter 64 . . . . **267**
More Layoffs
January 1982. 267

Chapter 65 . . . . **271**
The Protest
1982 271

Chapter 66 . . . . **275**
Trying to Stop the Layoffs
1982 275

Chapter 67 . . . . **279**

    The Maintenance Men from Garson Mine
    March 1982 279

Chapter 68 .... **281**
    Continued Harassment on the Job
    1982 281

Chapter 69 .... **283**
    The Strike and Me as a Ladle Tender
    May 1982 283

Chapter 70 .... **287**
    Maxie McGann
    1982 287

Chapter 71 .... **289**
    Talks Collapse and the Strike Deadline Nears
    1982 289

Chapter 72 .... **293**
    Every Miner Had a Mother
    1983 293

Chapter 73 .... **299**
    Whitewater Rafting and Merv
    January 1984 299

Chapter 74 .... **303**
    More Men Killed in the Mines
    June 20, 1984 303

Chapter 75 .... **305**
    Be Careful Whom You Ask for Help
    August 1984 305

Chapter 76 .... **307**
    The Harassment Came into My House
    September 1984 307

Chapter 77 .... **311**
    Stalkers ... Who Are They?
    October 1984 311

Chapter 78 .... **315**
    Brass Candlestick Holders
    November 1984 315

Chapter 79 .... **319**
    Sleeping with My Shotgun
    December 1984 319

Chapter 80 .... **321**
  Christmas with Merv and the Gang
  1984 321
Chapter 81 .... **323**
  The Stalker Gets Bolder
  January 1985 323
Chapter 82 .... **327**
  The Intruder
  May 1985 327
Chapter 83 .... **329**
  Merv Sells His House
  July 1985 329
Chapter 84 .... **331**
  Accident
  1986 331
Chapter 85 .... **333**
  More Men are Killed at Inco
  1986 333
Chapter 86 .... **337**
  Modified Work Centre
  1987 337
Chapter 87 .... **339**
  Meanwhile 339
Chapter 88 .... **341**
  More Men are Killed at Inco
  1988 341
Chapter 89 .... **343**
  My Mom Passes
  1988 343
Chapter 90 .... **347**
  The Flood 347
Chapter 91 .... **349**
  Light Maintenance: Some Men are Just Mean
  1989 349
Chapter 92 .... **353**
  Proposal, and We Lose One of Our Sues
  1990/1991 353
Chapter 93 .... **355**

    International Women's Day
    1991 355

Chapter 94 .... **357**
    Turmoil for the Women in the Offices
    1991 357

Chapter 95 .... **359**
    First Aid Instructor
    1991 359

Chapter 96 .... **363**
    They Called Me ... Troublemaker 363

Chapter 97 .... **365**
    Fighting the Harassment and More
    1992 365

Chapter 98 .... **371**
    The Psychologist, and
    Sudbury Women Stand Behind Me
    1993 371

Chapter 99 .... **375**
    No Job Description,
    CBC Radio Station 375

Chapter 100 .... **377**
    Maintenance Department
    1994 377

Chapter 101 .... **379**
    Stress, A Place to Cry,
    My Brother is struck by a Drunk Driver
    1994 379

Chapter 102 .... **383**
    My Union Brothers Fight Me the Same Way the Company Did
    1994 383

Chapter 103 .... **387**
    Men Should Keep the Lights on When They Are with a Woman
    1995 387

Chapter 104 .... **391**
    Other Women Stand Up, and The Inco Club
    1995 391

Chapter 105 .... **395**
    Merv and I Get Married
    1996 395

Chapter 106 . . . . **399**
    Meeting the Women Who Worked at Inco During the War Years
    1997 399

Chapter 107 . . . . **403**
    Big Changes at Inco, and Michael McDonald
    1997 403

Chapter 108 . . . . **407**
    Day of Protest March
    1997 407

Chapter 109 . . . . **409**
    Jennifer Has Another Lump, and I Run for Vice President LU 6500
    1997 409

Chapter 110 . . . .**415**
    Another Operation, Fights with Home Care, and Inco Layoffs
    1998 415

Chapter 111 . . . .**419**
    Thanksgiving and Christmas Party. 419

Chapter 112 . . . . **421**
    MIMS
    1999 421

Chapter 113 . . . . **423**
    My Dad and My New Boss
    1999 423

Chapter 114 . . . . **425**
    Jennifer and Mercedes
    1999 425

Chapter 115 . . . . **427**
    Y2K: No Worries
    2000 427

Chapter 116 . . . . **429**
    Divisional Shops and Gassing, and the Frat Boys and My Balls
    2000 429

Chapter 117 . . . . **435**
    My Twenty-Five-Year Service Party
    2000 435

Chapter 118 . . . . **437**

Women in Motion
and 9/11
2001 437

Chapter 119 . . . . **439**
Could They Make It Any Clearer That They Hold the Power?
2001 439

Chapter 120 . . . . **441**
Different Kinds of Women, and
Saying Goodbye to Jennifer Keck
2002 441

Chapter 121 . . . . **445**
Dad and the Nursing Home,
and Bruce and Brenda Get Married 445

Chapter 122 . . . . **447**
Cancer
2002 447

Chapter 123 . . . . **449**
Strike and Elections,and the Gang from '78/'79 get-together.
2003 449

Chapter 124 . . . . **453**
The Day the Lights Went Out 453

Chapter 124 . . . . **457**
The So-Called Strike Is Over 457

Chapter 125 . . . . **459**
Raging Grannies Protest 459

Chapter 126 . . . . **463**
Dad's Death
2003 463

Chapter 127 . . . . **467**
My Last Stand
2004 467

Chapter 128 . . . . **477**
Still Fighting, This Time for My Life 477

Chapter 129 . . . . **479**
Anger and Magma 479

Glossary **483**

This book is dedicated to my best friend and lover, Merv McLaughlin.

Merv, your patience and kindness slowly removed the many layers of distrust I had in my life. You stood beside me all these years, tirelessly supporting me, and never wavering when the conflict of events occurred. You treated me the way a woman should be treated: with respect and love. You believed in me and saw first-hand the injustice that was happening at work.

You were my caregiver for years when illness struck. Then you encouraged me to get the book done knowing how important it was to me to tell my story. When I relived the stories and became emotionally drained, you lifted me out of dark places. You reassured me that it was okay to be sad and angry, then helped me to let the hurt go.

I love you,

Cat

Acknowledgements

Dorothy Wigmore: Photographer. For the wonderful picture she took during the strike in '78/'79.

Janet Kobelka: Artist in Sudbury. Thank you for the wonderful painting that made the cover of my book.

Filmmakers of *The Wives' Tale*: Sophie Bissonnette, the producer; Martin Duckworth, the camera person; Joyce Rock, the sound person.

Bruce MacKeigan: For being my best friend (next to Merv), and for always being there for me.

Dave Patterson: Great leader and great friend, who stood by me all the time.

Women of LU 6500: Great friends, back-up, support.

Jennifer Keck: Great friend who always believed in me.

Joan Kuyek: Great friend, great leader.

Susan Kennedy: Very best friend, great supporter.

Mercedes Stedman: Great friend.

Doug Bornn: Photographer of Janet's painting.

Jennifer Penny: Author of *Hard-Earned Wages*, and for her pictures.

David Leadbeater: Economics professor at *Laurentian* University of *Sudbury*, Editor of *Mining Town Crisis: Globalization, Labour, and Resistance in Sudbury*. Thanks for helping get *The Wives' Tale* on digital.

Val Ross: Author of "The Arrogance of Inco" in the May 1979 edition of *Canadian Business* magazine.

All the Wives: They made up a big part of my life and my story.

Amy Henson: Personal organizer, editor. For her help with editing my story before it went to the publishing editor.

The Sudbury Star: Information from article.

The Northern Life: Information from article.

Mick Low: For writing the articles.

RD Wilson: The artist in the anode.

Laurie McGauley: For her photos.

Austin Lane/Gaetanne Gladu: For answering questions. And the picture of women cutting down the stack.

Dr. Joao Rezende-Neto: Surgeon at St. Michael's Hospital in Toronto. This doctor saved my life. *Big thanks*.

Inco Triangle: For the pictures.

Tellwell: A self-publishing company in Victoria BC, for the publishing of my book.

Simon Ogden: Editor at Tellwell.

Caitlin Ing: For all your help organizing at Tellwell.

Derek Ford: For taking my headshot.

Norris Valiquetttte: His art drawing.

Mackenzie Marshall: Organized all the journals and bits of paper.

Keith Lovely: Helping win the 147 WSIB

Sharon Murdock: helped with English at the beginning of the book.

Cindy Babcock: For supplying additional information for the book.

My Mom and Dad

Prologue

Kicking that man in the balls was not intentional. It was a quick reaction to his inappropriate actions as I stood in the pouring rain in the middle of January in 1979. I was cold, wet, and tired; holding a five-gallon plastic pail and asking for monetary support from the workers at an automotive plant in Oshawa, Ontario. The mining giant Inco in Sudbury had forced us to strike and we had been out since September 15, 1978. Our union was running out of money to support the workers and many needed it for life-sustaining drugs. We had to ask other unions for their support to survive and win this fight.

My dad told us a story about a meteorite or comet hitting the earth billions of years ago where Sudbury now stands in Northern Ontario. No one knew which one it was, because it disintegrated on impact and destroyed everything in its wake, leaving a crater 39 miles long, 19 miles wide, and 9.3 miles deep. It was so strong it pushed through the layers of the earth all the way to its core. This triggered a volcanic eruption to the surface. The crater filled with molten metal and bubbling gases, leaving a lake of lava. It slowly cooled and solidified to rock containing nickel, copper, palladium, silver, gold, and other precious metals. The earth healed itself and the lakes and trees returned. When these resources were uncovered, large mining companies came in to stake their claim.

In 1974, Inco—the world's largest Nickel producer—hired a few women. We were the first females to work full time as hourly employees since World War II. It was illegal for women to work there both before and after the war up to that point. At nineteen years old I was second in line waiting to be interviewed in front of the Inco employment/hospital building. My life was about to change forever.

Throughout my thirty years at Inco, I was labelled a troublemaker for standing up for what I believed in. As the years went on, I carried the name like a badge of honour. I kept journals of all the events that were happening through the years.

Some of the names in my story have been changed to protect the guilty.

Chapter 1

In the Beginning

Three stacks in Sudbury Ontario

What do you mean rocks aren't black? Of course they are! Just look around.

– I was 23 years old when I found out real rocks are not black.

I was nine years old, and again some invisible power was inviting me to climb the huge blackened mountains that surrounded my neighbourhood. I scrambled up one of the rugged cliffs to get a better look at my surroundings. My mom told me I was too little to be up on those mountains—it was too dangerous. But I didn't really think about it and I went by myself anyway.

A hazy blue poison gas draped over the three-block area that made up my neighbourhood. We lived in the north end of the city of Sudbury, Ontario. The gas burned my eyes, my nose, and my throat.

"Sulphur is bad today," I said out loud, as if talking to some invisible friend.

I could see our yellow house on the corner nestled in an area surrounded by railroad tracks and the blackened hills we called the mountains. Beyond the tracks sat more blackened hills, no trees, no shrubs, no grass, no flowers, not a living thing, only black barren rock. I covered my mouth with my hand, as if that would stop the sulphur from entering when I breathed, but all I managed to do was leave dirt on my face from the black soot I had acquired from the rocks. I wiped my hands on my pants, leaving more evidence I was once again up in the mountains. My mom would be mad.

Chapter 2

Kindergarten
1959

A teacher and a nun stood in the doorframe of my kindergarten classroom.

"Cathy, please come here." The teacher summoned me with her curled index finger. I limped towards them, fixated on how the nun was dressed. Her long black robe went all the way to the floor; black granny-type shoes peeked out from underneath. My eyes homed in on a very large cross that hung from a beaded belt she was wearing. I was spellbound by the dead Jesus attached to it. It was creepy. I curled my lip.

"Cathy! Cathy! Are you listening?" I nodded, shaking my head to clear the daze. "We noticed you have a lot of bruising on your face and you're limping. Can you tell us what happened to you?"

"Of course I can," I said, pointing proudly to my black eye. "I fell off of Bev's shoulders. She's my sister Sandy's best friend. We were running away from the neighbour's kids we were fighting with when I flew off." I was dynamically motioning my hands and making a swishing noise. "My mom took me to the Inco hospital. They put special bandages on the cut but said it was going to leave a scar."

"Okay, what about the limp?" The nun's eyes narrowed

"Oh, that!" I lifted my skirt to reveal the blue, green, and yellow bruising with six scabbed-over puncture wounds. "I tried to break up a dog fight and one of them bit me. My mom took me back to the Inco hospital." I kicked off my slip-on shoe and pulled off my sock. "I stepped on a rusty nail that was sticking out of a broken piece of fence, hiding in the long grass when I went to check on a cocoon. But Gail, my friend, pulled it out. My mom took me back to the Inco hospital. The doctor said I should be more careful, that this was becoming a habit. Oh … I had to get a needle too; the nail was rusty." I stretched the sleeve of my sweater to show the needle prick.

"Hmm … what are we going to do with you?" the nun said.

I smiled up at her. "That's what my mom always says to me."

"You can go sit down now. We hope you enjoy kindergarten." The teacher pointed to my chair. As I walked away, I heard the nun say, "We will have to keep an eye on that one."

Chapter 3

Oratory Speeches 1963/'64

My mom yelled from the screen door, "Cathy! You have to come in and work on your speech."

I stood, brushing the sand from my pants and mumbling in protest, fixated on the sand castle by my feet. My intentions were good until a piece of pink plastic caught my eye. At eight and a half years old, my attention span was short. I sat back down to place the door to my castle. Once again, the yell from the screen door—this time "don't make me come out there and get you" was added. I knew then it was time to go. My small feet stomped up the stairs, hoping to get a reaction from my mom … nothing. So, when I opened the screen door and hopped in, I let the screen door do its usual *bang bang bang*. She yelled, "Don't slam the screen door!" All of us five kids let that screen door slam. Satisfied at getting the reaction I wanted, I kicked off my shoes and spilled sand all over the floor.

My mother shook her head. "What am I going to do with you?"

"I thought you wanted me to work on my speech?" I said with a smile.

"You always have an answer. One day that mouth of yours is going to get you in trouble."

She handed me a pencil that she had sharpened with the butcher knife, and the pointed end looked like a beaver had been gnawing at it. We sat down at the kitchen table and began to write. "*My Summer Vacation*, by Cathy Mulroy, Grade 3."

We decided it would be about my summer vacation at my grandparents' cottage, nestled among massive white and scotch pine on Allumette Island on the Ottawa River. I had many great memories with them.

The nearest town was eight miles of dirt road heading one way, and twenty the other. Yet I always felt safe there, mostly because of Granny and Grandpa, and a dog named

Smoky. My Granny Katie (Mooney) Kennedy and my Grandpa Sandy (Alexander) Kennedy were my mom's parents. Their dog was a large collie and German shepherd mix—one of the loyalist dogs I have ever met.

Grandpa was a log driver, a member of the RCMP, and he worked at Inco as a chemist and groundskeeper. Granny made homemade bread and raspberry preserves. Grandpa was a great storyteller, telling us tales like how the Algonquian tribe lit the island on fire so Samuel de Champlain and his men would not come ashore. It forced them down the river to some really nasty rapids. They had to come ashore where they saw a large rock in the shape of a hat, and so they called this place Chapeau, Quebec.

I practiced and practiced my speech until the night of the competition. My hands were sweaty, so I wiped them on my skirt. I asked if I could put my hands behind my back like the boys, but the principal, a nun, said no, girls cup their hands in front. I thought it looked stupid.

It was my turn. My heart beat fast in my chest. I gulped, feeling a dryness in my mouth. All eyes were on me. During the speech people laughed and smiled. They were enjoying my stories. Extra energy ran through my body. When I finished, they clapped and yelled, "Bravo!" I was on top of the world. I had won a trophy for my speech.

The next year at the competition, my speech was titled "My Canadian Heritage." The principal announced the winner, but instead of my name, she announced that Pamela Duguay had won for her own speech titled "My Canadian Heritage."

Pamela wore a big smile. I was happy for her because we both now had a trophy. However, there was some commotion as my teacher pointed to something on the paper she was holding. The principal shrugged her shoulders and went back in front of the crowd. "There's been a mistake." The crowd went quiet. "Pamela did not win." Her voice seemed to echo. "It was Cathy who won." Pamela's face went white and her eyes widened just before she ran out of the room. I sprinted after her as she ducked into the girl's washroom, slamming and locking the stall door.

"Are you okay?" Sobs came from the other side of the door. "You can have my trophy; I already have one."

"No, I don't want yours," she moaned. My mother came into the bathroom. She told us that we had both won and each of us would get a trophy. That was my mom's doing.

Chapter 4

The Plague Motorcycle Gang 1969

Summer of '69, and school was out. I pulled my sunglasses off their usual spot on top of my head and placed them over my eyes. My hair was down to my waist, parted in the middle like so many other girls at this time. I strolled through Memorial Park, radio in one hand and a kitten I had found in the other.

Three grubby-looking men were sitting on a grassy hillside drinking beer. One wore a black leather jacket and the other two dirty jean jackets. All had vests on over their jackets, each with a picture of a skull and the word *Plague* on the back.

"Hey little girl, let us listen to your radio," one yelled out.

He wore brown cowboy boots with steel tips on the toes. I remember thinking these guys were way overdressed for that warm weather.

"No," I said, holding the radio tighter in my arms. He let out a raspy chuckle and peered over his half-rimmed sunglasses. His eyes were small and black like a bird's, but cold as a snake's. His hair was long, black, and greasy. Long sideburns, a dirty mustache that drooped down both sides of his chin, and a matted beard. I couldn't tell where the mustache ended and the beard began. I curled my lip and felt a shiver run through my body.

The other one was dirty blond, and I don't mean a dirty colour. He chugged his beer and threw the bottle on the storm drain they were sitting around, and it smashed.

"You're not supposed to be drinking beer in the park," I said.

He let out a hearty laugh and grabbed for my leg. I jumped back and fell onto the drain cover. The kitten went one way and the radio another. I stood up and checked myself for damage, feeling no pain when my fingers entered a four-inch gash on my shin, revealing layers of tissue just below my knee as blood poured out and down my leg.

"I have to get to a hospital," I whispered. I felt dizzy.

The bikers jumped up, looks of horror on their faces. I glanced at the drain cover—broken beer-bottle glass covered the area.

"This is all your fault!" I cried out.

The man with the half-rimmed glasses picked me up in his arms and ran toward a taxi. The dirty-blond man ran alongside him.

I could see the look on my face in the half-rimmed glasses: it was one of terror. The cab driver leaned against his car door, arms crossed, shaking his head. No, he didn't want blood on his seat. The biker carrying me handed me to the dirty-blond guy. "Here, Harley Charley, hold her." He removed his vest; the skull was facing up as he placed me gently on it. The other biker, named Tramp, held my radio. I'm not sure what happened to the kitten. We drove to the closest hospital, St Joseph's, a French hospital.

"I am going to call her parents, Cat," Harley Charley said.

"Okay," we both replied.

"You're called Cat too." He laughed, displaying a row of yellow teeth. I curled my lip. It must have been a sight to see: two cruelly sadistic, evil-looking characters entering the emergency department, one carrying a fourteen-year-old girl, blood dripping from a large gash in her leg.

We met a doctor on the way in and his eyes narrowed, suspicious of what he saw. He wanted to know what happened. I told him most of the truth, leaving out the beer the bikers were drinking. He asked me if there was more to the story and if he should he call the police. I shook my head no.

He told me my doctor didn't work at that hospital so I would have to go to the General Hospital. They did bandage my leg and, again, the bikers put me in a cab, then they called my mom.

When the freezing came out that night the pain was agonizing. We only had aspirin in the house for pain, so I suffered. It took forty stitches and I almost lost my baby toe. The doctor said I was lucky: if it would have cut an inch higher up my leg, I wouldn't have been able to walk again. That summer there was no biking, no swimming, no skipping, and no running. Over the summer, Harley Charley called to see how I was doing and got my friend to return my radio. He sent flowers and chocolate and asked if he could take me to a show. When I asked my mom, she said, "You know what the rules are: if a boy wants to date you, he has to come to the house and ask your dad."

I watched intensely through the window as a black Chevy four-door sedan with four bikers in it pulled up to the side of the house. Harley Charley jumped out of the front seat and a biker from the back took his seat. The car drove away.

My heart leaped when he knocked on the door. My mom let him in, and there stood a genuine biker in our kitchen wearing a heavy black leather jacket with a jean vest over it, the skull still on the back. He took off his grey toque and shoved it into his pocket, and clumsily pulled off his cowboy boots to display grey work socks. He hung his jacket on the back of the kitchen chair just as my dad opened the door from the basement. He looked the biker up and down.

"Hello, Mr. Mulroy. My name is Leon Miskowski; I'm known as Harley Charley." He extended his hand to shake my father's, but my father did not accept the greeting.

My dad looked the biker in the eyes. In a calm, composed voice, he said, "Boy, your feet stink." I was stunned at what my dad said. I had never seen or heard my dad be rude in all my life. He moved past us and we followed him into the living room. A sickening wave of panic welled up from my belly. My dad shut off the TV and motioned for us to sit on the couch. He sat in his armchair, brought his large miner's hands together—not clenched, only the tips of his fingers touching.

"Mr. Leon Miskowski." My dad was unruffled by this man. "My daughter is fifteen years old, and you are how old?" The question was clear.

"I am twenty-three, sir," Charley replied.

"Yes." My dad nodded once. "You are not to talk to my daughter, you are not to call my daughter, you are not to get anyone else to call my daughter on your behalf, and you are not to correspond with my daughter in any way. Do you understand what I am saying?" He did not take his eyes off of Harley Charley's.

"Yes, I understand, Mr. Mulroy," he responded.

"Good." My dad stood. "You know the way out. You can join your friends waiting for you in the black car outside." The car had driven around the block and my dad had spotted it at the side of the house.

He left the room without looking back and went down the stairs. I walked Harley Charley to the door, and we said our goodbyes. I ran to the living room window in time to see the black car pull away with the four bikers in it.

After school, a handful of girls went to town for a pop. The bikers were always there, and my friend Trudy, who was three years older, asked me to join them, and I did. Harley Charley told me he was going to jail for three months. When I asked him why, he said it was for possession of LSD. I was really mad because he said he didn't do drugs as he liked his beer. Tramp had the drugs, but he had already been in jail and would go away for a long time if Harley Charley didn't take the rap. That's how it worked in the gang. It seemed stupid to me. I never knew whether Harley Charley was actually guilty, but at the time I believed him. While he was in jail we wrote back and forth, and I got to know him better. He was a good man, but he was still a biker. After he got out, we saw each other until I found out he had started doing drugs with needles. I didn't want anything to do with that. He told me his dad was dying, and this made him forget. To me that was a poor excuse.

We had a big fight when I told him I didn't want anything to do with him or the bikers. I ran out of the apartment they were in and he came after me, stopping just outside the door. He wasn't wearing any boots, just those grey work socks, and it was January and incredibly cold.

"You get back here," he yelled, "or I will go after your family." I stopped dead and turned. My heart was beating very fast; I was scared. My mind was racing, wondering what to do.

"You had better not!" I yelled back, taking my stand. "Remember, I am only fifteen." The look on his face said it all. He didn't come after me. This was not over.

Chapter 5

My First Protest 1970

I stood behind my dad's chair watching the TV over his shoulder. Images of the war in Vietnam plastered the screen. Young men in the jungle trudging through chest-deep water, terror on their faces as they carried a wounded man on a stretcher. Another picture of a dead woman and three dead children lying outside a grass hut. The camera panned out to a hospital where boys, and I mean *boys*, lay on beds with missing limbs and bandaged eyes.

"This war should never be." My dad's voice was almost a whisper. He had been a paratrooper on the front lines during WWII. I backed away from his chair as quietly as I could, not wanting him to know I heard, but the next story stopped me dead in my tracks. It was May 4, 1970, and there was a shooting at Kent State University in Ohio after the fourth day of protests by students following President Nixon's announcement that US troops were being sent into Cambodia. Hundreds of students were tear-gassed and four were dead. "How could they shoot kids?" I whispered.

I stared at the clock on the classroom wall; it seemed to be running slower than usual. My first protest was against the Vietnam War. Kids from all over North America were walking out of class to let the world know we wanted the troops from the United States to come back home. The clock struck the time we were to leave. I got to my feet, only to be stopped by Mr. Hand, my teacher. His six-foot-two large-build body filled most of the doorframe.

"Where do you think you're going?" His words were hot on my face, his eyes unblinking as he stared into mine.

"I am going downtown to join in the protest against the war." My voice shook. "I know I am allowed to go; my parents said it was okay. My dad was a paratrooper and I am doing this for him too. Not just the young men who are over there fighting a fight that's not even their business. That's what my dad said." I waited.

"Well, if you have to, you have to." Mr. Hand stepped aside. I could have sworn he smiled.

The warm sun was inviting as a bunch of us headed to Memorial Park in the heart of downtown Sudbury. It was packed with long-haired boys wearing flowered T-shirts and blue bell-bottom jeans, some barefoot. Most of the girls, including me, wore our hair down to our waists, parted in the middle with buckskin ties around our heads, some with flowers sticking out of them. Girls passed out beaded peace necklaces and pamphlets denouncing the war.

A stage had been set up. A boy of about nineteen years old spoke to the group and told us about a drop-in center that was going to be set up in the basement of St. Andrew's United Church just off the park, and that volunteers were needed that summer.

Chapter 6

Draft Dodgers, Summer 1970

Summer was here. Last exam and I was off to the lake to meet some friends. Trudy sat on a rock, her feet dangling in the water.

"Hi." She glanced over at me, smiling. "You don't ever have to worry about Harley Charley anymore. He did something to his brother bikers and has left town. The bikers said if they find him, he will be one sorry son of a bitch. Unfortunately, you still can't hang out with the band or that guy you have your eye on—they threatened to break all the instruments if you go near them."

My heart sank. "I'll find something else to do. Besides, there won't be too many more dances now that school is out."

Another friend, Andrea Murray, and I read a notice on the board at Laffyamy's Restaurant. The drop-in centre at St. Andrew's had opened and they were now looking for volunteers. With a quick glance at each other we ran down Durham Street and into the alley, and headed to the back of the church. An old wooden door was opened, and we could hear voices coming from inside and music playing in the background: *the Age of Aquarius*. We both bobbed to the rhythm.

A full-figured woman ascended from the basement, holding tightly to the heavy wooden rail as she climbed.

"Hello Andrea!" she said, her voice soft but firm, her eyes round and friendly.

"We heard you need some help. This is my friend Cathy. We call her Cat," Andrea said.

The woman smiled and turned to me. "Hi Cat, glad to meet you. So, you two want to help around here." We followed her up the stairs to an office that used to be the priest's. I know that smell anywhere; every time we had to get our rosaries blessed when we were kids, we would go see the priest waiting at his door and that was the smell that came out of that room.

She asked us to sit and offered us a pop. "Well, we need workers to clean and sweep the floors in the drop-in centre. We need others to go out to Mine Mill camp and get it ready for …" A knock at the door interrupted her. A boy of about nineteen with long blond hair stood in the doorway. He had an animated smile, his eyes sparkled, and he wore tight blue jeans very low on his thin hips, along with a flowered shirt and a beaded buckskin necklace. "This is John," the woman said. "These girls are willing to help." He said that was great and that he was leaving in ten minutes, so we followed him out and piled in the back of his white van. I had no idea at that point how that summer was going to impact my whole life. We climbed into the van; four other kids were already sitting on the floor gabbing about something. One boy sat at the back wearing a brightly coloured poncho draped over his knees. He had a bushy mustache and his skin was light brown like a Mexican's. I didn't think he was from around there because we didn't have many people in Sudbury that weren't white. He was from the USA.

We laughed as we headed to Mine Mill camp; it was situated on Richard Lake, eight and half miles from Sudbury. The Mine, Mill, and Smelter Workers Union was the union my dad was in before it was taken over by the United Steelworkers. We turned off the highway and onto a dirt road, bouncing up and down in the van all the while. I was glad to get out. Four long screened-in lodges dotted the campgrounds, along with a building for showers and washing facilities.

John unlocked the camps and we went to work. It was very dusty. I disturbed a family of spiders as I wiped away the cobwebs. Many bunk beds were pushed tight against the walls. On each bed sat a rolled-up mattress tied tight with rope, exposing the metal weave of the bed. We washed the floors and pushed the beds into place. Shelves were built to house large cans of peanut butter and jam, and many loaves of bread. It took us a few days until all the cabins were clean and the mattresses were back on the beds waiting for the next lodgers.

We sat outside waiting for John and his white van. When it finally arrived, the door slid open revealing a group of boys, all around the age of eighteen. Andrea and I looked at each other and smiled, eyebrows raised. Jerry, a red-haired freckle-faced boy from Nebraska, was the first to step out of the van. Behind him, boy after boy looked sad, uneasy. They each had a packsack and sleeping bag. One boy even had a Dalmatian. This boy was Doug, eighteen with soft curly shoulder-length hair and nice brown eyes. My heart skipped a beat, but he had his eyes on Andrea. He limped as he went into the camp.

Andrea and I made peanut butter and jam sandwiches as the boys settled in, choosing their beds and putting their belongings on top. We had made a high-rise of sandwiches, the contents oozing out all sides. The boys each grabbed a sandwich and we all sat in a circle on the floor. Each boy gave his name and where he was from. Jerry the red-haired boy said he could never go back home again—he would be put in jail because he wouldn't go to Vietnam. Boy after boy told his story. Some said their parents would never talk to them again because they took off to Canada instead of going to war.

Another boy said that his father told him it was his duty to go and that he was a coward for leaving. He cried when he said he didn't believe in that war. Then it was Doug's turn to speak. "I have a dog with me; his name is Bone, and I have something wrong with my foot. I have to see a doctor."

Doug stayed with us for five days while he made arrangements to meet his father in Vancouver to have his foot operated on for the gangrene that had seized hold of it. Bone stayed with us. Over the whole summer boys came and boys went. Meeting them made the Vietnam war more real to me. These were great memories and a learning experience I would never have gotten from a book.

Chapter 7

Getting Married 1970

I went to Sheridan Technical High School instead of Sudbury High. Most of the kids' dads at this school worked for Inco. The girls huddled in circles in the school halls, our books pressed close to our chest. Boys shook their long hair and smiled at us, and we smiled back. I was growing up. As the girls moved toward the staircase, we stayed as close as we could to the wall. Our skirts were so short they just passed our butts. The boys would hang out under the stairs to get a glimpse up the skirts until Mr. Hand ordered them to keep moving. I was sixteen years old. This meant I could learn to drive, if my dad allowed me. I didn't care; I liked taking the bus.

At that year's Halloween dance, I was hoping to hook up with Lloyd Duhaime now that Harley Charley had left town and most of the bikers were in jail. Lloyd played bass in a band called The Village Steps. His older brother Mike played the drums and Billy Irwin was on lead guitar. Danny Dubai was also on drums and Ray Servant played the electric piano/organ. His other brother Marc did the lights.

Andrea convinced me it was okay to go all the way with Lloyd. Girls that wanted to keep their boyfriends did *it*. It was Christmas and Lloyd bought me a ring—we were going steady.

"It's not an engagement ring," he said and we both laughed. This was soon to not be funny anymore.

Sometime in January we were parked up at the blue water tower. It was too far to go to the slag dump where people would park to watch the glowing red lava flow down the black hills. The windows of the car steamed up. We were using the calendar safety net, and this was not a safe time to have sex. He promised to pull out but didn't. Six weeks later, Valentine's Day, I handed the nurse a pee sample and headed back to school. My hand shook as I dropped a dime into the pay telephone that hung just outside the school lunchroom. "Congratulations! Your test was positive," the receptionist said.

I couldn't think or function at that moment. I felt disconnected, cut off from reality as I watched other students laughing with each other as they headed into the lunchroom, while others leaned against the wall talking about what teenagers talk about. My mind raced as I tried to process this bad information. What were the consequences of my actions? I headed for the guidance office. What was I going to do? What have I done?

A woman invited me into her office. For a minute my mind was drawn to her shiny gold-framed glasses that took up most of her face—they weren't flattering. She asked if she could call someone. My friend Vickie came to mind; after all, she was pregnant with Lloyd's brother's baby. I called her and we headed for the Woolworths food counter. Miserable, I plunked myself onto the round seat and ordered a chocolate milkshake. We entered one of those photo booths and took pictures of ourselves to remember this horrible day.

I handed Lloyd a Valentine's Day card that had a tiger in a cage on the front of it. I didn't know how symbolic this card was to my future. He asked me to marry him. I said yes.

My mom answered the door and let Lloyd in. When he removed his coat, I began to laugh when I saw the enormous wet marks under his armpits on his lilac-coloured shirt. Nervously, we sat across from my dad; he lowered his newspaper. After we told him the news, my dad said not to worry and that everything would be taken care of. I thought it went rather well.

A few days later, my mom told me to be at Holy Trinity Church on May 1st at twelve o'clock. She and Lloyd's mom set up a wedding and a shower. I was told when to be there.

I thought at any moment I was going to wake from this bad dream. My wedding dress was a size seven. Not the dress I wanted.

Rain poured down as I stood at the screen door looking out. I kicked the screen door open and listened to the *bang bang bang* it made. My mother didn't say a word. She was worried about the flowers not showing up.

"Flowers for what?" I mumbled, feeling buzzed on a yellow pill called Valium that one of the girls had given me.

There was no reality to what was happening when I walked into the church. Lloyd's mom met us at the door to inform us that Lloyd's dad had gotten drunk the night before and would not be there. The rest of the wedding was a blur. There was a small reception at a hotel in a room called the Penalty Box. Little did I know this was another message from the gods.

I had no idea where we were going for our honeymoon. The only part I played in this wedding was to show up.

I was now Cathy Duhaime. My life changed forever.

Chapter 8

Our First Apartment 1970

Lloyd and his mother found an apartment for us. I had nothing to do with that, either. So, like the wedding, I went along with it. It was in Minnow Lake, his area of town. I wanted to be closer to my mom and dad, but he said he would not live in my part of town.

It looked great from the outside of the building, until I realized we had to go through a garage to get to the apartment. It was dark and gloomy and the door to the apartment was at the very end. He didn't carry me over the threshold like they did in the movies. I felt sad.

It was a long room, wider than a hallway. I counted thirty-one cupboards and drawers, all painted dark brown. A table from the 1950s sat against the wall. It had chrome legs, as did the two vinyl chairs.

Why would a large plywood box be sitting in the kitchen beside the table? It was to cover half the bathtub that extended under the wall from the washroom. If I were to take a bath, the wall would be in my face and my legs would be in the kitchen. I was feeling overwhelmed but didn't want to look ungrateful—after all, he had married me. I remember thinking I should be thankful. Once I saw the bed, I couldn't hold back my tears. The bedroom dropped down from the kitchen, making it even with the floor of the garage. An old dirty mattress full of lumps sat on a weaved metal frame, similar to the ones that were at the Mine Mill camp. One of the legs didn't even reach the floor. I felt doomed; this was not how I had pictured my life going. In fact, I had never thought about tomorrow—I was only sixteen years old.

"I am not sleeping on that," I protested. The next day we were given a better bed by a friend.

Lloyd got a job at the university, working in the print room—he was trying. He still played in the band, out every night to practice. I stayed in the apartment.

Day after day I sat on our prickly couch, part of an old sectional. It wasn't too bad when the old TV worked, but most of the time it didn't.

All my friends were in school and I didn't know anyone in this area. I didn't drive and I had no money for a bus. My days were filled with depression, a feeling of hopelessness. I had no idea who I was anymore. I didn't even have my own name. It wasn't long before Lloyd became very verbally abusive. He began calling me stupid because I didn't wipe the counter off right, leaving water behind. He would complain I didn't make the bed properly, or that I didn't know how to cook. Well, I never had to do any of that before I was married; I was a young girl going to school. That was it. With the mixed-up hormones and the life I was now in, I felt trapped, imprisoned. I thought I would wake up from this nightmare, but I didn't.

I remember crying and calling my mom. She told me things would get better. They didn't.

One day the apartment was infested with small silverfish. They scurried all over the floor. The lighting was poor so they didn't mind coming out during the day. When the spiders came, they terrified me. I always had an intense fear of spiders, especially large wolf spiders like these ones. I stayed on that prickly couch for three days, only getting off to go to the washroom. Lloyd was mad I didn't do anything, called me lazy and stupid for being afraid. I used a whole can of Raid on one spider and it still walked under the fridge. The landlord investigated the spider problem and found a large nest in a tree just outside our only window. He destroyed it, but I was always on the lookout for more spiders.

Chapter 9

Having My Baby 1971

My son, Peppy as a baby.

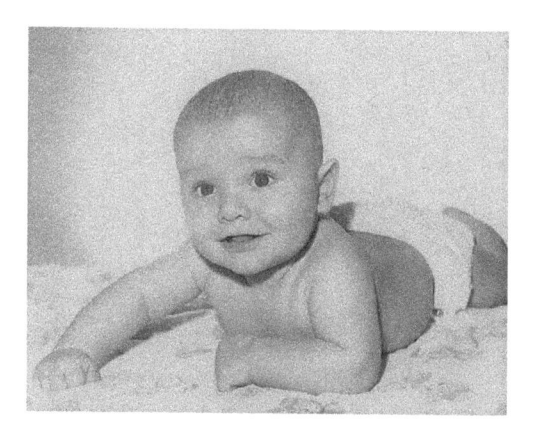

On October 7 I began to have cramps in my belly. The baby was on its way. That night I walked the floor by myself while Lloyd slept. He was starting his first day at Inco. His alarm clock went off. I was happy to have some companionship: pain loves company.

He walked past me in a groggy morning stupor and told me to make him some breakfast—he wanted bacon and eggs.

The smell of the eggs frying upset my stomach and I made a beeline to the bathroom and vomited. He knocked on the door, not to ask if I was okay but if I was going to finish making his breakfast.

"No, I can't. I'm sick," I moaned. I heard the loud smack of his lips; he was disgusted with me. I begged him to ask his boss if he could start work the next day. I was sure the boss would understand. He said it was his first day and he couldn't do that. Instead, he dropped me at his mother's. I waited for her to make the family breakfast before she drove me to the hospital. Again: fried eggs. The smell turned my stomach.

After twenty-six hours of labour a baby boy was born. This was the happiest I had been in the last year. My boy was perfect.

Silverfish still occupied the floor of the apartment. It was time to move before the baby started to crawl.

We moved to the Kingsway apartments above a second-hand store. What a difference. Now it was time for me to get my first paying job, and I secured a position at A.L. Green's Department Store in New Sudbury. I was a sales clerk and took my job very seriously, and finally I had my own money.

We had put our name into Sudbury Housing to be considered for a geared-to-income residence. We had only been in the apartment for two months when we got the call. It was a town house, brand new, at the end of the row, and it was down the street from my mom and dad's. Life may get better, I thought.

Chapter 10

Not the Real Meaning of Christmas
1972

Not long after that I was laid off from A.L. Green's Department Store, I had to look for another job.

Lloyd's other brother got his girlfriend pregnant. Now there would be three little ones all close in age. This was a good thing for me. His girlfriend was only a year younger than I was and we liked hanging out. Now we would have something more in common: little cousins.

I removed the silver Christmas tree from its cardboard box. "I hate this tree. This is the last year we will have this ugly thing." I muttered my complaint loud enough that Lloyd could hear.

Between Christmas and New Year's my mom called to tell me a young man was at her door looking for me. She handed him the phone—it was Doug, the young draft dodger I had met in the summer of 1970. I was so excited to hear his voice. I cried happy tears as the memories of those fun-filled days played in my head. I wondered if he had ever gotten his buckskin jacket back that Andrea had stolen off of him. I asked about his foot; he said he had an operation in Vancouver, and it was good as new. He and a friend were travelling to Montreal after working up in the Yukon. He wanted to see me, so I invited him and his friend to our place. He said the car they were driving was falling apart—they didn't know how it had lasted this long and asked if they could crash for the night at our place. We had a pullout couch in the living room so I said yes, anticipating all the stories he would share with me. A storm was raging fiercely when I saw them drive up. Their passenger window was gone; they had taped a plastic sheet up to keep out the cold. I asked if they were hungry, and they said they had already had hamburgers. I gave them a tour of the town house I was so proud of.

We sat around and talked about his dog, Bone; Andrea stealing his jacket; the gangrene in his foot; and all those stories. He talked about what it was like living up in the Yukon. Lloyd glared at me and motioned me into the kitchen. He was not happy with my friend. He chastised me for bringing them into the bedroom. I defended myself by saying I just wanted them to see our home.

"They cannot stay overnight," he snapped.

Dumbfounded, I whined, "I told them they could. You can't ask them to go out in that storm, in that run-down car with the broken window. It's Christmas; you're going to tell them they have to go?"

"No, you're going to tell them they have to go. They can sleep in their car. They made it this far like that; one more night doesn't matter." He turned and walked upstairs, leaving me standing in the kitchen in despair.

Doug asked what was going on and if they could spend the night. Embarrassed and sad, I looked down at the floor, shook my head. "No, you can't." A heavy quietness filled the room. It was very uncomfortable. Doug asked if I would point them to the closest church—they might be able to stay in their basement. Crying like the world had ended, I mouthed "I am so sorry" over and over as he and his buddy climbed into the beat-up car with the plastic sheet for a window. I knew I would never see him again. The car disappeared into the blizzard. Thoughts of the story of Mary and Joseph being turned away from all the inns mirrored what just happened. I felt this hurt would never be forgotten.

Chapter 11

Peppy Gets the London Flu 1973

April brought its usual rain showers. I sat my eighteen-month-old son on the couch. He didn't look well; he was pale and running a fever of 103°. He didn't have enough strength to sit, and toppled over.

I called my mom and I was sure she was at the door just as I hung up the phone. My dad drove us to the hospital and Peppy was admitted. We were told he had the London Flu and he was very sick. Over one thousand people in North America alone had already died from this flu.

They put him in isolation for nine days. I had never been so scared. They said it was better if we didn't visit him because he just got upset. They also said they didn't want us carrying the flu bug around.

When he was released I held him tight in my arms. We could have lost our little boy. Something inside of me had changed. I looked down at him and told him how much I loved him. I would do anything for him, stand between him and a tiger if I had to. He was the most important person in my life.

It was time to get another job, again at a department store, this time at Silverman's in downtown Sudbury. There were no good-paying jobs for women in Sudbury, even if you had a good education. I was out of the house and had my own money once again. It was only a few dollars, but I could take the bus downtown and go for a coffee.

The verbal abuse in my marriage was now the norm. "You're stupid, you're fat," and so on and so on. I believed everything he was saying about me. I was no good for anything. Yes, he was a good provider and he had a job. I had a roof over my head and food to eat. I should have been thankful. That's what I heard.

Lloyd was now a letter carrier for the post office. He had been laid off at Inco after the company announced that it would be shutting down the smelter in Coniston just east of Sudbury. It had closed down as the Government of Ontario implemented stricter environmental restrictions, and the smelter in Coniston was not as efficient as the one in Copper Cliff. A handful of employees were laid off, and Lloyd was one of them.

Having a little money of my own made me feel better about myself, but the job at the department store didn't last either. I got another job at Canadian Tire. I was fed up with this lifestyle, but I couldn't change it without an education. Back then I believed in God, Jesus Christ. So, I prayed and sang all the words to *Jesus Christ Superstar*. This was how I got through the days.

Deep down I knew something would happen someday. I would be saved.

After Christmas of 1973, we finally got rid of that ugly silver Christmas tree. I was over at Lloyd's parents' house when his dad came in early from work. He had a large bandaged gash on his head. He said he'd had an accident at work. He worked underground as a miner in the same mine my dad was in: Creighton. A large piece of rock had hit him in the head, and he may have had a concussion. He asked me to get some ice from the freezer and wrap it in a towel. I did as he asked. I noticed he had changed after that: he didn't drink as much and he was nice to the grandchildren. Not that this erased the person he was before, I just noted that something in him had shifted.

Maybe all that is needed is for one to be hit in the head with a big rock to change. I can think of a few who could benefit from this …

Chapter 12

Getting Hired at Inco 1974

At the Copper Cliff copper refinery, safety instructor Luis Fay (left) explains basic lifting techniques to Susan Vallier, Bob Floyd, and Cathy Duhaime. Safety school is a must.

I was laid off at Canadian Tire after Christmas. This was becoming a real drag. I decided to make our geared-to-income townhouse more like a home, painting walls and wallpapering. I was a real little homemaker. Taking a break, I turned off *Jesus Christ Superstar* on the record player and turned on the TV.

Special announcement: Prime Minister Pierre Elliott Trudeau reported that Inco, the giant mining company in Sudbury Ontario, will be hiring women as hourly-rate employees. Women had not held jobs like this since the war years.

Inco was one of the largest mining companies in the world. Mining had long been perceived as a man's domain, largely due to its past requirement for heavy manual labour. But I had seen women who worked on farms that could put a lot of men to shame when it came to bailing hay. In the 1930s, legislation stated it was too dangerous for women to do this work.

"What? And not dangerous for a man?" I said to the TV.

The announcer went on to explain that labour code stipulated that discrimination was based on colour, race, national origin, or religion—there was nothing in it about discrimination against gender. But during World War II it was okay for women to work at Inco. On August 13, 1942, the Order in Council PC 7032, "Employment of Female Persons by International Nickel Company of Canada Limited in the vicinity of Sudbury," was issued. Over 1400 women were hired to work at Inco's surface operations. They all lost their jobs after the war ended. The Mining Act of Ontario stated that women were no longer legally employable in mining operations.

"They must have thought it was too dangerous again!" I said sarcastically.

"In 1974 the laws have changed again, and Inco will be hiring women. Put your resumé together and go down to the employment office for 7:30 a.m." I felt as if he was speaking right to me.

I pulled the kerchief off my hair, covered the paint can, and cleaned up. The warm shower hit my face and thoughts of getting hired at Inco entered my mind. Wrapped in a towel, wet hair dripping, I called my friend Carmen. Carmen was dating Ronnie, a good friend of Lloyd's. I told her the news and asked if she was interested in the job as well. She said yes, and that she would borrow Ronnie's car and pick me up at 6:30 the next morning.

Giddy and a little scatterbrained, I sat down at the supper table and told Lloyd I was going to apply at Inco as an hourly-rate employee. He raised one eyebrow, gave me a cold glare, and told me Inco doesn't hire girls.

"They do now. Trudeau just said so on the news." My face was beaming. "It was so funny: a reporter had asked Inco why there were no women on hourly rate, and their answer was that women hadn't applied. So, the doors are now open." I knew this is what I was supposed to do.

"Well, why would they hire you? You have no qualifications, you're not the right weight—you have to be at least 145 pounds. I know, I worked there." He always had to find fault.

"I don't care if I am only five-foot-one and 105 pounds, I am going to apply anyway. Nothing like bursting someone's bubble," I muttered to myself. "Oh, by the way, Carmen is going to apply too." He never said anything about her applying.

After supper he took his usual place on the couch to have his nap before heading out with the boys in the band.

Carmen picked me up and we headed to the Inco employment office, the same building I saw the Inco doctor in when I was little. There was a woman already waiting at the door. We introduced ourselves; her name was Sue. She was tall and strong-looking with long brownish-blond hair, the same style as Jacqueline Kennedy's.

It wasn't long before the line was extensive. One by one we entered a room. A man sat behind a desk and asked for our previous employment and told us that we would get a call for a medical examination if we were chosen. A few days later, I received a call to come back in a few weeks for an exam. When I told Lloyd, he said it didn't mean I got the job, that it was only a medical.

Meanwhile, the doctor had taken me off the birth control pills because they didn't want women to be on them for more than three years. We would follow the calendar days. All I will say is that he promised to pull out and he didn't.

I told my mom I was following in my dad's footsteps. My dad was a miner at Creighton Mine; I wondered how he was going to take this news. He was frightened for me, but said, "Give it a try, little one." He always called me "little one" because I was so small.

The day of the medicals I ate four bananas—I was told it would make me heavier. I was now 106 pounds and had terrible cramps. Each woman was handed a yellow paper hospital gown. It was a long day with pee samples, blood work, etc. Through all this, Carmen and I got bored and revamped our yellow dresses, tearing them and making them into very short V-necks with no sleeves. The other women laughed as Carmen and I modelled this new fashion. By the end of the day, ten of us were hired. They took our pictures and put them on cards called passes. On the pass was our badge number; this is how we would be identified. Mine was 35554.

Time to celebrate our new jobs. Carmen and I watched the sun go down behind the blackened mountains with the view of the Inco Superstack. I toasted our new boss, holding up the second empty bottle of wine. My words came out slurred and I actually toasted our new "bus." The Superstack was erected on the blackened hills. It towered over our city. It allowed the ground-level pollution to be lower and so we shared the sulphur dioxide and nitrogen dioxide gasses over a much larger area. The emissions were black at this time of day. During the day, the smoke emissions were white when the sun shone on it. It's funny how people didn't complain about white smoke. It was still the same poisonous gases. My dad said they always let out more at nighttime.

I always felt a connection with that 1250-foot Superstack; maybe it was because it was fully completed on the evening of August 21, 1970, and August 21 is my birthday.

Carmen and I laughed, rolling on the blanket I put down. Since that afternoon we had watched swimmers come and go to cool off in Ramsey Lake. They were all gone now, and we were both very drunk. "It's time we go home," I said. "We have a big day tomorrow—our first day on the job." I struggled to get up and find my balance. Carmen was having just as much trouble standing as I was. I reached over to lend a hand, but when she took it we both fell back on the blanket. We giggled like schoolgirls.

"Shall we try this again?" she said, squishing the blanket and empty wine bottles into her bag. "Can't leave a mess," she slurred, and laughed some more. We stood but were not very steady as we leaned on each other, surveying the steep climb up the berm of the railroad tracks. We began to climb—one step, two steps—gravity won, pulling us onto the ground. We both felt the sharp slag rocks that draped the berm of the tracks, knowing this would hurt in the morning. Time and time again we tried to get up that hill but kept falling back on the jagged slag. We were laughing like fools and the night was now black—we couldn't see anything. One more step and we were falling again.

"Get off me," Carmen mumbled. "You're on my head."

"Sorry. Let's not stand up. Let's crawl up the hill."

So that's what we did, one knee at a time, as the sharp slag cut into our knees and hands. "Okay, we have to be careful. We are very drunk and we have to cross the railroad tracks. We will stop when we get to the top and look both ways," I said.

"You're right, we are really drunk. Are we going to crawl over the track too? If we stand up, we might fall all the way back down the tracks," Carmen said. So that's what we did: fast as we could we crawled over the tracks. The light from the street lamp was great to see. Under it sat Ronnie's car, the convertible top still down.

"I can't drive," she said. "I'm too drunk."

"I can't drive either, because I really can't drive. I don't have a license. I don't know how to drive." We laughed as we crawled into the back seat.

"I think I'm bleeding," Carmen said, lifting her legs.

"Yep, you are. I'll check mine when I get home. Can't lift them now," I said. A friendly face appeared—it was Ronnie, and he commented that we were a sight. He drove me home first and helped me into the house. He was right: we were a sight. I laughed when I saw my black face in the mirror. It looked like I had been working in a coal mine. I washed it the best I could, looking at the black on the facecloth, knowing I would get shit for that.

The sound of the alarm clock was not a friendly noise. Lloyd exited the bathroom as I leaned on the wall for some support. He was not happy with the way I had looked the night before and told me that I looked like a whore with my boobs hanging out, the blanket all covered in black soot.

I shook my head, wondering what having black all over my boobs had to do with being a whore. I didn't care.

Carmen picked me up and we were off for our first day. I was shocked when I saw she was wearing a skirt and flip-flops. She said she had no choice—her jeans were black and she didn't have another pair. Her legs and arms were scratched pretty badly, and I said that she looked like she had been in a fight with a few cats.

"So ... did Ronnie give you shit?" I asked.

"No, he washed me up and put me to bed. Did you get in shit?"

"Oh, that was nice of him," I said, remembering what Lloyd had said. "No ... all was okay." I shook my head as if to free me from the memory of being called a whore.

Ten women sat around a large wooden table. A man entered, very clean-shaven, hair combed to the side with a part so straight it looked like he used a ruler. He removed his suit jacket, rolled up his sleeves, and sat at the head of the table. He was not friendly as he gave his instructions on what was expected of us. One of the women said something to another and they laughed.

The man slammed his fist on the table. "This is not a laughing matter!"

The women looked startled; I bent my head down and looked at the table, not wanting anything to do with this. We were instructed to stand and go outside. We followed a man in work clothes for a tour of the plant. We came to a place called the tank house. The smell of this area burned the inside of my nose. We were instructed not to put our hands in the tanks, as the acid would take our flesh right off. Copper slabs called anodes were hanging in this acid. I looked down at the floor covered with this liquid acid, then to Carmen with her flip-flops splashing through the puddles of acid on the floor. We made eye contact, both of us with worried looks.

After the anodes are solidified they are sent to the tank house. We had a lot of pride in our copper and our tour guide claimed it was the best in the world. The copper anodes are sent by narrow gauge trains to the tank house. They are removed by a crane and placed into tanks or a cell with an electrolyte solution.

A charge is added. The charge slowly dissolves the copper ions. They are attracted to the copper starting sheets. They become pure copper 99.999 percent. The Copper Cliff Copper Refinery (CCCR) produced about a 250 million pounds a year.

The anodes and starting sheet sat in this bath for about 14 days. There were over 1300 tanks. Each held about 4000 liters of this electrolyte solution (acid). So you can imagine how much this would burn your nose and throat. Not to mention what your lungs would look like. Especially if you were a crane operator always working directly over the tanks or if you were a worker who walked on top of the tanks to make sure the anodes didn't cling to the starter sheets.

Each cell or tank held 33 anodes and 34 cathode starter sheets. 16 to 46 cells formed a section. Each day 2 to 4 sections would be pulled out of the tank, adding up to about a million pounds a day. They would be washed off and now the 99.999% cathodes would be sent to the Fine Casting Area. They would be charged into the vertical furnace, continuously casting and made into shapes like wire bar and billets. He told us there used to be 23 different kinds of shapes back in the day.

Then we went through the casting areas. The roar of the furnaces was deafening; fire seemed to be shooting out of everything. We finally reached the training room at the far end of the refinery. The instructor pointed to Carmen and me. He said we were to be transferred out of the tank house because there were no steel-toed rubber boots to fit us. We were to go with another man. We followed him back through the plant, past the roaring furnaces. The cranes beeped, sirens went off, horns and trains and whistles blew. A cab was waiting to take us to the Soucie Salo Safety supply store. The sales clerk said we had very small feet as she handed us some boxes. I sat and another clerk removed a pair of work boots from the box. I lifted my foot so he could put a boot on me.

"These are the smallest work boots made. We will have to improvise and tie the metatarsal guard to the boot using the shoelace. The metatarsal guard will help protect the top of your foot. Those bones are easy to damage if something rolls or falls on them," he said.

"I'd know your voice anywhere. You're Santa Claus," I said. "You're the Santa Claus from the Steelworkers Hall. I went there as a child and you are on TV at five o'clock every day close to Christmas."

"Ho! Ho! Ho! So I am." He tied the guards onto the boot, but they were too big and flopped around when I walked.

The cab driver dropped us off where he had picked us up and we had to find our way back to the training room, going through all the different departments. We were both so scared we hung onto each other's arms. A man came up to us and said he would take us through.

We were in safety talks for the next couple of days. They told us horror stories of a man getting his foot cut off when a train ran over it, and a man whose long hair got caught in a machine, tearing off his scalp and part of his brain.

The next day Carmen quit. I was on my own.

Chapter 13

Working for the French Diefenbaker 1974

A man named Gerry drove men to work. He lived in our area and charged by the week. He would pick me up at 6:30 a.m. I felt proud that I had organized a ride despite having no driver's license, no car, no Carmen.

Lloyd was not happy I would be travelling with a man I didn't know.

There was a terrible smell in this man's car, kind of like garlic. Gerry said he worked in the silver building. This is where Inco produces all its precious metals. Everyone who worked there smelled like this. It got into your pores. It took his wife a few years to get used to it and he wasn't sure she really did. I wrinkled my nose, thinking that I didn't want to work in the silver building.

I watched out the window as we passed the blackened hills, the Superstack bellowing out its tons of sulphur into the air. The next thirty years were going to be trying.

I climbed the stairs to the women's dry—the shower and changeroom—just above the foreman's office. I remembered a friend asking me if the women had their own showers. I told her no, we had to shower with the men, but we'd wear paper bags over our heads so the men wouldn't recognize us. What a stupid thing to ask.

Two other women were already changed. Sue, the woman I met the first day waiting in line at the Inco employment office, and a little French woman, whose name I don't remember. She quit only a few weeks in—she was pregnant. We were to meet the boss at the bottom of the stairs.

A man wearing a very heavily starched white shirt stood at the bottom of the stairs. He ordered us to follow him; there were no introductions. We walked past high piles of copper wire bar, shaped like sausages, three hundred pounds each. Loud banging startled me as the bars came over a conveyor machine. Using large two-pronged forks, men flipped them upright. These men glared at us as we walked past. The next department dealt with the casting of the wire bar and other shapes. The roar of the furnaces was loud. Fire seemed to be everywhere. We kept following the man in the starched white shirt. We passed small train lines called narrow gauge tracks. A small engine sat idling. It was like a miniature freight train hump yard. We stopped at a large wooden door, something you might see on a barn. It slid to the right—a stop bar on the other side was there to remind the person to look around before entering an area called the anode department because of the overhead cranes. Three of us were going to the anode department. The noise was intense: sirens, horns, roaring furnaces, blaring gas burners blowing. We just looked at each other, scared.

My work boots were heavy and the metatarsal guard kept flopping around on them. A tall, lanky man approached and told us we would be working out in the yard for a few days, cutting the grass. I was okay with that; it was a beautiful day.

Two silhouettes stood in a huge doorway. It was big enough for transport trucks filled with logs to drive into.

One of them, a large man, eyed us up and down, snorted his disapproval, and grunted something at the stiff-shirt guy that I couldn't hear over the noise.

"No talking. You will only talk when I say so." His French accent was very thick. His eyes were cold and indifferent, his face inches from mine, and I could see the deep wrinkles in his dark skin. His heavy jowls wiggled back and forth from his jerky motions.

He reminded me of a dark-skinned John Diefenbaker, the thirteenth prime minister of Canada, or a bulldog. I shook my head to get the images out.

We walked to a shack outside and he told us we would be mowing the lawn, pushing a mower sideways on a hill. As we worked, my feet began to get sweaty and they slid around in my boots. We were in front of the main office building, and every once in a while a face would appear in the windows and watch us.

Sue warned me to be careful what I said around this boss. He ruled with an iron fist and enjoyed making people feel uncomfortable.

One time, about three days in, we were having a break. I removed one boot, checked out the blister on the back of my ankle, and asked if anyone had a Band-Aid.

The boss shot me a dirty look. "No! You don't need any."

One of the employees spoke up, said I could get a few in the first aid room. "Shut up," the foreman scowled at the man. "Mind your own fucking business."

I couldn't believe it was okay for a boss to swear at the man.

"She has a right to go and get some Band-Aids," the man continued.

"Get back to work." He motioned the man out the door.

We didn't get paid for our lunch, so I thought I would go at lunchtime. The first aid attendant handed me a handful of Band-Aids and told me to use them until the boots broke in. I shoved them in my shirt pocket, and as I was leaving I came face to face with that bulldog boss. He was steaming. "What are you doing here?" he demanded as he swung open the door to the first aid room.

"I'm getting some Band-Aids for my blisters," I replied.

"I didn't give you permission!" he yelled.

"I'm on my lunch. I was told this is my time. I didn't know I needed your permission." I was scared.

The first aid attendant came over to the counter. "Did he refuse you first aid?" he asked with some implication in his voice.

"No, I didn't," the foreman grumbled. He grabbed my arm and led me out.

Wow, what have I got myself into? I thought. This was a world I never knew existed—power over people. When we got back to the shack I put the Band-Aids on.

"You're not much of a worker, crying about blisters on your feet. I've been here for twenty years and my boots aren't even worn," he grumbled.

I spoke before I thought. "No, but the seat of your pants is worn out." This was not a good move. His eyes narrowed with contempt, his face turned red with resentment. Quickly I apologized for my joke and said that it wouldn't happen again. One man held back his laughter, another chewed on his own lip, anticipating the boss's reaction. "Break is over," the foreman growled. "You two stay behind." He pointed to Sue and me. The men left.

"How would you girls like to come to my camp after work?" His voice was now softer, but cunning. My stomach turned.

"No thanks," I said swiftly. "I have to go home; my husband will be waiting for me." Sue said she would think about it. She stayed behind in the shack, undoing knots in a rope. I was out in the sun asphalting the road. No one showed us how to do anything. I stood behind a truck that was full of asphalt and smelled horrible. I pushed the shovel into the hot pile and it stuck. I tried to lift it; I tried to pull it. Nothing worked. When I finally freed my shovel from the stuff, not more than three inches were stuck on the end of it. The men were not impressed. After I watched them work from the bottom of the pile and applied their technique, it wasn't that much easier. At the end of the day the boss asked Sue if she was going. She told him she would some other time. The following week we three women were shipped to the anode.

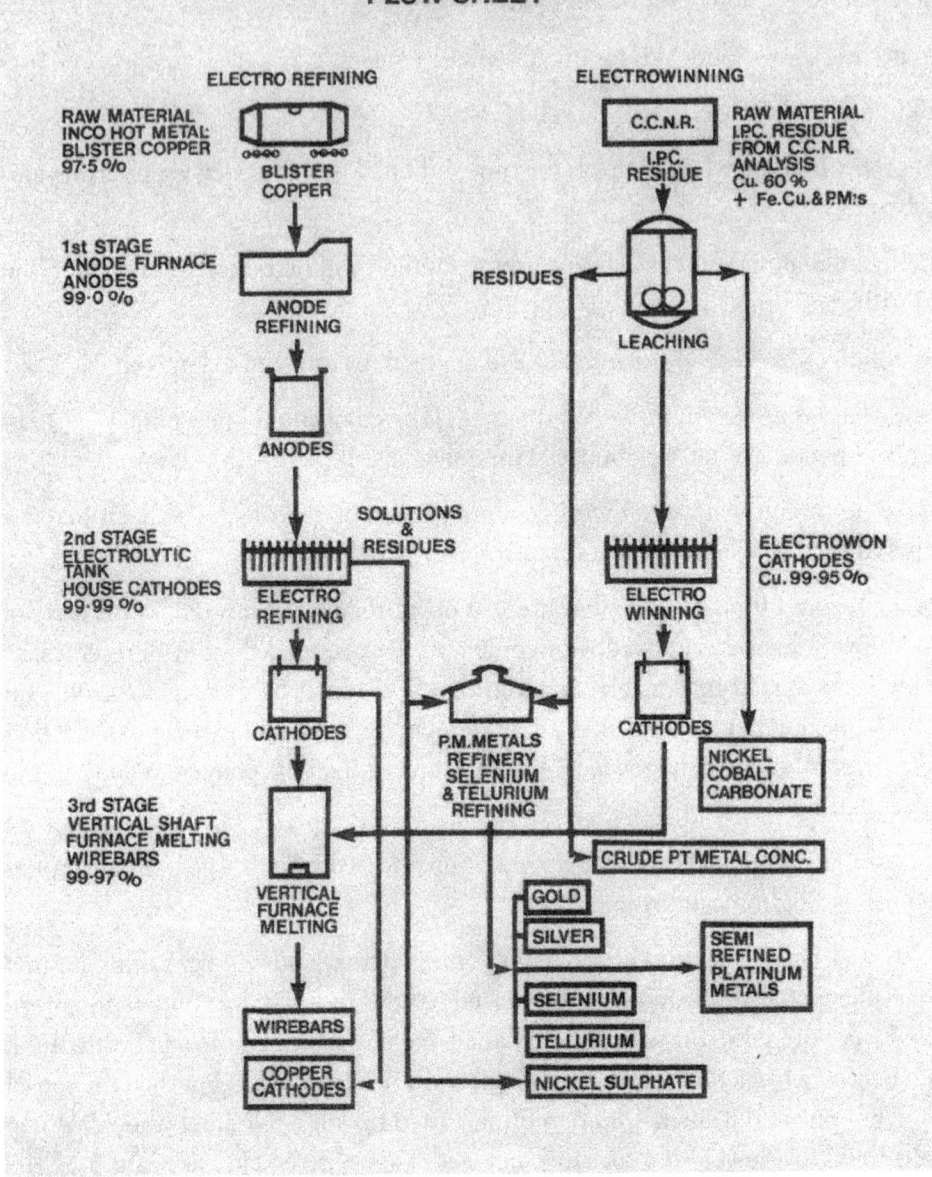

An explanation of the copper refinery process as described in an information pamphlet by Inco in 1980.

Chapter 14

The Anode Process

This was the anode department: three big furnaces, five carousel wheels, with twenty-two molds to make anodes that were five to six hundred pounds each. It was dirty and very noisy.

At first, all of us newbies were put on the broom. We swept, making a lot of dust, until an old man came and showed us the proper way to sweep dust. Who would have known there is a proper way to broom dust? Short jerky motions: less dust.

It was good to see Ray working in the anode. I'd known him since I was twelve, from the Donovan days at Victory playground. Sudbury was broken up into different neighbourhoods. Our family lived in between the Donovan and the Flour Mill neighbourhoods. Our school was in the Flour Mill and our church was in the Donovan. Ray lived in the Donovan and we were part of a bunch of kids that hung out at Victory playground, where we danced to a band that could play three or four songs.

He took us under his wing and told us about the anode.

"The first thing," Ray shouted over the noise, "is to charge or fill the furnaces. We will use cold charge and then hot metal or blister copper. Cold charge is just that: cold copper. We get it in cold skulls from the ladles." Ray knew we were oblivious to what he was talking about when we eyed each other with confused looks on our faces. He went on to tell us that skulls were the frozen copper that was left in the ladles, and he pointed to a large bowl-like container with a lip on it for pouring the molten copper. He said that any copper that ended up on the floor, in the pit, or in front of the furnace doors, or any anodes that are too big or to small, or any broken lugs were all charged back into the furnace. This was a language none of us knew.

A very large yellow machine that looked like an enormous forklift was suspended from the ceiling. He told us to step closer to the wall as he swung himself up into the charge crane with ease—very impressive. The charge crane jerked as he manoeuvred it to a skull of copper that sat on one of the train cars. He pushed the forks under it, picked it up, and moved it to an open door on the side of the furnace. He then drove the forks into the furnace and, using a hydraulic hoe-like blade, pushed the copper skull into the furnace, then backed out and over to the next skull that was sitting on the following car.

When there was enough cold charge, the rest of the furnace was filled with molten metal that came in a hot car (a torpedo) from the smelter; it's like lava or magma. This is poured into the furnace. There are two sizes of hot cars: one held 150 tons and the other thirty-five tons. Later that day, a hot car arrived. Blue gas and smoke spewed out of a big hole of the top of the white egg-like car. It hurt my throat. It was sulphur; I would know that taste anywhere. It covered the city when we were kids. It hurt and burned my throat and nose. Some days my mom would make us come in the house so we wouldn't breathe it in.

The furnace crew was not ready for the hot car yet, so a large arm swung into the hole and natural gas was blown into it to keep the molten metal from freezing. It wasn't long before the anode department was full of sulphur gas, and I found it hard to breathe.

After a while, the furnace crew was ready for the hot car. A crane man got into the crane above our heads and dangled a four-legged chain that hung from a large hook. The crane man blew his horn and brought the chains over to a gigantic spoon. The spoon was like a huge ladle that had small steel train wheels on the bottom of it and a large lip.

It was placed on short rail tracks in front of the side door of the furnace, the same door Ray had charged the copper skulls through. The hot car would be dumped into the spoon and the molten metal would pour out the lip into the furnace. There was so much gas I wondered if I would ever get used to it. Another man climbed into the train and hooked up the hot car. He then climbed onto the car, put on his face shield, and motioned to the furnace crew that he was ready to pour. The golden molten metal was beautiful as it poured out the top of the hot car and into the spoon. Sparks of molten metal flew out of the spoon, reminding me of fireworks. After the hot car was empty it was ready to be sent back to the smelter. With the chains, the crane man lifted the spoon at the back and emptied the copper that was still in the spoon, which was then hooked up and put back at the end of the anode. It took about fifteen to twenty hours for this process to be ready to cast. During this time the heat in the furnace built up and the solid material inside transformed into molten bath at about 2100 to 2200 degrees Fahrenheit.

We followed Ray into a room that looked like a cow stable with two divided areas. One held concrete mixed with sand and the other was wet Magna-Crete (this cured faster than concrete, and unlike concrete it bonded to new and old concrete as well as most construction materials, including wood and steel.) He filled a wheelbarrow with thick paste cement, pushed it out the door and up a small ramp, and stopped on the rail tracks where the hot car had been, in front of the side door of the furnace. Each one of us took a turn throwing a large handful of the sticky, pasty cement at the six-inch open space all around the door. It was like caulking or sealing. It must have been six feet away from us. This was a strange way of doing things. Ray grabbed a handful of cement, threw it, and it stuck; it was obvious he had done this many times. He grabbed another handful of cement and let it fly. On the third try, mine stuck. Most of ours landed on the floor in a big blob. Ray told us that after we were finished we could have used rubber gloves, as our leather ones were now ruined. I ran my gloves under the water tap, trying to get the pasty cement off before it dried. We had to buy our own gloves.

After all the copper was melted in the furnace, it was ready to skim. All the foreign substances that were in the copper would rise to the surface of the molten bath, like slag or loose bricks from the inside of the furnace or the hot car. Then it would be skimmed by the furnace crew using a long hoe-like instrument to drag out the chunks. They worked from a window at the end of the furnace called a skim bay, filling up eight or ten square pots and letting them cool. The frozen skulls would be smashed into pieces in a place called the pig storage. At a later date the copper would be charged back into the furnace. Copper was not wasted; it held precious metals like gold, platinum, selenium, tellurium, and nickel sulphate. All extra money for Inco.

Chapter 15

Poling Stage

A load of poles coming in on a truck.

    The next part was the most violent stage of the refining cycle, called the poling phase. Ray pointed to a pile of large green logs; he said they were usually maple. The average logs (poles) were twenty-two inches wide and forty-two feet long. The furnace crew inserted a pole into the bath through the skim bay window to two thirds of its length and the rest of the log was hung from a support chain or lever. The end of the pole was submerged into the molten metal bath. The purpose was to detoxify the molten metal by taking the oxygen out of it; this process released a tremendous amount of energy. Ray handed me a pair of dark glasses so I could peer into the furnace. It was exciting to see the molten bath bubble and splash. The furnace was filled with smoke and fire—it gave off a tremendous amount of heat. I can't explain how I felt, but it raised an emotional attachment to the molten copper, which we called blister copper.

I handed him back his dark glasses and told him it looked like hell in there. We sat on the tracks and waited for the pole to burn. He said this was the most dangerous part of the process. If there happened to be a pocket of snow or water within the pole there could be a violent explosion, which might damage the wall or the roof of the furnace or injure one of the furnace crew.

Copper did spill out through the skimming bay window at times and workers would get burned. He raised the sleeve of his shirt, displaying burn marks on his arm. He shook it off as part of the job. He told us it took about six to eight hours of poling, and they could use up to eight to fifteen poles to get the copper just right for casting. Samples brick (ingots) of copper would be taken out so the head furnace man could tell when the copper was ready. Once the copper was ready to cast, it sat still and quiet like a hot yellow lake.

The newbies followed Ray to the other side of the furnace opposite the charge door. The next stage was the casting cycle. This was where we were going to be working.

The copper came out of the furnaces from a vertical slit known as the tap hole. The blister copper flowed into a small pool and down a short streamway we called a launder. It looked like a trough for molten metal in the shape of a V. Two large carousel wheels turned at the same time. Two ladles resembling huge buckets sat on the floor below each launder. Each one had a lip so the molten metal could be poured into the molds. Natural gas burners blew into the ladles and along the launder so the copper would not freeze.

I watched as the copper flowed down the launder into the ladle and then into flat rectangular molds; the molds were made of copper too. Twenty-two molds were held on a large rotating carousel. Each one had an indentation eight inches thick, forty-two inches wide, and forty-eight inches long. The mold had two little arms called lugs to hang them by. The carousel weighed two hundred and twenty tons. It ran by a steel cable that was five hundred feet long and all one piece, the same as the steering mechanism used in big ships.

Water was poured onto the copper and under the molds to cool everything down. We can put water on top of molten metal, but we can't put molten metal onto water, or it will violently explode.

A man picked up the 500- to 600-pound anode with a manual air hoist. He placed it in a tank of water and the wheel turned, another anode lined up and was popped up by a hydraulic pin under the mold, and he picked it up. As the wheel turned, another man who was sitting on a steel chair on top of a stand stuck a small mop into a bucket of paint and spread some on half the mold, making sure the part the molten metal hit first had a lot of paint, then painted the rest with an air gun. This was so the anode wouldn't stick to the mold. I curled my lip as I saw the paint vapour rise as the paint hit the hot molds, and the paint man breathed it in.

A man came up to the newbies; we were still beside the tap hole. He wore asbestos coveralls and coat, heavy mittens, and a face shield at all times. He was a tapper, the one who controlled the flow of copper from the furnace to the ladles. He asked us to step back as he pointed to a six-inch opening. It was about twelve inches thick during the poling stage, and it remained sealed with putty-like cement. In order to drain the furnace, the tapper removed part of the cement plug at the top of the slit, allowing the copper to flow into the launder and the ladles. As the level of the bath drained down, the tapper chipped away at the tap hole. He controlled as much of the cement seal as was necessary to maintain the desired flow—it was like he was standing next to a narrow dam. I couldn't believe that this little dam was holding back three hundred ton of molten metal. If too much cement had been chipped away, or something down on the casting floor caused a slowdown, the tapper had a handful of cement ready to plug the runout and push it in with his bar.

Down on the casting floor was a high stand, higher than the casting crew. It was erected between the two water tanks that held the anodes for cooling. Two wheel *men* sat in their chairs and were in contact with the tapper at all times by hand motions or an alarm.

I watched as they moved a lever and the wheel turned. They moved another small lever and the ladle tilted to fill the molds. Hand signals were used to communicate. If a mold was cold or wet the wheel man would set off an alarm to warn everyone there would be an explosion, which was common.

We were told a story about a tapper who lost control of the flow of copper when the bottom of the tap hole failed. A red spot appeared, called a hot spot. Two hundred tons of molten copper flowed like Niagara Falls out over the launder and onto the floor. The tapper fought hard to get it to stop but it was out of his hands. The wheel man laid hard on the alarm button. It was every man for himself, and they ran as fast as they could to get to a safer area. The whole area filled with smoke. So many explosions—some men had burns, but most were very lucky. The tapper finally got it under control, but what a mess after the copper cooled—it had solidified onto everything: cables under the wheel, all the hydraulics, etc. I hoped I never would see this.

Ray poling the furnace.

Chapter 16

My Accident on August 9: Meeting the Union and the Company 1974

Why was money coming off my check? It read "union dues." Was this a savings account at the credit union, like I had when I was a child? No. I was to be enlightened.

Graveyard shift, 11:30 p.m. to 7:30 a.m.; we were casting. I was glad to be out of the daytime heat. I had been feeling rather sick and the boss gave me some salt pills that made me feel sicker.

I was on the hoist with the anode lined up in front of me. Part of its lug wasn't formed right. I stared at it, unsure what to do. The wheel man motioned for me to pick it up. The five-hundred-plus-pound slab of copper was almost in the tank when the lug broke. The manual air hoist handle flew up and hit me in my abdomen. The anode fell and an alarm went off, telling the tapper to minimize the flow. I went flying backwards off the stand and down three feet onto the floor. It hurt and I didn't want anyone to see me cry, so I ran away and hid among the trains. A fellow employee found me and took me to the first aid room. From there I was transferred to the hospital. After blood work, the doctor came back to tell me I was pregnant and they could not take X-rays. But from the bruising the doctor said there could be some damage.

Now my eyes were about to be opened. I was introduced to a whole new world of the union and company politics. I was told to go down to the union hall. My dad drove me and said he would wait. When I arrived at the Frood Road office of the Steelworkers union, a man in a suit ushered me into a room where a bunch of men in suits were sitting. They gave me cold glares. I was told to sit in a certain chair. They began to talk about me as if I wasn't there, something about keeping my pregnancy quiet. They didn't want to make a precedent over this incident. They talked and talked, and my eyes wandered around the room at the books on the wooden shelves with gold writing on their spines. I was told to go home and not to tell anyone I was pregnant. Then I would have X-rays after the baby was born.

I didn't know what the big deal was; I was married. I was put on something called "compensation." And someone paid me while I was off.

It was a hard pregnancy: heartburn and many attacks. The relationship with my husband was terrible. He was very verbally abusive, adding on top of the name-calling that the baby wasn't his. I never could understand why he was so mean.

We had moved to Copper Cliff, renting a house not far from the smelter. The view from our living room window was the base of the Superstack. It was enormous. On the other side of the house was a building called the oxygen plant.

I needed to get my driver's license. Lloyd said he would teach me, but that wasn't a good idea. I signed up for driver's education, passing with high marks on November 11, 1974, and won a free helicopter ride.

It was the most exciting thing I had ever done. We flew over the Donovan, Flour Mill, the town hospital, and Ramsey Lake. Then came the best part: we flew to Copper Cliff. The land was so barren: no trees, lots of blackened rock, pools of water with strange colours of orange and red that was more like slime. This was called the tailings, where Inco dumped all kinds of toxic waste left over from its production. We flew very close to the opening of the Superstack; I was captivated by its enormous size, its power. I was spellbound by it; it felt personal, like the stack and I had a connection. It was a strange feeling. The helicopter turned and we headed back.

When we landed, the Sudbury Star newspaper was there. They took my picture as the winner of the ride and I was on the front page. What a great experience.

My happiness was short-lived. My Granny Katie Kennedy died on November 22, 1974. I held her hand and told her if I had a girl I would name her Melanie Catherine, because I was named after her.

Chapter 17

Having Melanie 1975

Cathy and daughter Melanie

This was a tough pregnancy. I was sure some of the impact from the hoist could have had a contributing factor. Along with that came heartburn and a lot of acid reflux. Sometimes when I sneezed, yellow bile came up from my stomach. I would sit in the bathroom, making myself throw up to ease the burning sensation in my stomach. Lying down was impossible, so I would prop up pillows all around me.

On March 8, 1975, I began to have some spotting. I hoped the baby would be born on that date: International Women's Day and International Women's Year. The contractions were not as bad as the damn heartburn.

Lloyd and I watched the first two periods of the hockey game, then I was brought into another room. Lloyd stayed to watch the last period. The doctor informed me he was going to break my water to speed things along. He inserted a long fishing-rod type of instrument. There was a quick reaction and I felt a horrible pain shooting through my back. Then came a gushing flow of water and the doctor jumped back, but not in time: the water splashed his arms. Luckily, he was wearing gloves and scrubs. He said he would return in the morning; the baby wouldn't be here for a while.

The contractions were very heavy, like someone had kicked me in the privates. The baby was coming. The nurse said it wouldn't be for a while, and I told her the baby was coming now. "Call the doctor back!" I protested.

"Lay down." The nurse pushed me to the pillow. "You have to relax."

"Just check me out!" I yelled. She did, and the baby was coming. At 1:45 a.m., Melanie Catherine was born. Dark-skinned with fine black hair on her back—she was so cute. *What beautiful skin*, I thought.

The next morning a nurse told me the baby had too much mucus on her lungs, so she would stay in the nursery room until later on that day.

"Do you have a mirror?" I asked the nurse.

I held it so I could see my privates. It revealed a huge bruise on my vagina; it had to be three or four inches around.

"Oh, a nasty one. The baby hit your wall," the nurse said.

"Can I have an ice pack or a bag of ice?" I asked.

She came back with the ice and some pills. "This is for your pain." She handed me the pills and poured a glass of water from a plastic container. The pills were called 692 painkillers; she gave me two.

This was when I found out painkillers and I don't like each other. When Lloyd came in to visit, I had no idea who he was. The pills made everything out of sorts. He had shaved off his beard, so I didn't recognize him. You would think I would have recognized him after he told me I was being stupid.

The nurse came in with two more 692s, and I took them. That did it—I was hallucinating; the paint was peeling down off the walls. I felt I couldn't breathe well. They brought my baby in wrapped in a towel. I unwrapped her and took a look; the peach-fuzz black hair that was on her face and body was magnified. I screamed—she looked like a monkey baby from the *Planet of the Apes*. Paranoia set in—someone had exchanged my baby for a baby monkey!

"Nurse! Nurse!" I yelled. "Come in here quick!"

A young nurse came running into the room. "What is it?"

"Look at what's in there; look at that ugly thing! Where is my baby?" The nurse went over and opened the blanket.

"This is your baby," she said, puzzled.

"No, it's not; get it out of here, now." She picked up the baby and left. A few minutes later the head nurse came in. I was still standing; I hadn't moved. "What seems to be the matter?" she asked.

"Where is my baby?" Terror filled me.

She asked me to calm down, but how could I?

When they looked at my chart, they saw I was supposed to be given 292s, not 692s, and the best thing for me was to sleep it off. No wonder I felt like that. They closed the curtain around my bed and put up a sign that read: "Do not disturb."

When I got up to use the washroom, I fainted. What a horrible feeling that was. I slept until the next day and returned to normal, apologizing for my outburst. No one apologized for giving me the wrong medication.

I got a roommate; her baby was born in the doctor's office in Chelmsford. She didn't even have time to take off her boots. He was born right on the doctor's desk. The baby was born with a clubfoot; they fixed it and put on a very tiny cast. The mother was very religious, so I thought I would have some fun with her and told her that the baby was the mailman's. She gave me a very shocked and judgemental look. I began to laugh. "Don't go praying for me; my husband is a mailman."

Chapter 18

Rebuilding a Furnace
1976

I returned to work six weeks after the baby was born. The bosses and men were mad that I was off work having a baby. One man said he saw my picture in the newspaper and told me I should have been at home and not taking a helicopter ride. Some said they expected me to get pregnant every year so I would be off. Little did they know there was no maternity leave.

Sweat trickled down between my shoulder blades. It was a sweltering day in the anode department. The foreman came into the lunchroom and announced that we would be rebuilding the number-two furnace that summer. He barked out a few more orders and left.

The furnaces in the Copper Cliff Copper Refinery held their own mysteries. It's difficult to fully understand or explain to the outside world. People who work around furnaces know exactly what I'm talking about. There's a connection between the worker and the furnaces, a mystical partnership that is beyond human understanding. We learn to understand what the furnace is saying. Its actions reflect the way things are or the way it is feeling. It roars and bellows a certain way when running right but cries and howls when something is wrong. There may be a feeling in the air, a different smell or sound, or it grumbles from deep down inside when it has a complaint. Call it intuition, call it a sixth sense, there is something one acquires after being around them for a certain amount of time.

"What do we have to do to rebuild a furnace?" I asked an older man who sat beside me at the dirty lunchroom table. He was a bit odd, and gave me the willies. He looked up from his newspaper. A chill went up and down my sweaty back at what he said, his voice low and rough.

"We Christians have known this for the last 2000 years. It's a fact that hell bubbles and brews right under our feet. If you don't believe it, read the Bible." He pulled a small black book from inside the newspaper. He was reading his bible hidden by the paper.

"God told us in Revelation, chapter fourteen." He shook the Bible in front of my face with his gnarled fingers, probably damaged with rheumatoid arthritis from years of working in the anode. The book was well worn and had many dog-eared pages marking all the ones he liked to read. His voice rose as he continued his sermon. "God is going to torment the people with fire and brimstone. Do you know what brimstone is?" His leathery complexion was inches from my face. My eyes widened with fear as I shook my head. He stood, hovering above me. "It's sulphur," he whispered, putting a firm emphasis on the s's like a snake sound. "Ssssulphur comes from the centre of the earth. It's Satan's calling card." My arms blossomed with goosebumps. I was brought up Catholic; I know all about Satan. He stared in my eyes waiting for a response. I didn't give him one.

"You've smelled sulphur," he muttered. "You've been here for over a year now. The sulphur is in the brick." His eyes narrowed. "That's what we will be taking out of the furnace. It comes in with the molten metal, taken from the belly of the earth. The demons merge into the ore before it comes to surface so they can escape their never-ending torture in hell. Millions of demons will escape. You will feel them when you remove the brick." he sat back down, put his bible back inside the newspaper, and continued reading.

My heart thundered in my chest. "Okay, ahh, that's a very interesting story, never heard that one before, time for a coffee." I got up, grabbed my lunch pail, and joined the men on the other side of the lunchroom.

One of the men who was listening told me not to worry about the old man, as he was always going on about God and devils. He handed me a chocolate bar, telling me this would make things better. *Chocolate always makes things better*, I thought. I smiled, said thanks, and took the chocolate bar. Little did I know this was his devil's calling card.

The foreman entered the lunchroom and gave us our orders. "Two minutes in and two minutes out. Everyone grab their safety equipment and head to the furnace." The doors of the furnace had been removed and it looked unusually bare and quiet, no roar. The foreman handed me a chipper gun and ordered me into the furnace. I took a look inside and could see that the bricks were still red hot.

"You want us to go in there? This can't be safe. Why can't we wait until the furnace cools down?" I asked.

He said that this is the way it was done, that cooling down was time-consuming, and time was money. He pointed for me to get in there. Each type of air-power tool requires knowledge of specific operating instructions. Inco's instructions were: here's the chipper gun, this lever activates the air and this one cause the ten-inch chisel bit at the end of the gun to move like a drill. Go to it. That was the training.

The foreman ushered us up the eight-inch-wide plank. It was laid from the tracks to the opening where the doors used to be. He told us to be careful, that he didn't want any injuries. This was one of the most bizarre things I had ever done. I walked up slowly and Marc, the man who gave me the chocolate bar, took the chipper gun from me, freeing my arms to balance myself. Another plank was on the inside of the furnace so we could go down into its belly. I could see the end of the plank smoldering because it was touching the hot floor. Some guys had made wooden shoes that were tied to their boots. They too were smoldering. The old gnarly-fingered man's voice played in my head: "Ssssulphur: the Devil's calling card."

"Hot" did not describe that heat. I felt dizzy, scared; I thought I might faint. I began to panic. I scrambled back up the plank ramp and down the other side, out of the furnace. I needed to catch my breath; my heart was beating so loudly I could hardly hear the foreman yelling at me. I stared at him wide-eyed. His lips were moving but I couldn't understand what he was saying. I felt a hand on my shoulder; it was Marc, and my head began to clear as he told the foreman to give me a minute. The foreman shook his head and grumbled about why I was even there. I walked away from the furnace with Marc and he told me to take a few big breaths. He comforted me, and I was grateful when he said, "It's only two minutes. Do whatever you can in two minutes; just stay in there." The foreman's arms were crossed over his chest and he had a scowl on his face as I walked back up the plank and into the furnace. I think he would have liked to have sent me home.

"Two minutes," Marc said, handing me the chipper gun. I began chipping away at the hot brick. I could smell the rubber in my boots burning. *Two minutes*, I repeat to myself, *two minutes*. This went on all shift. I didn't do very well at this job. Coffee break—time for a cigarette. I pulled my pack out of the inside of my hardhat. That's the best place to keep cigarettes; they don't get all dry from the heat and they don't fall out. It's okay to have a Bic lighter at work but I always worried that with all that heat and molten metal it might explode.

I once saw a man who carried matches in his shirt pocket. A spark of copper landed in it, igniting the matches. We watched as he hit his chest trying to put out the flame. I'm not sure what was safest.

I placed my coffee thermos back in my lunch pail and noticed a small yellow sticky note with a smiley face drawn on it. I turned it over: no name. I placed it back in my lunch pail and headed to the parking lot. I just couldn't wait to get home. Two days off, wishing I could sleep for those two days. My husband wanted me to hurry with supper because he had a ball tournament starting that night. I put supper on and cleaned out my lunch pail, finding the yellow smiley-face sticker. I tore it up into little pieces and threw it in the garbage. If Lloyd saw it, he would have asked who had given it to me; I didn't know, and he wouldn't have believed me.

On Monday, I felt miserable having to go back to work on the furnace repairs. I was sore all over my body.

This day we were cleaning and repairing the dory—the top part of the furnace where the black ashes collected. Men were already there chipping away inside.

I climbed the ladder that led to the top floor, catching the too-big metatarsal guards on the rungs of the latter, which caused me to stop to shake my feet free every time it happened. Everything up on the top was covered in a blanket of black soot, a powdered form of carbon, produced when the furnace was running. Respirators were provided to protect us from inhaling harmful dust. Marc showed me how to put it on. I felt a little claustrophobic and began to breathe very fast. He told me to calm down and breathe normally. Then he handed me the chipper gun. I entered the dory, which was about the size of a garage, and began to chip away at the wall. Each person took a turn. Black soot rose and blew all over; I could hear the men yelling. I turned and saw one of them frantically pointing at the floor. The hose for the compressed air gun was swelling like a balloon, and then it burst. The hose broke in half, the chipper gun went dead, and the other end of the hose twisted and curled, blowing high-pressured air all over, black soot sailing high into the air. Marc ran to shut off the valve. The hose lay still like a dead snake. I fumbled out of the dory to see everyone covered in black soot. We walked away so we could remove our masks. We looked so funny: white teeth and the whites of our eyes stood out against the black soot on our faces. We looked like coal miners from Nova Scotia.

The men in the lunchroom had a good laugh when we entered. I smiled; Marc commented that he didn't see me smile much, and that's why he had put the little yellow smiley face in my lunch pail.

"You put ..." I began to say, and he covered his lips with a finger to shush me. I stayed quiet.

I took a long shower to get all the soot off. I laughed at the hose breaking; it was funny.

"You wouldn't believe what happened today." I told Lloyd the story; he didn't laugh. "I guess you had to be there."

The furnace was almost finished; now came the hanging bricks: carbon refractor hanging bricks, two in one encased by a metal sheet, and a rebar hook coming from the middle of them. These bricks can withstand high temperatures, sudden changes of temperatures, and the action of molten metal. They were so heavy I could only carry one at a time up the plank. One man yelled at me, wanting me to do more. I didn't care. The floor of the furnace had been laid down with silica bricks with silica sand in between them. I was so glad when this job was finished. I might not have done as much as the next guy, but I gave it all I had. I felt proud that I had helped rebuild a furnace.

Some days I stopped at Lola's Restaurant for breakfast. It was in Copper Cliff town. Lots of men stopped there, most of them Inco workers. Lola's was a dirty greasy spoon restaurant that served great food, if you could keep the flies away. It had a long blue counter with vinyl-covered stools, the kind you would see in the 1950s.

Gail, the waitress, made the place. A large, loud, red-headed woman who loved the Sudbury Wolves hockey team. She had a one-of-a-kind personality. Her favourite saying was: "Just eat it, sucker, and stop complaining." I loved watching her interact with the men.

Chapter 19

My Gallbladder

Melanie's first Christmas: I was happy because the kids made me happy, but my marriage was horrible. Nothing I did was right. I felt he resented me for being married to him. Between the name-calling and insults, I felt hurt. I got it at home and again at work. This is when my health began to deteriorate. More attacks from my gallbladder. After making onion rings one night, I got the worst attack ever and ended up calling an ambulance while my husband slept on the couch. The doctor said I had to get my gallbladder operated on, as there was a large stone.

I told my foreman I was on the list to get a gallbladder operation. I would be off work for at least six weeks. His mouth quivered in annoyance, making a smacking noise. He shook his head back and forth, repulsed at what I had just told him. With that curled finger he told me to follow him to the superintendent's office. Like a little sheep, I followed. A man sat behind a desk; his looks gave me the willies. His face was white as milk, his eyes were blue but had pink around them. He was balding with white hair making a half circle on his head. He had large pink puffy lips that looked wet. He made my lip curl and sent a shiver up my spine.

"Not more women problems!" he shouted. His words made his lips wetter and I shuddered. I gave my head a shake so he wouldn't see me staring at them.

"Excuse me, men have gallbladders too," I said.

"I don't like your attitude," he growled and stood up.

"Well, I don't like yours, either." My words came out rudely, covering the panic that was brewing in my gut. This irritated him even more; I softened my tone as I tried to explain that all humans have gallbladders. In a businessman's voice, he told me to leave his office. I followed the foreman back to the anode, wondering what the fuck was wrong with everyone.

My operation was scheduled for April, on a Monday, the same day Lloyd was leaving for Toronto on a course for six months, but he would be home on the weekends. I asked him to ask his boss if he could go on Tuesday so he could be with me the day of the operation. He said he couldn't, because the post office was doing him a favour. I guess he forgot how I was at the hospital every day while pregnant to see him when he had his gallbladder out.

Chapter 20

The Rifle

On the Friday afternoon shift before the operation, the men were joking around and singing the song "The First Cut is the Deepest"; it was funny. Marc asked if I could join a bunch of them for a drink after work. This was the first time I was asked to go with them, and I felt very excited, even though I was not a drinker. I called home—Lloyd was out, and I told the sitter to tell him I would be home late as I was going out with the guys for a beer. A dozen of us or so sat around a table at the hotel and a drink was put in front of me called a Slow Comfortable Screw Against the Wall. We all laughed at the name. Southern Comfort, vodka, orange juice in a Harvey Wallbanger.

After I drank it, I became very ill. Marc walked me to my car, and on the way I had to vomit. I leaned against a truck and threw up. Again and then again. I started laughing when I saw that I had vomited right beside a flat tire on the truck. I felt better and drove home. It was about one in the morning.

My stomach knotted as I entered the quiet house. I was going to be in so much trouble. I tiptoed into the living room and headed for the bedroom.

"Where the fuck have you been?" His voice was deep and husky coming from the darkness, dripping with spite. Lloyd was sitting in the dark in the corner of the living room.

"Out with the guys." I swallowed hard. "They invited me out before my operation." I could make out his silhouette sitting in the chair, the light from the streetlamp barely squeezing through the slit in the curtains. I could see he was wearing his rusty-orange terrycloth housecoat. I froze when I made out the .30-06 rifle sitting on his lap. My heart pounded hard in my chest; I thought I might be seeing things. I reached over and turned on the lamp, asking him why he was sitting in the dark. No mistake: he had a rifle sitting across his lap. This rifle was designed to take down a moose weighing 800 to 1500 pounds. I was 117 pounds.

I remember him bragging to a friend about his new toy, that this rifle can produce greater penetration and less bone and tissue damage.

"What are you doing?" I said, my voice raw, my body trembling.

"I'm going to shoot you," he said matter-of-factly, but with some hesitation. But he hadn't yet, so that was a plus.

"Why?" My voice was strained; my eyes were fixed on the rifle. He said a woman had called and said I was with her husband. I told him I was with twelve men and asked which one he was referring to.

He told me the name: it was Marc's wife. I looked up the number in the telephone book and cradled the receiver in between my ear and shoulder. My hand shook as I put my pointing finger into the rotary dial. I hoped to get some help with the predicament with my crazy husband and his rifle. She was no help; she said her husband talked about me all the time; she thought I was sick in the head for working with guys. I interrupted her to tell her about the rifle, but Lloyd's hand came down on the cradle and the phone hung up. We yelled at each other. I went to leave, and he tore the back pocket off my jeans to get my keys and headed out the door.

To my great relief, he was gone. Great, because I wouldn't want to leave the kids with this maniac.

I didn't know what to do. Should I tell my mom and dad? Should I call the police? If I did, would he shoot me? Would he shoot the kids?

I decided I wouldn't tell anyone.

On Monday I went to the hospital alone. I felt lonesome and abandoned as I watched the needle go into my arm. The nurse told me this would calm me down. Thoughts of the rifle were still fresh in my mind. She wheeled my gurney just outside the operating room. The nurses were at a meeting when I felt the drugs kick in. Instead of it slowing me down, I became enraged. I jumped off the gurney and began to kick the wall, then a garbage can, swearing like a sailor about how much I hated my life. They calmed me down and got the operation done. When I came to I was still swearing. What was happening to me?

One of the younger men from my shift came to visit me in the hospital. He was the same age as me, without as much mileage. He asked if I had gotten in trouble for going out with them the other night. I lied and said it was okay. I thanked him for coming to see me but told him not to come back.

A 30-06 rifle like the one Lloyd threatened me with.

Chapter 21

The Hot Car

The boss entered the lunchroom and yelled out, "Hot car! Cathy, you want to learn how to dump a hot car? You'll be working with Marc." A feeling of excitement soared through my body; I jumped to my feet and followed Marc out the door. A hot car, or "torpedo car," sat at the end of the railroad track. It was full of molten copper. Blue smoke, full of sulphur dioxide, bellowed from the hole in its top, filling the charge aisle. The hot cars were built in Sorel, Quebec. When they arrived in Copper Cliff, they were nothing more than a metal shell. Inco's masons made the refractor brick that lined the inside of the hot car. Molten copper has to be really hot to stay in that form and it would melt the steel egg without that special brick.

The hot car was filled at the smelter, poured from the converters into a ladle and then poured into the hot car. A converter was a horizontal cylinder of steel, thirty-five feet long and thirteen feet in diameter, protected by Magnafrit bricks to withstand the heat of the molten metal. The molten metal produced by the nickel reverberatory furnace in the smelter comes from crushed and concentrated ore. Copper, nickel, and iron sulphate make up the molten metal. The nickel and the copper are recovered, and the iron sulphate is regarded as an impurity; it is the job of the converter to remove it. By removing the impurities, the copper-nickel content of the matte goes from 20 percent to

75 percent before it goes to the next stage of the smelting process. The next cycle takes about thirty-six hours, and then it is transferred to the next department of the smelter for the separation of the copper and nickel sulphide. The furnace matte is blown to blister copper, which is casted into ladles, poured into hot cars, and transported to the copper refinery. Typically, a *matte* is the phase in which the principal metal being extracted is recovered prior to a final reduction process (usually *converting*) to produce a crude metal. Mattes may also be used to collect impurities from a metal phase.

The hot car was one hundred and fifty tons. It travelled on a train track that went over the highway—now that's a scary thought. Each furnace had the capacity to hold 350 to 400 tons, depending on how much brick had fallen off the walls or roof inside the furnace, and how much cold charge was in there.

My hard hat was heavier than usual because I had mounted earmuffs on it, and it got even heavier when I attached the shield to protect me from splashing molten metal and the bright rays given off by the magma.

My throat burned as the sulphur made its way through the charge aisle. The spoon was in place by the door of the furnace—that's what I would be pouring the molten metal into. Marc showed me how to unhook the hot car from the regular train and hook it up to our engine. I then drove it down the track. I jumped down from the train and headed for the ladder on the side of the hot car. Getting up on the hot car was not going to be easy. I'm five-foot-one-and-a-half inches, and weighed 117 lbs. The first rung of the ladder was higher than my shoulders. I thought that if I could just get one foot up there, I could swing the other one up. I grabbed hold of the second rung and tried to swing. It was a failed attempt and I laughed. I swung my leg up again and it reached, but how was I going to lift myself up? Then I felt someone push my butt and give me a shove up. I climbed to the top of the train and turned around. It was Marc, and he saluted me. I felt a wrench, an alarm in my gut. I ignored it and climbed up to pour my first hot car.

Ray, the head furnace man, placed a wedge on the wheels of the hot car so it wouldn't roll. I could feel robust power surge through my body when I grabbed the lever to dump the car. The hot car had a commanding presence deserving respect. I admired its danger.

Ray gave me the okay to start pouring. Slowly I moved the handle and the big egg began to rotate on its axis. Copper magma flowed out of the large hole from its top and into the spoon. The heat that radiated from the pour was exhilarating. The spoon, pushed by a hydraulic pin, allowed the copper to transfer into the furnace.

Once the car was empty or the furnace was full, I heard the horn blow and I put the torpedo egg back to its upright position, drove it back down the track, and hooked it back up to the other train that was waiting to bring it back to the smelter. I removed the spoon and put it back in its place. A proud grin was planted on my face when I entered the lunchroom.

I poured a cup of coffee, walked over to Marc, and told him never to touch my butt again. He apologized and that was that ... so I thought.

Later, Marc and I threw the clay around the furnace door. I was getting pretty good at it. The other part of the job was making sure the furnace stayed at a constant temperature, so I followed Marc up the ladder to the top floor above the furnace, and yes, I got my metatarsal guard caught in the rungs of the ladder again. It was so hot and dusty up top. Marc showed me the valves, gauges, and labels, and told me what each one was for. Water ran through pipes to keep everything at a good temperature. The problem was that most of the labels were unreadable. Marc hit the gauges and the needles spun around, but some didn't even register. I found this disturbing.

One day when I was up there, a hot car came in. The sulphur was so heavy I couldn't breathe. We all knew how dangerous sulphur was. I brought it up to the boss and asked if we could get an alarm installed, so that when anyone was up there and a hot car came in, the alarm would go off to let them know they should vacate the area. He shrugged it off.

Chapter 22

My First Car 1976

After the rifle incident and his not staying with me during my gallbladder operation, I didn't have much love left in me for Lloyd. I was frightened and afraid he might kill me. I had heard of a husband shooting his wife, his kids, and then himself. Most of the time I was in a daze, going through the motions of day-to-day living. Deep down, I was angry that he had pulled a gun on me. I resented him for not being with me during the operation. It was against my principles to hate, but I was really close. He acted like it was nothing, because he said the gun wasn't loaded.

We had an unexpected visit from our landlady. She informed us Inco wanted the land back that her house was on, so we had to move. I didn't want to buy a house; I wanted out of this marriage. Buying a house meant I would be trapped tighter than I already was.

Lloyd's mother lent us five thousand dollars for a down payment on a house in Minnow Lake: his part of town. Lloyd was still going to Toronto and would look for a car for me. He called and I took the bus down. It was a beautiful 1970 Oldsmobile Cutlass with a black vinyl top and yellow body. 350 cubic inch, four-barrel carburetor. My first car.

So we moved. All the friends we had were Lloyd's friends from Minnow Lake and his family.

Chapter 23

Innocence Lost
1976

Lloyd was still going to Toronto and coming home on the weekends, and that's when my heart rate elevated and my whole body shook, fearful of the criticism he was going to throw at me this time. *You're fat, you smell like a refinery, I don't want to touch you, that baby is not mine* ... the words cut through me like a knife. I heard this all through my pregnancy. I hated being married to him. I hated my life.

Disapproval and harassment at work, only to come home to the same treatment. All this stress caused more attacks. The muscles tightened and locked at the end of my esophagus. I suffered in private agony.

I lost all hope of my life ever changing. Sleep didn't come easily as my mind raced through everything that was going on. After the graveyard shift, I would come home and pass out and sleep the entire next day. By Wednesday my gut would be in spasms. No one to talk to; no one cared.

The rebuild of the furnace was finished. We would be ready to cast in a few hours. The previous night's fight at home ran through my mind. I didn't feel like staying in the lunchroom, so I went down on the wheel stand and watched the furnace crew pole.

Deep in thought, I felt the tears welling up. Then a tap on my shoulder startled me. It was Marc. He asked me if I was okay as I wiped the tears away.

"Your husband again. Do you want to talk about this?" His voice was loud over the roar of the furnace.

I shook my head. "I'll be okay, and he's gone for the week. I just want some time to myself." He left and I watched the pole being shoved into the furnace.

I trudged back to the lunchroom to get a coffee before casting. When I opened my lunch pail, I found another small yellow stick-it with a happy face on it and a chocolate bar sitting beside it. I knew it was Marc. I smiled at his kindness.

It was two o'clock in the afternoon when I was woken by the phone ringing. Marc was on the other end asking how I was. Groggily, I said okay, but that he shouldn't be calling me—I could get into trouble. He said he knew Lloyd was out of town so he thought it was safe to call.

Exhausted, I began to cry, emotionally drained. I told him about the rifle incident that happened the night we all went to the hotel before my operation. He asked if I had told anyone about this, and I said, "No, I was afraid." He said I should talk about it, that he was a good listener and he wouldn't tell anyone, that I shouldn't be holding this in all by myself, that I should meet him for a coffee at Tim Hortons.

"No! No. Thanks that's not a good idea. If Lloyd ever found out I went for a coffee with a man, he would shoot me for sure." He went on to say it was okay to have a friend, and it was only coffee. He said I would feel much better getting all this off my chest.

The kids were at my mom's. I didn't have to pick them up until six o'clock. I agreed to meet with him. I drove into the back parking lot of Tim Hortons; he was standing outside his car with two coffees in his hands. He said he thought I would feel safer if we just drank the coffee in his car. I agreed—it sounded like a good idea. I told him everything about the rifle. I went on about how much I hated my life. By then I had to use the washroom. I asked if I could bring him back another coffee and he said he would rather have a beer. We all knew at work how much he liked his beer. I told him I had to get my kids and thanked him for listening.

"Just one beer," he said. "I listened to you, now we can go for a beer and I will tell you about my life. I need to talk, too." I felt guilty about leaving, so I said okay, but that I needed to get home and pick the kids up by six. He drove for thirty minutes to a small hotel in Dowling, a little town just outside of Sudbury. I had never been to Dowling before.

The hotel was a dump. The smell of stale beer that had accumulated in the rug turned my stomach. Marc ordered a screwdriver and two beer. I sipped on the screwdriver while he downed the beers. Washroom again. When I got back, he had two more beer and another screwdriver. I glanced at my watch and told him I had to go home to get the kids. He said he would drive me back to my car after I finished up the second drink, so I did.

I remember feeling dazed; my head felt heavy. I leaned it against the window, and the world started spinning. How was I going to drive? The next thing I remember was him opening the passenger door and giving me his hand to help me out. I tried to focus. I had no idea where we were, but it wasn't the parking lot of Tim Hortons. He said I was in no shape to drive, that I should rest. He pulled me forward. Like a bad dream I felt him kiss me, then everything went blank, then flashes of his hands on my body, then blank again, off and on. I felt him on me then I was gone again. It was morning when I came to. He was in the other bed. I was terrified. I panicked and asked what had happened. He said that nothing had happened, that I had just passed out. Flashes of the night flickered through my mind like an old black and white movie.

I began to cry; he kept saying that nothing had happened. I told him I wanted to go home, asked him to please drive me back to my car. My mom would be worried that I didn't call. He told me to take a shower and then he would bring me to my car. It was like my mind had left my body. I showered and got dressed and we went down to the restaurant. I followed like a lost puppy, sat at a table, and a waitress brought us coffee.

I asked again what had happened, what he did to me. I had flashes and needed to know. Just then, a woman charged into the restaurant and headed to our table. Her face was red, her lips were suppressed with fury, and words sputtered out of her lips, but I didn't hear anything. She picked up Marc's coffee and threw it in his face, yelling something. I went deaf, a stunned silence. Marc's eyes widened with alarm as all the people in the restaurant stared at us. She left as fast as she had come in. Dazed, I stood up and told Marc to take me to my car, *now*. I didn't say a word when we pulled into the Tim Hortons and there was my car looking lonesome in the light of day—as lonesome as I felt.

Marc once again said that nothing had happened. He went to grab my hand and I jerked it away, not wanting him to touch me. I got into my car and watched him drive away.

I sat there for a while trying to compose myself. I knew I had been raped; I knew from the bits and pieces from the flashbacks in my mind. He must have spiked my drink. I thought back to the night I went out with the guys, how sick I got—he was sitting beside me that night too, and maybe my drink was spiked that night as well.

I called my mom from the coffee shop phone. She was worried and angry with me, but she didn't ask what happened and I didn't tell her.

I felt strange when I picked the kids up, kind of like a robot. I felt detached from reality. I wasn't even sure that was my mom and those were my kids. Nothing happened, I told myself, which was a lie. I told myself I would put it at the back of my mind, never to think about it again. Monday was a holiday, time and a half, but I called in sick. I didn't care about the money. I just couldn't go to work and face that predator, the person I thought was my friend. I told myself it was all my fault: I should never have told him Lloyd was out of town, I should never have told him about the rifle, I should never have gone for a coffee. I was terrified Lloyd would find out and kill me with his .30-06. He might even kill the kids to get back at me. I couldn't tell anyone. I went to the doctor and told him my gut was bad, and he gave me a week off. During that week I had many conversations in the mirror. I told myself to bury this, to just leave it alone, to not think about it anymore.

It was hard to go back to work. I was still in a dreamlike state—nothing felt familiar, the men in the room were people I didn't recognize, and everything I was certain about had no meaning. Marc entered the lunchroom, grabbed something, and left. He didn't even look my way. It was like I was looking through a fog.

I needed to get out of the anode department. I needed to get away. I didn't feel safe.

I prayed a job posting would come up and I could bid out. A training job for a casting crewmember in another department, fine casting, came on the board. I had the seniority to win the posting. I bid on it, but the job was cancelled. A few weeks later it was up again. Again, I bid on it and again it was cancelled. I was told the general foreman in that department had said no women were going to work in his department. There was no grievance because I couldn't prove that was why the company cancelled the training job.

One day while having lunch, Ray came in.

"Hey Morin, you and McDonald going out this weekend?" Most people in the anode called each other by their last names—it was a compliment. The next month when the job posting came up, I didn't tell anyone I was bidding on it again. While filling out the paperwork, I put in my badge number—35554—but where it said "name," I put C. Mulroy, my maiden name, my real name, not Duhaime. People called me Duhaime and assumed I was French, so on the spur of the moment I wrote Mulroy instead.

The next week I was awarded the job. The foreman came into the lunchroom, his voice strained as he ordered me to go to his office. He yelled at me about how much trouble I was in. I could hardly hold back my laughter.

I peeked through the grimy window. I could see the general foreman at his desk. I entered and sat down; his round fat red face quivered as he frantically gnawed on the remnants of an old cigar, drenched with saliva in between his thin shapeless lips. This made my lip curl; it looked disgusting.

He banged his fist on the table and shouted at me that I was in deep trouble.

"For what?" I asked with a hint of sarcasm. I knew why I was there.

"You committed fraud; you lied on these forms." He shook the papers in my face.

"I did not lie." The words came out calm and slow.

"Yes, you did!" He was now screaming as the paper crinkled in his hand. The unlit wet cigar stub rolled around; I thought it might drop out. His fat face jiggled like a bulldog's. "This is not your name. It said C. Mulroy. This is fraud and we are going to make sure you pay for this. Your name is Duhaime. You have deliberately deceived the company." He sat back in his chair, so arrogant, so sure of himself.

"Let me see that paper; let me see how I deceived this company."

Again, I was out of my body—not scared but calm. "No, Duhaime is my husband's name. My name is Mulroy, Catherine Patricia Mulroy, and I can prove it. That's the name on my birth certificate. So, I didn't lie." I stood to leave. "Besides, we are just a number here at Inco, a number you gave me. We are identified by numbers, and my number is on that sheet. 35554, that's me. That is my identity: first, last, middle name. It doesn't matter. It's all the same." I could tell he was really fuming, but I didn't care. I would be moving to another department.

"We will see about this," he said as he slammed his fist on the desk, causing the job posting to flutter onto the floor. The foreman sat cowering in the corner. I slammed the office door just for theatrical effect.

The men in the lunchroom eyed me when I got back. "You had better talk to a steward," one man said. "They are out to get you." A steward is a union employee who represents and defends the interests of his or her fellow co-workers when the company violates the terms of the collective bargaining agreement. It is a voluntary position, but the individual needs about thirty signatures from other co-workers be a steward. They still work on their daily job but have time to be an advocate for the workers.

I headed back to the office; the cigar-toter was gone. I told the foremen I wanted to talk with a steward. We have to have permission, but he can't refuse me. I was learning the laws. He asked who I wanted to see, but I didn't know any stewards. He said there was one in the wire bar department. He would call over and set it up.

Another foreman met me in the wire bar department and walked me to the lunchroom. A good-looking man was sitting at the far end going over papers. He looked like Clint Eastwood. He introduced himself as Bruce McKeigan.

"Can we talk in private away from the others in the lunchroom?" I asked. We went to the weighing shack and I told him what had happened. He said maybe I shouldn't have done that. That was it—my anger went off the charts. "I am so sick of men here telling me I don't belong. I can't have the jobs in another department because one general foreman doesn't like women."

"It's okay, I'm on your side," he said.

"How long have you been a steward?" I asked.

"I just became one; you're my first," he said and we both laughed.

He filled out the grievance. *I, Cathy Duhaime Mulroy, have a grievance under the collective bargaining agreement.* The company general foreman decided to let it go, and I was on my way to my new position in the fine casting department.

Chapter 24

Fine Casting 1977

The symbol for copper is the same as the gender symbol for women. It consists of a circle with a small cross below it ... maybe a message that the goddess Venus was there to protect me. How fitting, on February 14—Valentine's Day—I started my new job in fine casting. I was working with pure copper, casting fine shapes like billets and wire bar. It was still three shifts but weekends off.

Inco bought the refinery from Ontario Refining Company but still called it ORC. This casting process hadn't changed in seventy-five years. Neither had most of the men's attitudes.

No celebration at home for me on my new job. My reason for leaving the anode will stay in the anode, fused into the bricks along with the devil's calling card and the memories of the assault. All I had to do was tell myself I was fine, plunk my hard hat on my head, smile at my reflection in the mirror of the women's dry, take a few deep breaths, and tell myself I could do this.

"I am woman, hear me roar, in numbers too big to ignore!" I sang the words aloud. "Yes, I've paid the price. Fucking right I've paid the price." I took another deep breath and headed to the fine-casting lunchroom.

Men were busy with their morning rituals of coffee or tea and a snack. Some gave me a quick glance, others nodded hello.

I placed my hard hat on the shelf and noticed this lunchroom wasn't anywhere near as dirty as the one in the anode. In fact, the tables had been wiped clean. I wasn't sure where to sit; some people are creatures of habit and I didn't want to sit in someone's place only to make an enemy. A man named Bill moved over and patted the seat beside him. I extended my hand and told him I was Cathy. He smiled and said he had figured that one out.

Next, I reported to the time office, a large room that had a few offices that branched off it. A man at the very end motioned me over. I glanced into the offices as I passed their doors. The general foreman, the one with the wet cigar in his mouth, the one that told me I had committed fraud, the one who didn't want women in his department, sat behind a desk, his eyes narrowed with contempt at the sight of me.

I continued on to the man who kept waving his arm in the air directing me to come to him. The day-shift foreman, a tall skinny man with a long, beak-like nose reminding me of a bird, told me I was to report to him. There were no introductions. He scribbled something in his book and got up from behind the desk, and I followed him out the door.

We met up with two men from the day-shift crew; one was not much bigger than I was with a smile from ear to ear, which I was happy to see. The other man was quiet.

The bird-faced foreman gestured to us with that beckoning index finger to follow him. It seems all foreman did this. I think it was disrespectful to workers, but I didn't care at the time.

Again, no introduction, so I took it upon myself by extending my hand to the others. "Hi, I'm Cathy, just came from the anode."

"Hi. I'm Ron and this is John," said the smaller man, pointing to the other one.

The skinny bird-faced foreman stopped abruptly and yelled that there would be no talking, as he shook his finger in my face. I gasped at his reaction, surprised by his anger. The three of us glanced at each other and didn't say another word.

We descended a cement staircase that brought us under the floor. Long vertical molds hung on a carousel.

"What is this place?" I asked, astonished at what I saw. The bird-faced foreman was quick to react at hearing my voice, giving me that *what did I tell you* look.

"I was told to ask questions." I tilted my head, trying to look cute. His face was red with anger; my sheer presence annoyed him. He told me to ask the men once he was gone.

"Okay!" I let out a giggle and a forced smile; I could see the veins on his neck bulging, looking like little rivers. My anxiety built, and I began to sing in my head. *I am strong, I am invincible, and I am woman.*

Ron gave me a little lesson on the number-two wheel. This was similar to the carousel wheel in the anode, except this one had long vertical moulds. "Number-two furnace holds pure copper, 99.999 percent. It comes down the launder in molten form and into handheld ladles. Then it's poured into the top of the moulds that are on a carousel about eight feet long. As the wheel moves, the next mould will line up to be filled. The moulds are cooled with water as the wheel turns. Once the copper is solidified as a billet, a trap door on hinges at the bottom of the mould will open in order to set the billet free. One of us hammers out a wedge that holds the door closed, which is attached to a chain so it won't get lost. The billet will slide out and into a tank of water. This is a warning that if the ballot gets stuck inside the mould, we hit the side of the billet with a large steel bar and it should release. Whatever you do, *do not* place the steel bar in the opening of the hinges. Once a man stuck the bar in between, and when the billet slid fast it hit the end of the bar and the other end soared upward, impaling the man in his throat. He died instantly. The company ordered the body to be removed, hosed down the blood in the area, and continued casting." Ron eyed me, making sure I understood.

"Now we will go over to the other side of the wheel. That's where the doors have to be closed so the moulds can be filled again." Ron pointed to an old brown steel chair whose life had seen better days. The legs were twisted and only three reached the floor. The fourth leg was bent up into the chair. The chair tilted and was tied to a wooden pole by copper wire. The pole was just leaning against the wall, not secured to anything. "You have to close the doors with your feet. It's not easy, especially for short people like us." He gave a demonstration. He sat on the chair, lifted his feet, and began to rock the door on its hinges. "Once it stays up you have to work fast. Get off the chair, take the copper wedge, put it through the latch and hammer it in. You have to make sure the door closes, or you may get molten metal splashes through the opening. If that happens, you have to warn the ladle tender on the floor above. You do that by hitting the pipes with the bar. You hope they will hear you through the roar of the furnace, the gas blowers, and the cranes. This is a really stupid job." He laughed. At that moment I had no idea how big a part this chair would play in my life.

Back at home, I got the silent treatment when I told Lloyd that the men I was working with that day were really nice. My anger built at Lloyd, but my children got the brunt of it. I was yelling at them all the time. I cried after they went to bed.

Friday came too soon, my last day of working with Ron and John.

The bird-faced foreman gave us our marching orders for the day, telling the men they were to work on the top floors while I was to work under the furnace steps in a crawlspace, again with that hooked finger summoning me to follow him. He pointed under the stairs. It looked like it hadn't been cleaned in fifty years. In order to clean under there I would be on my hands and knees. I crawled under, taking apart the broom and leaving the handle, hoping there were no rats. It was so dusty. I remembered wearing a respirator when working up on the dory furnace, and I had seen men wearing dust masks when sweeping the floor. I was told the dust was full of copper oxide and that it was a carcinogen—cancer-causing. I crawled back out and dusted off my jeans. Both the bird man and the cigar-toting general foreman (the CTGF) saw me and headed my way, wanting to know why I was out. I told them it was dusty and that I required a dust mask. The bird man snarled and said he didn't think I needed one. "By law you have to give me one. You can get me one or get me a steward; it's up to you," I said.

He stomped away and was back in a few minutes with a dust mask. He handed it to me with a little too much unnecessary force.

"Thanks." I put the mask on and crawled back under the stairs. After cleaning for a while, my back screamed, needing me to stand up and stretch it. It took about four hours and the place was cleaned—at least that's what I thought. I crawled back out, brushed off the dust, and headed for the lunchroom. I didn't even have time to take off my hard hat. The CTGF and the bird-faced foreman entered the lunchroom, beckoning me with that stupid finger to come out. The two of them wanted to know what I was doing when my job wasn't finished.

"I *am* finished, and I did a good job. That place hasn't been cleaned in years, maybe never," I said.

"Follow us," the man and his finger said, and headed back to the stairs. The bird-faced foreman shone his flashlight under the stairway. At the far end in a corner was a small pile of dust, not much more than a cup. He motioned me back under the stairs to get it, both men amused at their actions. The cigar hung between those skinny lips and I know I curled mine. He disgusted me. "Are you kidding me?" I asked.

"Are you refusing to finish that job?" the CTGF yelled.

"No, I am not refusing the job; I just thought it was clean enough."

"It's not clean enough. You go back under there and clean it." They both snickered at their behaviour.

Angry and frustrated, I crawled back under the stairs, crying as I brushed up the final little pile of dust. My tears turned to mud as they ran down my face, so I sang, "I am strong. I am invincible. I am woman."

I washed my face in the dry before going back to the lunchroom.

I stirred my coffee and watched the current in my cup. There was no way I wanted to go back to the anode with the rapist there.

The best thing for me was to fight back. So, my new mantra was *don't fuck with me*.

My eyelids felt heavy as I pulled into my driveway, and it took a few seconds to change from Cat the worker to Cat the wife and mother.

I didn't understand what was happening to me or how I could control my anger. I wished I had an invisible forcefield around me like they had on *Star Trek*.

Was I a failure as a mother, a worker, a wife? Who am I, what am I? So many questions, so much sadness.

In the lunchroom, some of the men were talking about how the women at Inco were taking away men's jobs. I had had enough of that shit.

"I have been here for three years now—this is my job, nobody else's, so stop saying I am taking away a job from a man. Just shut up about it." There were surprised looks on some of the men's faces.

My outbursts were explosive, like copper hitting water. How do I get in control? I became more depressed as the days went by; I wanted to sleep, that's all, I didn't want to be around anyone.

Bill always treated me with respect. One day, as he was headed to the lunchroom for morning coffee break, I was pushing a broom when he yelled at me to come and join him. I leaned the broom against the wall and followed the men into the lunchroom. I just had time to remove my hard hat when the CTGF entered yelling at me that it was too early to have a break, that my break was from 9:00 to 9:15 and it was three minutes to nine.

"You will be counselled for this," he warned me. "Come to my office." Again with that fucking summoning finger, he motioned me to follow. Bill stepped in and said it was his fault; that he told me to come for a break. The CTGF yelled at him to mind his own business or he too would get a counselling slip. I told Bill thanks, but that it was okay.

The CTGF gave me a counselling slip: a "step 1" for taking a fifteen-minute coffee break at the wrong time. I trotted over to the wire bar to find Bruce McKeigan, my steward. Once again he wrote down: I, *Cathy Duhaime Mulroy, have a grievance under the CBA* ... blah blah blah.

When Bruce and I gave our argument, I said my step was unjust because all the clocks in the refinery were all different times, so no one really knew what time it was. Just like the song, I sang the tune: *Does anybody really know what time it is ...*

The CTGF told me I should stay quiet or he would charge me with insubordination. He really wanted to get back at me for getting into his department.

Bruce added that this was the first time a general foreman had given out a step; they were always initiated by the first-line foreman. He said that the general foreman's actions were blatant discrimination.

The word *discrimination* played over and over in my head. So *that* was what this was called. There's a name for the way I've been treated. This was a game changer, for sure.

The next day I was back on the broom, and I watched the men file into the lunchroom. They all laughed as I marched back and forth in front of the CTGF's office, broom over my shoulder like a soldier holding a rifle, waiting for 12:00 to go for lunch. The CTGF busted out of his door, yelling, "Do you know how stupid this looks? Do you know how immature you are?"

"No, I don't. Do you know how stupid that step was? Do you know how immature you are for giving it to me?" The clock struck noon. I leaned the broom against the wall and went for lunch—I had made my point. I knew he wasn't finished with me; he'd be gunning for me now. But I had a new friend and he was a steward.

The next day I was invited by one of the women to have lunch with her and a few others in the women's dry. There was a small room with a table in it at which they ate. I ran and got my lunch pail, excited to be with women, making sure I was back in lots of time. Someone squealed on me and again I was confronted by CTGF. He told me I was not to eat anywhere else but the lunchroom, and I was not to socialize with the other women who worked in the other parts of the plant. I told him the other women's bosses didn't have a problem with this. A few days later, I was asked again to have lunch with them. I put my lunch in a brown paper bag, leaving my lunch pail open on the table to make it look like I would be right back. The floor was deserted when I headed for the women's dry. My eyes darted back and forth looking for the general foreman. I made my way past the dump car on the railroad tracks. Suddenly, the general foreman jumped out from behind the dump car and grabbed my wrist; the brown paper bag swung back and forth and I tightened my grip, hoping it wouldn't fall.

"Where do you think you're going?" His face was close to mine and I could smell the stinky cigar.

Fear and panic filled me. His grip tightened. "What's in the bag?" he demanded.

I gulped hard. "It's a used Kotex pad," I blurted out. "Do you want to see it?" My eyes met his in an uncomfortable staring contest. A strange look came over his face, which was a bit of a surprise. He stood there for a moment, not saying a word. Finally, he let his grip go, turned, and headed for his office. I continued on my way to the dry and sat down at the table. Sue asked if everything was okay. I dug a sandwich out of the brown bag, smiled, shrugged my shoulders, and bit into my peanut butter and jam sandwich. I knew the general foreman would be watching me from now on, so I enjoyed this last lunch with the women.

When I told Bruce what had happened, he said the general foreman had no right to touch me, and that he would have a talk with him. He told the general foreman that his actions could fall under the category of assault. He was surprised.

Bruce was getting married in May. I bought a ticket, but Lloyd said we weren't going.

Day shift. I adjusted the rear-view mirror to cut down on the glare of the sun.

The god-voiced announcer came on the radio: "In 1974, workplace health and safety concerns arose at Elliott Lake after many employees were diagnosed with cancer." I turned up the volume. "Silicosis! Due to radioactivity from the uranium. Workers went on strike over health and safety conditions. Management and the Ministry of Health were fully aware of what was going on, but they failed to notify or admit that workers were in danger. The government appointed a royal commission in 1974 to investigate health and safety in the mines. The commission was chaired by James Ham, a professor of engineering at the University of Toronto. It became known as the Ham Commission." *Sounds like a sandwich*, I thought as I shut off the engine, not thinking much about it.

Next morning, same broadcaster: "Inco Ltd. has announced a slightly higher fourth quarter earnings in 1976. Net sales for the fourth quarter were 578 million, compared with 444 million for the fourth quarter of 1975; sales for the year 1976 totalled 2.0 billion, compared with 1.7 billion for the previous year." I shook my head in response; I couldn't even imagine how much money that was.

That weekend, I visited my mom and dad. Dad was in his favourite chair reading the newspaper. I saw the front of the paper: "Inco" in large black letters.

"What's that about?" I asked, striking up a conversation. My dad liked it when I asked questions.

"Well, it looks like there will be a law for workers, a safety bill," he said.

"A bill, like we will have to pay for something?"

"No, no, not that kind of bill. This bill is a law; a law that will help workers. The right for a worker to refuse to perform their work if he or she has reasonable grounds of suspected health or safety hazards, without fear of reprisal."

"Wow, that's cool." I crunched my teeth into an apple. "You would think that's just common sense. Why would anyone work on something that's unsafe?" My dad smiled at my childish ignorance.

Bruce and I sat on the platform of the warehouse. We were both on our lunch. He told me about his wedding, and I said I was sorry I couldn't go. Rumours were going around that Bruce and I were sleeping together. Bruce and I were friends, that was it. We respected each other and would never do anything to hamper our friendship. We were best friends.

We were talking about the safety bill when the foreman came to the wire-bar door. There's that curled finger again, motioning me to come with him. He informed me that I was not to sit outside with Bruce anymore. He said that he was doing this for my own good. With slouched shoulders I waved at Bruce and followed the foreman back into the plant.

My stomach was in knots. My mom said all would be okay—Lloyd's mom didn't want to get involved, my older brothers had their own lives, my sister lived in Ottawa, and my younger brother was in Toronto and I had no girlfriends. Bruce was my friend.

Chapter 25

Coveralls

I needed some new work clothes. A lot of the men wore green coveralls. Inco's warehouse carried them and sold them to the employees for half price. A man behind the counter gave me the smallest size they had. I put them on over my clothes. The crotch of the coveralls went down to my knees and they were too tight on my breasts. This would not do.

I went to Silverman's, the place I used to work at. They had a large jean department. I found a pair of jean coveralls, the kind that farmers wore. A boys' eighteen fit like a glove, a tight glove, and I thought I looked good as I admired myself in the mirror. What twenty-two-year-old girl doesn't want to look good, even in jean coveralls? As the days went on, the coveralls broke in nicely. My foreman stopped me, and again with that summoning finger told me to follow him into the general foreman and superintendent's office.

I asked if I needed a steward; he shook his head no.

These two men were new bosses for me. I hadn't yet had any dealings with them.

This general foreman was in his late 40s. He had greasy black hair combed like Elvis, only longer. He sat behind his desk and motioned me to sit in a chair across from him.

I took note that the superintendent was standing to the general foreman's right. I said I would stand. I didn't want to look any smaller than I was. The general foreman had a smirk planted on his face that read: *I am more superior to you.* I was sure they had been filled in on this woman who had snuck into their department. They were going to show me they were in charge.

The new superintendent's face reminded me of a snake's. It made me smile when I thought that at any moment he might flick his tongue out of his mouth and begin hissing. My first impression was that he could not be trusted.

Two against one—what did these newbies want with me? Just as the general foreman began to start his rehearsed speech, I took my hard hat off and slammed it on the desk. Both men glanced at each other, startled.

"We feel your coveralls are not appropriate," the general foreman began.

The snake backed him up. "Your attire is not right for this plant."

"What's wrong with them?" I asked.

"We think your pants are too tight." Both men laughed, enjoying their approach.

"Yes, they are tight, but not *too* tight and I don't think there is a law that says I can't wear tight coveralls," I stated.

"It's distracting," the general foreman snarled.

"Who is being distracted? Has there been a complaint?" I asked

"Well … no," he stammered.

"This is stupid. There are men working here whose clothes are torn, have holes in them, some are almost falling off of them. These are the kinds of clothing that can get caught in the moving machinery. I am sure you have never talked to them about their clothes." I could feel my anger rising.

"Yes, we know that, but we are talking about your clothes now." The general foreman raised his voice, trying to get control of the conversation.

"How dare you!" I screamed. My anger was out of control again. I tried to compose myself. I looked at the general foreman's flabby beer belly hanging over the top of his pants. His white shirt was so tight the buttons were stretched, screaming as they hung onto the button holes. He saw me looking at his big belly.

"You think my look is distracting?" I said sarcastically.

He understood what I said, so he came back with more insults. He laughed as he said, "Your pants are so tight, we can see the date of the nickel in your back pocket." Both men mocked me, amused at their joke. The snake bobbed his head in agreement.

My rage surfaced. I grabbed my hard hat and hit it hard on his desk. I leaned over to get closer to the big-bellied general foreman.

"What the fuck are you doing looking at my ass?"

The words ground out between my clenched teeth. I didn't blink as I stared him down. I had no intention of being the first to look away. He glanced up at the snake.

"You boys keep your eyes in your head and off my body. As far as I'm concerned, this discussion is over. I will wear what I want, as long as it doesn't break any safety regulations. If my clothes are tight, I won't have to worry about them getting caught up in any rotating machinery." My heart thumped hard in my chest. I grabbed my hard hat, plunked it on my head, and walked out of the office. My clothes were never mentioned again.

Men and the wire bar.

Cathy and Roger

Chapter 26

Hamilton McMaster University

Bruce told me Dave Patterson, the president of LU 6500 Steelworkers, wanted us to go to Hamilton to a week-long course on safety and health. This would give me an opportunity to be a member of the OSHA, the Occupational Safety and Health Administration committee. This was a joint safety and health committee in my department. Five members from the hourly rated employees and five from the company.

I wanted to go so bad. This could be life-changing. I might get more respect. Driving home, I was filled with despair over how I was going to talk to Lloyd about this. My fingers played with the ends of my hair, twisting and untwisting as I told him about the course, and how I could make it onto the safety and health committee if I took it. He asked if Bruce was going and I told him yes. He wanted to know who was going to babysit. I suggested he and my mom could share the week. I reminded him of the six months he was away, and that this was only a week. He said I was not going.

"I am going to Hamilton for a week at McMaster University, and that's that." I even surprised myself.

"Don't think you can take the car," he snapped.

It's my car, I thought to myself. *It's in my name, my insurance.*

"No, I am not taking my car. I have a ride with three other men."

"Oh, that's nice, my wife and three men. What do you think my family will—"

I left the room. I didn't care what his family would think.

The university looked like a castle out of a fairy tale book. My mouth gaped at the sight, my body trembled with eagerness when I realize that I, Cathy Mulroy, was at a university, even if it was for only a week. Never had I dreamt of doing this.

The instructor started with the Ham report, the one I heard about on the radio.

In 1975 the Ham Commission report recommended joint committees. By 1976, this led to the creation of Bill 139, which established the Employee's Occupational Health and Safety Act, the minister of which can order joint labour-management committees.

The goal was that by 1978, Bill 70—the right to refuse unsafe work and form mandatory joint committees in the work place—would be law.

"Oh my, this is what my dad was reading about," I remembered.

The instructor went on to say that workers should be informed about all the safety hazards at Inco. Under the present system, the workers as individuals and the union had been denied participation in tackling safety and health concerns. Between 1960 and 1974, seventy-one workers were killed at the Sudbury operations.

Throughout the week we were to know the bill inside and out. The right to refuse dangerous work, the right to know about the hazards in the workplace, and the right to participate in the safety process. The following is from Ontario's Occupational Health and Safety Act:

RIGHT TO REFUSE UNSAFE WORK

Stage 1:

1. Worker has reason to believe work or task is unsafe.
2. The report shall be made to the Supervisor (preferably in writing) and should outline the worker's reason(s) for believing the work to be unsafe.
3. The worker shall remain in a safe place near his or her work station.
4. Supervisor shall forthwith investigate in the presence of the worker, a worker representative from the Steward, then a mining inspector.

5. The Supervisor shall respond to the worker in writing about what happened, should the issue be resolved and corrective action taken, outlining remediation timelines, if applicable.

6. Should the issue be resolved and corrective action taken, if required, the worker shall return to work. If the issue is not resolved proceed to the next step.

Stage 2:

1. Refused work may be offered to another worker providing it is offered to another qualified person, but he or she has to be told that there has been a work refusal.

2. There will be no reprisals, no employer or person acting on behalf of an employer shall, dismiss or threaten to dismiss a worker; discipline or suspend or threaten to discipline or suspend a worker; impose any penalty upon a worker; or intimidate or coerce a worker.

I became a member of the joint safety and health committee. It was interesting sitting across from management without being in trouble. My first assignment was to do an inspection of the wire bar and fine casting with a new foreman. We started at 7:30 a.m. It took all day, no stone unturned, everything from the missing toe boards on the catwalk going to the crane to any lights that were out. We were proud of the job we did. We had four pages typed up and ready for the next meeting. There was no "atta girl" or "atta boy" like we expected. Instead, the management side was very angry with us. They shook their fingers at us and said we were troublemakers, nitpickers.

I tried to interrupt, saying we thought that's what we were supposed to do: find things that needed to be fixed. The new foreman didn't say a word, he just lowered his head while his bosses said I had coached and charmed him into doing this.

One boss slammed his fist on the table and said I was nothing but a troublemaker and that I was irritating him. His face went red, showing his anger, and he spat out that he wanted a break.

Bruce said they were mad because we had brought up too many concerns and now the company had to address them.

I told Bruce that most of these were just minor things that could be fixed with no money, like changing the light bulbs or fixing the toe board. I watched as the bosses stood in a huddle, all convinced I was some kind of witch who had put a hex on the poor new foreman.

Chapter 27

Cassi Summer and History Layoffs 1977

While visiting my mom and dad, I was walking down the street when I saw a man with eight collie puppies and their mom. He asked if I was interested in buying one. When he found out that I was the daughter of Rita and Pat he said he would let me have one for ten dollars, the price of the dog food.

I asked him how he could sell them so cheap. He said he had an agreement with a farmer friend who owned a male. They had gotten into a fight and his friend refused to breed the male. When his friend was in town, he stole the male for a few hours and here were the pups.

This was my birthday gift to myself. We called her Cassiopeia after the constellation in the northern sky, a vain queen in Greek mythology who boasted about her unrivalled beauty. Why? Because she was the most beautiful dog I had ever seen. We called her Cassi.

The god-voice blared over the radio. Inco's sales of nickel and copper were below expectations for the first six months of this year. The company was continuing to carry a large stockpile. I wondered what a stockpile was, visualizing big hills of ore sitting out in the plant's yard, dark, wet, and musty.

The foreman did his lineup for the day, ignoring the men's questions, such as: "Were there going to be layoffs, or was Canada's Inco going to replace employees who were lost through normal attrition?" He didn't respond.

More hints of layoffs at Falconbridge (the other mining company in Sudbury), too. A slump in nickel prices caused both companies to acquire their own stockpile. Dave Patterson, our president, blamed Australia, the Philippines, Africa, and the Eastern Bloc for what had happened to the market. Their prices were substantially below producer prices, producing a similar product because the worker's wages were much lower. The company said there would be no layoffs ... this year!

Falconbridge planned a shutdown of its Sudbury production facilities from September 11 to October 9.

I feared I might get laid off after Falconbridge announced a reduction of its workforce by 350 employees by the end of that year, 1977.

On September 20th, Ottawa said the pollution standards might have serious consequences for the future value of ore prices, as the standards would result in lower rates of metal recovery. This was an old tactic the company tried before saying that if the government made them meet these pollution standards they would have to cut back on production and manpower.

Our 14,000 workers would be in the line of fire. There could be layoffs and mine closures in Sudbury. Our government didn't step in to help us. The company had poured 850 million dollars into the Indonesia operation and 224 million into the Guatemala operation. Sudbury received nothing.

Dave Patterson tried to organize it so that the entire nickel industry bargained at the same time. This would give us better bargaining power. For example, Local 8126 in Shebandowan with only 170 members would be in a better bargaining position with us than by themselves. It would take a few years, but it could be done.

Jack Gignac, the president of the Mine, Mill, and Smelter Workers Union, Local 598 (Falconbridge), thought this was a good idea, and he said he would bring it to his 2900 members.

On October 18, there were more rumours about layoffs. Patterson tried to contact Wally Greton, manager of industrial relations at Inco, and Frank Bennett, the vice president, but they would not comment. At a press conference, the LU 6500 executive board told reporters Inco would not confirm or deny rumours of next year's layoffs. The rumors were 2000 workers and a shutdown of a series of mines: North Mine, Crean Hill, Creighton, number-three shaft and Little Stobie.

Our collective agreement would expire on July 10, 1978. Dave asked the employees not to work any overtime—this included employees on bonus, fearing they would work themselves out of a job.

Mining was the main employer of Sudbury. On October 20, 1977 Inco announced 2800 jobs would be lost in the Sudbury area by the end of January 1978 and another 650 in Manitoba. In total 3450 hourly and staff throughout 1978. Employees were given a sixteen-week notice. There were more cutbacks in the first half of 1978. Copper Cliff North Mine in Sudbury was suspended, along with Birchtree Mine near Thompson, Manitoba. Production from Stobie Mine was reduced, while Creighton complex number-three mine ceased operations and production from Crean Hill Mine would gradually reduce its operation.

Then the company slapped us with a four-week shutdown on July 17; about eighty-five percent of the work force had vacation to cover this. I was terrified I would lose my job. What would my life be like if I did?

Dave tried everything. Sudbury may be among the first communities in Canada to benefit from the work-sharing provisions of the federal government's Employment Act. There would be a meeting with the union, company, and the Canadian Manpower and Unemployment Insurance commission to discuss work sharing of the employment act which would shortly become law. Under the work sharing program, some could retain their jobs and some jobs could be divided. The work week would be shortened by twenty-five percent. There was no way that the union was going to accept this. Why should the taxpayers subsidize what Inco should be paying for? I had no idea what all this was about.

On October 24, a labour support rally was held at the union hall. The new national New Democratic Party (NDP) leader Ed Broadbent, Ontario NDP leader Stephen Lewis, and Sudbury area's three NDP provincial members, Floyd Laughren, Elie Martel, and Bud Germa, were all there. Ontario Members of Parliament Jim Jerome and John Rodriguez were there also. The citizens of Sudbury were invited because this layoff was definitely going to affect the whole community. Jack Gignac joined in with his union. The Sudbury and District Labour Council suggested that the way to prevent further layoffs and destroy the worker's constant fear of uncertainty was public ownership.

The union hall was jammed. There was not much room to move around; people were standing on tables. I found Bruce and sat down on the seat he had saved for me.

Patterson was at the mic. "We are here to protest 3300 layoffs at Inco and Falconbridge." His voice was strong. I noticed his long blond hair curled over the collar of his shirt. When he asked our government to intervene, everyone was up on their feet and thunderous applause and foot stomping greeted him. The energy in that room was exhilarating.

The NDP members, especially Ed Broadbent and Stephen Lewis, drew the greatest applause for their call to nationalization.

I yelled at Bruce over the noisy crowd. "What does nationalization mean?"

He yelled back. "It means we want Inco to be transferred from private to governmental control. We in Canada would have a say in how the company is run and the money would stay in Canada, instead of sending it to other countries."

That sounded like a good idea to me and I hollered along with the rest of the crowd. There was so much power in the union hall it felt like everything was vibrating. Never had I felt this kind of energy. Anything was possible. Empowered, a wave of confidence filled my body. I felt hope—something I hadn't felt in years. I was excited yet terrified. My life was going to change forever.

A few days later, I sat in Country Style Donuts eavesdropping on some men talking about a cartel. I wrote it on a napkin so I could ask Bruce. He told me it was a combination of independent commercial or industrial enterprises designed to limit competition or fix prices. I had no idea what this was all about. Everywhere people were talking about the layoffs and how they would impact our city. What about all the spin-off jobs that would be lost, like sales people, waitresses, and so on?

Our local civic leaders asked people not to panic because of the announcement of the 2800-employee job loss at Inco. Sudbury regional chair Doug Firth made an announcement about how much of an effect a six-month strike would have on the community. It would be tough, he said, and we were just going to have to buckle down and things would come back in the long run. This announcement was a joint effort with the mayor.

"What the fuck?" I said to the radio. "How can you tell us not to panic, that everything is going to be just fine? I don't want to get laid off and neither do the other 2800 people. Who are you to scare the people about a six-month strike when we are not even there yet?" Who was this clown? I shook my head.

Inco announced to the staff employees that there would be 350 more layoffs in Canada the following year.

Prime Minister Pierre Trudeau rejected suggestions that the government should intervene by purchasing Inco's excess stockpile of nickel and sell it later when the market improved.

John Rodriguez (NDP, Nickel Belt district of Sudbury) complained that while Canadian workers were being thrown out of their jobs, Inco was expanding its operations in Guatemala, Indonesia, and New Caledonia.

A community group called "Women Helping Women" released a letter to Dave Patterson stating that the company was not a neutral agency—it served the needs of the men who owned it. Inco had milked millions of dollars from working people in this area to feed the owners in New York and Toronto. The company told us they couldn't afford the high wages in this area, and they had a higher profit margin in Guatemala and Indonesia. These countries are dictatorships infamous the world over. The Women Helping Women organization was funded by the secretary of state and was studying the extent of health and crises services for women in the Sudbury area. I felt withdrawn when I heard these women talk; I had no idea what the hell they were talking about. They were so smart. But I was ready to learn.

Premier William Davis was to meet with Inco's chairman Edward Carter on Thursday to talk about the layoffs. Davis rejected the demands from Stephen Lewis to force Inco to rescind the layoffs. The federal government proposed a four-day work week. Patterson said there was no way we were going to accept that. That would mean the people of Canada would further subsidize the company directly through unemployment insurance commission. Inco already owed $378 million in deferred taxes.

The layoffs started with 2200 workers in January, another 600 later, then 650 in Thompson, Manitoba and 384 in Port Colborne, Ontario. The company said they had enough stockpiled ore to last eight months, but PM Trudeau said it was more like twelve to fourteen months.

It was sad to see the people who were going to be laid off enter the hall. They were filled with anxiety, worried about what they were going to do. People who were hired in 1975 were going to lose their jobs. A man with tears in his eyes said he had a wife and five kids and asked how they were going to survive on $145 a week from unemployment insurance. Another man yelled out that he had been laid off at Falconbridge in 1975 for fifteen months and had just got back to work that year. He went on to say he should have gone to Elliot Lake or Algoma Steel. Others complained about moving their family to other areas, saying they were not pack rats. Bruce said that after the 3000 were laid off, just as many would lose their jobs in the secondary industry, like supermarkets, clothing retailers, restaurants. Layoffs may even double in these areas. This was just the beginning of what was ahead.

Over the next little while, the union fought hard. They thought Inco might be willing to delay the layoffs, but Inco said they had no intentions of doing any such thing. The union fought harder, proposing better deals on pensions and a better severance pay to encourage older workers to retire. They also wanted Inco to stop contracting out some of the jobs that could be done by our people. There was no hope. "The 650 employees will be gone this year," Jack McCreedy, Vice Chairman of Inco, said. "There are more to come next year."

Our government was not going to help with the massive cuts here in Canada. Walter Curlock, Inco's President, said the company had received $79 million from our federal government in the form of exports to help build the project in Indonesia and Guatemala. It employed 3000 in Indonesia and 900 in Guatemala. Here in Sudbury they were laying us off. It was a crime. Sudbury has always funded Inco's operations somewhere else and not in Sudbury.

Chapter 28

The Bombing December 1977

December 6, 1977, afternoon shift. All work was done and we were sitting in the wire bar lunchroom waiting to go home. No one wanted to leave early for fear of getting our pay docked.

I always got a chuckle out of the cat and mouse game that played out every once in a while when we came out of the anode. A man or two would sneak out, hiding behind rail cars, lunch pails tucked tight under their arms like a football, their heads darting back and forth looking for the boss. It was funny to watch. I could never leave early because the women's dry was just above the office of one of the foremen, and I stuck out like a sore thumb. This night was different. The foreman came into the lunch room and told us we could leave a half hour early. We didn't have to be told twice; we grabbed our lunch pails and the room emptied in less than a minute. I showered quickly and was out of the plant heading for the parking lot by 11:40, the time my shift usually ended. The cold snow blew into my face and I tightened my grip on my hood. I could never remember a boss letting us out early in all the years I had been there, but I was happy to be going home.

On the radio the next morning: "Last night at midnight there were three bomb explosions at Inco's hydro substation at the Copper Cliff copper refinery. Two power transformers were knocked out, plunging the plant into darkness, forcing graveyard shift employees to be sent home."

My coffee spilled while my hands shook. "What! Bombs at the copper refinery at midnight. Shit, I walked really close to those transformers twenty minutes before they exploded! I hope no one was hurt."

The announcer continued. "The company said it was sabotage. No doubt about it—the fence wasn't cut but tracks in the snow indicate someone climbed over the fence."

I chewed on my bottom lip. "What! Someone actually set bombs. Who would do that? Why would anyone do that? Someone could have been killed." The next day shift, 350 employees were sent home. 170 supervisors and staff shipping personnel were kept on the job. I thought it odd that they would keep staff employees. Why would they be shipping out copper if there was danger; why would they let the truckers in the plant if there were bomb threats? I was suspicious.

The radio reporter when on. "All afternoon shifts are to report to work today. The Sudbury police would not comment on the explosions or whether they were linked to a bombing at Clarabelle Mill [an Inco operation] Ontario hydro substation, which happened nine days earlier. This explosion plunged ten thousand homes and businesses into darkness for two hours. The bombers had gained access to that station by cutting a hole in the fence. Police say three separate explosions caused a half a million dollars damage to the transformers in the substation." The new reporters were interviewing people; this gave the union a chance to report safety and health concerns in the silver building. The workers claimed the polluted air in the building was responsible for an unusually high mortality rate. The safety committee claimed the building exposed the employees to magnesium, nitric, acid, cyanide, chlorine, fluoride, arsenic, and metal dust. It didn't have anything to do with the bombing, but it was great to get that message out. I remembered the man who gave me my first rides to work when I started—that was where he worked. I remember how he smelled. I wondered if he was sick or maybe dead.

Over the next few weeks our lunch pails were checked going in and coming out by security guards. Did the company think we were carrying bombs in our lunch pails? It was like pointing a finger that the bomber was one of us. I still wondered why we were allowed to leave a half hour early that night.

The company came out with statistics that the average age of laid-off workers was 22.5 years and that 25 percent of them did not have dependants. As if they were justified because some had no dependants. I was twenty-three years old.

Chapter 29

Layoffs
January 1978

Bruce looked troubled when he told me a letter had gone out to some of our members. This was to inform them that the sick leave granted to them in accordance with the provisions contained under article 1124 of the collective bargaining agreement had expired December 31, 1977. It drew their attention to the fact that an absence of over fourteen days beyond this date would be dealt with in accordance with the provisions contained under article 1101: termination of employment. It was signed "Wally Gratton, Industrial Relations." Dave Patterson said that this was new.

The company was laying off 1800 hourly rated employees before February 13, 1978. Dave and his committee fought to decrease the numbers and got an early retirement plan for 250 workers. There was a last-ditch effort to prevent the layoffs, but that collapsed in Ottawa. On February 13, 1978, the last of the 1800 minus 250 hourly rated employees, both men and women—walked through the gates for the final time. We had our own Valentine's Day massacre. They started bargaining in April and our contract expired on July 10, 1978. Dave believed that taking away rights was high on the list. This stress was hard on my gut. Life at home was terrible and now it looked like I would be on strike.

Chapter 30

Bill 70 (139): The Right to Refuse Unsafe Work

"Fuck the bill!" he shrieked, inches from my face. I could feel the force of his voice on my cheeks. It's obvious he's irritated with me, shaking his hands in the air as if shooing away flies.

"I have the right to refuse. This is the law!" I shouted as I charged after him.

Making an abrupt stop, he turned, spitting the words at me. "Grab your lunch pail and go home."

At the start of my shift in the wire bar, I checked the graveyard shift bulletin board. My gut knotted as I reacted. *Here we go again, there must be a mistake.* I marched to my foreman's office, hands planted firmly on my hips, ready for a fight. "I don't work in the fine-casting department anymore, yet you have me working on the doors for the fine-casting foreman." There was no discussion. No argument. Just report to the foreman in fine casting.

Over to fine casting I went. The foreman reminded me of a French Elvis wannabe (referred to hereafter as the FEW). He leaned far back in his chair. He was expecting me, that smug smile on his face showing he had some satisfaction with my misfortune tonight.

"Why am I on doors?" I demanded.

He sat up straight and, using the side of the desk, aggressively pulled himself up with more force than necessary and leaned over the desk. "I'm short a man and you're the next qualified." My lip curled as I heard the word "man" instead of "worker."

"I don't work for you," I said.

"You do tonight." A superior grin replaced the smirk that cried out *I am the boss*. At the same time, he ran his fingers through his black, greasy hair. It made me shudder.

"Since when do you get someone from another department to fill in?" I asked.

"Since now," he chuckled, amused at this dialogue.

"I demand to see a steward."

His hostile response was instant. He roared, "You're going on the doors!" He stood up all the way.

My stomach clenched. My muscles tightened. He was known for his anger and for flying off the handle.

When I was nervous my cockiness surfaced. It didn't fail me this time. "Well then, is the new chair there?" For a second or two nothing was said.

"I don't know anything about a fucking chair!" he yelled.

I pulled all my strength from within. "Well, the OHSA committee agreed that a proper chair be installed on the door-closing side of the number-two furnace wheel. They all agreed that the brown steel chair was unsafe."

He came from behind his desk, peered down at me sitting in the chair. He leaned over, taunting me. "I'll make you half qualified," he said, being spiteful. "I guess you will have to stay on the door-opening side all night." A broad smile crossed his face, reminding me of the Cheshire Cat in *Alice in Wonderland*.

Shaking my head, I couldn't believe this guy. *He's as stupid as a stone*.

"You can't be half qualified." I stood up too. He moved. "You're either qualified or you're not." The palms of my hands faced upwards. "Besides, the job description clearly states that workers must change sides every half hour because of the heat. I am going down now to check if the chair is there." He followed, stopped, and waited by the furnace. The old brown broken steel chair was still there, still attached with copper wiring to a pole that was not anchored, still just leaning against the wall. This was so stupid. The furnace hadn't run in a while and they had done nothing to fix this problem.

Memories of working down there came flooding back: the times I sat on that stupid brown chair whose three legs reached the floor while the other leg was bent up under itself, having to position my shoulder blades on the seat of the chair in order to reach the doors with my feet. It was a hard balancing act.

Scared doesn't begin to describe how I felt when I didn't get those doors closed tight. Fearing I might get splashed with molten copper, I banged frantically on the water pipes, hoping to get the ladle tender's attention on the floor above, hoping they heard it over the roar of the furnace, gush of the gas blowers, and rattling of the crane. What a stupid way to communicate with the workers on the upper floor. It was just like Ron said it would be.

The FEW was still beside the furnace, arms folded tightly across his chest.

"Well, the new chair is not there," I cockily stated in my usual way.

"I don't know anything about a fucking chair!" he bellowed.

"Don't you read the minutes from the OSHA committee? They said months ago a chair would be installed that could be adjusted for tall people, and for short people, like me," I said, hitting my chest.

"There are not enough men qualified for tonight and you are next in line. I need a man and you're it, end of story."

"That's not how it works. You have to call in overtime. I. Don't. Work. For. You."

Fuming, his face red, he said, "You are going down on the doors! Are you refusing to work?" More spit spouted out of his mouth. "Then you can go home!"

"I want to see a steward!" I shouted.

"No, you can see one tomorrow!"

"Are you refusing me a steward? You can't. It's in our collective bargaining agreement." I felt amazingly calm and controlled, no fear.

He turned and began to walk away. I followed. Nervously, my voice squeaked out, "I am using Bill 70 (139)." He didn't stop. I raised my voice. "This bill gives me the right to refuse unsafe work."

"Go fuck your bill!" he yelled.

"This bill is law," I said as a matter of fact. For the first time, workers in Ontario had won the right to refuse unsafe work. "It's called Bill 70 (139), and it's one of the biggest wins for the labour movement. It means I have the right to refuse if I feel the job is unsafe, and you can't penalize me." My words were clear. He walked faster. I pursued him, feeling like that little dog in the cartoon show, bouncing up and down trying to get the bulldog's attention.

Frustrated, my hands were flailing in the air. "You leave me no choice. Under Bill 70 (139) I am refusing to work because I deem this job to be unsafe." My heart thumped hard; I could feel each beat. "Call in a safety engineer." I was claiming my right, standing my ground. I knew the law from my safety training in Hamilton and it was kicking in.

Again, he refused. "No. You're not seeing anybody." His anger was alarming. I hid my fear.

"Okay, call in a mining inspector," I said.

"No!" His hands now clenched, and I am sure he wanted to hit me at that moment.

We were face to face. "So, what you are saying is you are refusing me a steward, a safety engineer, a committee person, a mining inspector, *and* you are sending me home." My voice got higher and louder at each point.

He glared at me. "You just fuck off! You and your fucking bill! Get your lunch pail and go home!" He was acting like a madman. I could see the hate in his eyes. I felt it too. This time I didn't follow when he walked away.

Immediately, I reported the entire incident to the chairperson of the Safety and Health Committee. He agreed that I should go home, saying he would contact the union and we would see what tomorrow would bring.

Climbing the stairs to the women's dry, I mulled the whole thing over, second-guessing myself. *Did I do the right thing? Did I follow the right steps?* My heart thumped hard in my chest; my hands shook. Then, looking in the mirror, I took a deep breath. A broad, crafty smile filled my face and I giggled. No one had ever used the bill at Inco. How was this going to play out? I just couldn't wait to tell Bruce.

Lloyd got up when he heard me in the kitchen, squinting from the light and interrupted sleep, wanting to know why I was home. Like a floodgate opened, I babbled out all that had just happened, feeling breathless when I finished.

"You're going to get yourself fired," he sneered as he headed back to bed.

Under my breath I whispered, "I don't care what you think." I wasn't in the mood to sleep because I had slept all day, and I was excited. I didn't want this feeling to end. I let Cassi in and we proceeded to the rec room to listen to the song that made me feel good:

Say It Ain't So, Joe, from my Murray Head album. As it played, I relayed everything to my dog that happened that day.

Bruce and I attended a meeting at the Steelworker's Hall, where we were told criminal charges under Bill 70 (139) would be laid against the company and the FEW. Also, my last night shift would be paid.

Later that day, we met at the copper refinery with the company. The FEW looked pitiful sitting slouched over in the chair, fear in his eyes, much different than the hateful rage from the night before. The company's defence was that he should not be responsible for his actions because he didn't know about this new bill.

Bruce and I glanced at each other, knowing this was as far as it was going to go. We nodded, accepting it. The point had been made.

Before we left the room, I had to get the last word. "Do you think this would work on a traffic cop?" I paused. "Sorry officer … was I going too fast? Oh my, I didn't know the speed limit. Would he let me go? I think not."

Intense stares, but not a word.

A month later, two thumbs up, I watched them install the new wooden chair for the number-two doors. I had a big smile when I saw it could be adjusted.

This was one victory in many battles yet to come.

Bruce McKiegan

Doors on fine casting wheel.

Chapter 31

The Strike Vote September 1978

Over a thousand Steelworkers, mostly men, jammed the union hall in a forceful show of solidarity. Ninety percent of our members voted; 83 percent (8320) turned down the one-year contract and gave the bargaining committee the power to call a strike. Only 2005 voted to accept it.

Sixty percent rejection in Inco's Port Colborne.

Thirty-year-old fair-haired President Dave Patterson told us clearly that we were all to go back to work on Tuesday or we would not get paid for the Monday holiday. We were to do this while the bargaining committee attempted to reach a settlement.

"If we all stick together, we can win this fight!" Dave shouted. He carried a sign that read "83% proof Inco." Two men carried him high on their shoulders into the atrium of the Steelworker's Hall where we all cheered.

The old contract expired the following Friday, after two extensions. The average worker made six dollars an hour plus the cost of living. An Inco spokesman said the offer was fair, reasonable, and responsible under the existing economics. He tried to intimidate us, planting fear that Inco had 300 million pounds of nickel stockpiled. The company would be good for a year. He concluded the company had no further proposals. Dave Patterson was firm: we weren't moving on our position, so let's sit down and negotiate.

Friday came. The bargaining committee had been negotiating since April in Toronto and were tired of all this stalling. By the end of the day, if there was nothing on the table they would be headed back to Sudbury. The company reminded the committee that there was a verbal agreement that the union would give them five days' notice of any strike action so they could shut down operations.

"If the extensions run out, there won't be any five days' notice," Dave stated.

On September 11, the committee negotiated for three days around the clock. They wanted improvements in wages and pensions, a supplementary unemployment benefit fund, long-term disability benefits, and a cost-of-living allowance clause. They also wanted removal of provisions in the earlier company offer that would erode workers' rights in the grievance procedure over job postings and transfers.

Inco supervisors had been staying overnight in the plants as normal precautions for the safety of the operation. I watched as they carried in beds, freezers, and boxes and boxes of food. They would all be eating steaks and we would be eating bologna, if we would be eating at all.

The company offered ten cents an hour. That would bring our hourly rate to $6.10 an hour; however, we would lose six cents cost-of-living allowance so all we were getting was four cents. Inco employed about 33 percent of the Sudbury region's workforce, so if we were to go on strike for a long time it could have devastating effects on our city.

I was surprised when a strange thing happened in Port Colborne LU 6200. A wife of a worker asked to speak at the membership meeting. She voiced her concern about possible financial sequences of rejection of this proposal. Leaders of both 6200 and 6500 were recommending that the members reject the settlement.

On September 14, Inco took out a large ad in the Sudbury newspaper. It was an open statement to Inco employees and interested citizens. It went on to say how bad their situation was, and how good they felt the contract was. Our union leaders took out a large ad as well. It showed the outstanding issues and the four cents we were offered. A war was brewing.

Remember, over 80 percent of us did not want a one-year contract. The day before the vote in the Sudbury newspaper, Stew Cooke, International Steelworkers District Six director, also put an ad in the newspaper. He recommended that we accept the offer, because he felt a long strike would not result in reasonable success for the union. I was introduced to shitty politics.

"Stew who? And why was he speaking for us?" These were the questions on many of our lips. Dave Patterson was furious as he told Stew to mind his own business. "How dare you make a statement like that contrary to what the bargaining committee is telling its members. Our bargaining committee was elected by its members to make decisions for them, not you." Friday came, the votes were cast, 60 percent rejected the offer and we were on strike.

Immediately, picket lines were up at the plants and mines. Union members paraded outside the union hall with signs saying, "support our strike," car horns honked as they passed the steel hall.

On September 18, 1978, LU 6200 in Port Colborne accepted the contract. They had listened to Stew Cooke. 397 voted in favour of that shitty contract and 288 against, going back for four cents.

Chapter 32

Getting Involved 1978

Loading sandwiches for the picket line

I was on strike, whatever that meant. Lloyd was still working and playing in his band and curling and whatever else he did. Another fight—I complained that I never got to do anything. He quickly reminded me I didn't have any friends because I work with *only men*. His remedy for my dilemma was to get off my ass and do something, because no one was stopping me. Energized by his criticism, I took that as permission. Watch me now.

I felt a little apprehensive when I entered the huge kitchen off the main hall at the Steelworkers building. A blond woman, about twenty-six, met me at the door, introduced herself as Betty, and told me she worked in the mills. I introduced myself and proudly told her I was from the copper refinery. I had a feeling of self-importance when I identified myself with my plant. She showed me around the kitchen, which had a large walk-in freezer—I had never seen one before. I was impressed. My job was to make egg salad sandwiches and coffee for the strikers on the picket line.

Using an ice cream scooper, I plunked the mashed eggs onto a buttered slice of white bread and covered it with another. We had a good assembly line going. After a few days I felt sick to my stomach from all those eggs. Little did I know at the time, but I have an egg allergy.

Betty brought me upstairs to Dave Patterson's office. I knew who he was, of course, but I didn't remember meeting him before. He was a long-haired blond man, and at present he was standing behind his desk talking on the phone. He motioned me to have a seat.

"Okay. Okay." He gritted his teeth, agitated with the person on the other end. "Look, we are doing our best. No. No. No. Don't let anyone cross the picket line. This is a strike." His voice was powerful. "Well, if the company wants an injunction, then let them get one. No one crosses the lines." The long telephone cord dragged across his desk as he walked around. He rummaged through a cigarette pack, pulled one out, and then gestured to me for a light by flicking his thumb up and down. I pulled out my lighter and gave it a flick. "Yes, yes. I hear you," he went on. "We'll cross that bridge when we come to it. Okay. Okay." He sucked back hard on his cigarette and let out a heavy sigh as if I had just given him a drug.

"Hi, I'm Dave Patterson," he said, extending his hand, cradling the phone with his shoulder as the lit cigarette hung from his lips. He wore blue jeans and cowboy boots; I wasn't sure what to make of this guy.

"It all takes time," he continued into the phone. I let his conversation fade out. I stood up to explore the room, the books on the shelves with the gold writing on the binding. They felt familiar to me, as memories of men in suits and ties talking to me about my pregnancy in this very room four years ago streamed through my mind.

I peeked into the other room, an open-concept with many desks. Busy people swarmed around. Phones rang. People chatted. Papers were handed back and forth. A man carrying a box of file folders sailed by me, followed by another man with the same type of box.

Dave hung up the phone. I extended my hand and introduced myself. "Hi, I'm Cathy Duhaime."

"You're here to help?" he asked, not waiting for an answer. "Myrtle!" he yelled over my head. "Would you get John Rodriguez on the phone for me please?" A proper-looking woman in her late 50s sitting at a desk just outside the office nodded and picked up the phone.

"Well," I began, "I was working in the kitchen and ..." Myrtle yelled back to give John five minutes and he would call.

"Okay, so you were working in the kitchen," he said as he moved papers on his desk. I was surprised he had even heard me, let alone paid attention. "You're a 6500 member, right? You don't want to make sandwiches; you would rather be doing something else. Come with me. We can use you on the vouchers." His high energy was overwhelming.

"I got John on the phone," Myrtle said.

"Okay, give me a minute," he yelled back, and motioned me to follow him into another large office. The people there were also high energy as they bustled about.

"This is Cathy; she's here to help. Introduce yourselves and put her to work." He was gone in a flash.

I was unsure I was in the right place—what the hell was a voucher? A tall man with black curly hair motioned me over. He explained how our members were going to get paid.

"Okay. Are you ready?" he asked. I nodded.

He explained that each plant or mine was identified by its name on the front of the box. This one was Creighton Mine. He explained there were about twenty-five different sites that had to be covered. All plants and mines within an area of 65 km by 30 km. Each box contained file folders with a sheet for each member. On the sheet was the member's name, badge number, what plant or mine they worked at, address, phone number, spouse's name, and number of children. He said there were 11,700 members. Most would receive thirty dollars a week and three dollars per child. Members who were working were not eligible for the thirty dollars. If their wife was making good money they were asked not to pick up the thirty dollars. Drivers picked up the boxes and brought them to their destination. Members lined up, proved who they were, signed their names, and after they received their voucher their names were ticked off. Their paper went back into their folder and into the box. The driver brought them back to the hall where we rechecked everything. This was all done by hand.

"That's it. Got it? Okay, you will get it soon enough," he laughed

"My husband's working," I said, "so you can keep my share." He smiled.

Some people were putting labels on us, like rebels, troublemakers, even communists, whatever a communist was. I was an NDP member.

Maybe it was because we rejected what Stew Cooke, the international director, told us to do: accept Inco's offer.

Or maybe it was because we agreed nothing and no one was entering the plants or mines. The company had threatened an injunction, a court order that would refrain us from stopping people from accessing the picket lines. They wanted a say in who and what went in and out of the plants or mines. Ronald Macdonald, the vice president of LU 6500, admitted "there could possibly be confrontation on the picket lines if there was an injunction. The union stood firm on its current policy, no access, that's the whole idea of having a picket line."

McDonald was in charge while Dave was at a Steelworker's convention in Atlantic City, NY, trying to secure financial support from other Locals. Meanwhile, the company was flying personnel in and out of the plants by helicopter, which cost thousands of dollars, and Inco staff were receiving their full wages even though they were not at work.

An article in the Sudbury Star caught my attention. Wives of the strikers wanted to be involved and were in the process of organizing a committee and calling themselves Wives Supporting the Strike. The leader was a twenty-one-year-old red-headed woman name Linda Obonsawin. She wanted to provide a better understanding on the contract dispute and practical assistance for weathering the financial impact. She would stand with her husband and was asking other wives to support their husbands too. Twenty-five women attended their meeting and passed out leaflets to get more wives involved. They planned to set up parties for the children, a clothing depot, toy exchanges, car pools, and babysitting. Linda wanted to set up a skills service exchange. Fix something for someone and someone will fix something for you. She knew this might impact some businesses in Sudbury but said they couldn't afford it anyway. I found this really interesting.

It was the fifth week of the strike and it was bitterly cold for October. Frost had already formed on the roofs of the houses in the mornings. I hoped this was not an indication of what the winter was going to be like.

It might have been cold outside, but it was heating up in the Steelworkers Hall. It was a daily beehive of action—coordinating picket duty, strike assistance, budget planning strategy, telephones always ringing, and a steady stream of people coming and going. There was a strong feeling of solidarity among these volunteers. We believed if we stuck together there was no reason why we couldn't hold out for a good contract.

Food donations came in for the picketers, like pizzas, coffee, donuts, etc. Many companies were joining our fight. This was smart because their names would be remembered after the strike was over.

A local dealer gave televisions to the picket lines so the picketers could pass the time, but Inco threatened to shut off the electricity to the picket shacks unless they were given the right to enter and exit the plants and mines. We held our ground; they didn't shut the power off. Other picketers passed the time by playing ball, horseshoes, and cards while others fed the foxes that visited the lines with scraps. Guitar and fiddle music filled the night air with stomping music.

The union started its own newspaper called *The Striker* to keep everyone informed. Other Sudbury citizens started a group called the Citizen Strike Committee to help the union raise money.

We organized a free corn roast to mark the third anniversary of the imposition of federal wage price controls, when workers across Canada had vigorously opposed the program with a national day of protest. We used the large Sudbury Star parking lot across the street from the Steel Hall. Hundreds of people gathered, mouths watered for the golden buttery vegetable. While volunteers husked hundreds of ears of corn and others cooked them, Dave and I filled his truck, driving the cooked corn over to the parking lot and coming back to be refilled. It was a great day of solidarity.

Chapter 33

Queen's Park 1978

A tedious job, wrapping those yellow labels on all those cans, but someone had to do it.

Dave and a few others spent hours secretly labelling cans that read: "Dollars for the Nickel Strikers." They piled them high in the shape of a pyramid, then took them to the Ontario Federation of Labour (OFL) convention to be held at the Sheraton Centre in Toronto. Over 800,000 unionized workers across Ontario voted unanimously to organize all-out financial support for our 11,700 Steelworkers' fight against Inco. They condemned government for allowing Inco to expand into Guatemala and Indonesia. Then they called for the nationalization of Inco under public and democratic control.

The delegates shook the yellow-labelled cans—they each held four cents, Inco's offer. For several minutes the reverberating sound of the clinking coins filled the air.

A few days later I boarded a bus with thirty other people. We were off to Queens Park, the Ontario legislation building in Toronto. Bruce explained that most laws originate with cabinet government bills and were passed by the legislature after stages of debate and decision-making. Members of the legislature vote on the bills that come before the House of Commons. However, individual members are able to introduce a private member's bill. They usually get defeated after the first reading. It's the power of the people to elect the people who have the power to pass, amend, and repeal laws. I was happy he was explaining all this to me. We were going to upset the legislature.

The secret of what we were going to do was revealed once the bus was on its way. Dave explained they didn't want the House to find out our plans. I was so excited.

Dave stood at his usual spot in the front of the bus and gave us our marching orders. He told us that members of the public are welcome in the House, but we had to be quiet. We were going to observe the House in session, so we had better not get caught before we had a chance to disrupt the House or enact the plan.

I was thrilled when I was handed my yellow can and four pennies. We were to keep the cans empty for quiet's sake and hide them on our body. I placed mine inside my coat and the pennies in my pocket. My body trembled all over as we entered the building; it looked like a castle from the 1600s. Silently, half our group went to the left the other half to the right. Our half faced the south part of the House where the member who would be speaking would be. We sat quietly as the House began to fill with the legislated Members of Provincial Parliament (MPP). Then the nod signal was given and we began to put our pennies into our cans. There was a problem with it being so quiet in there: the sound of *clink, clink, clink* could be heard every time someone dropped a penny in their can. I wasn't the only one holding back the laughter. Every time I looked into a friend's face their lips were pressed tight together as if they were ready to explode. I had to look away. My eyes darted back and forth to see if any of the guards heard us, but no one did. That made me want to laugh even more. Bruce gave me a nudge that snapped me back.

The House began. A speaker stood and began to talk about the price of nickel. That was our cue. All of us stood up in unison and began shaking our cans with the four cents in them. The thunderous clinking noise echoed through the chamber. We shook and shook as hard as we could. Our smiles showed how much we were enjoying this.

The legislative people looked terrified and confused, not sure what to make of us. Some froze on the spot, looking bewildered, while others scurried out the exit door like mice running from a cat. We continued shaking our cans and more guards showed up. One by one we were escorted out. We did not put up a fight. We just waited for our turn to be marched out the door. The House was adjourned. I felt exhilarated.

A lunch was made up for us in another building by Bud Germa, who was MPP for Sudbury at the time.

An exhausted group of radicals boarded the bus to head back to Sudbury. Dave stood at the front and told us that support was coming in from all over Canada. Gordon Lambert of the United Automobile Workers said, "Inco steelworker children will get gifts this Christmas. We will unite. Workers have to win this battle, not just for steelworkers but for the auto workers and everyone else that is working for a multinational corporation. The OFL must demand nationalization of Inco." A few cheers came from the tired crowd. I sat back in my seat and watched the reflection of Toronto's tall buildings in the window and went to sleep.

Chapter 34

Steelworkers Benefit in Toronto December 8, 1978

Everyone's money was running low. How were we going to pay for our member's insulin, heart medication, cancer medication on thirty dollars a week? It was like trying to feed five hundred people with a few loaves of bread and fishes.

Bus trips were arranged to drum up support from other unions throughout Canada. We knew it was going to be a long strike and that we would need help.

Being on the voucher committee made me feel important, that I had value, something I had not felt in a very long time. The men on the committee treated me like I was part of the group. With this attitude I was driven to do whatever I could.

The power of the strike began to grow, taking on a life of its own, emitting energy—a living, breathing thing that kept us motivated. But it was early and we were young and full of hope.

Soon there would be no money to cover life-sustaining medication for our members. We needed to set up benefit fundraisers with other unions and organizations to help us.

Meanwhile, the bargaining committee negotiated at the Royal York Hotel in Toronto, four hours away from Sudbury by car. The company wanted to keep the bargaining committee isolated from the membership. I think their belief was *united we stand, divided we fall*. With all these new beliefs I thought of myself as a knight of the round table or a musketeer: *all for one and one for all*.

The frost on the windows and roofs in Sudbury indicated a very cold December day. I walked down the stairs of the Steel Hall and Dave handed me a folded green eleven-by-seventeen paper on his way up the stairs. I stopped, opened it, and read:

INCO

SOLIDARITY BENEFIT

Speakers:
Cathy Duhaime—*Inco Striker*
Joan Kuyek—*President of Women Helping Women*
Linda Obansawin—*Wives' Strike Support Committee*

Entertainment & Party

OISE Auditorium
252 Bloor St. W., Toronto

$2.00 Cover Charge

Friday December 8th
8 P.M.

Sponsored By:
United Steelworkers Local 6500
Organized Working Women
International Women's Day Committee
Ontario Federation of Labour
NDP Women's Committee

"Wait, Dave, my name is on this paper. It says I'm to speak in Toronto," I said, with fear in my voice—not so much of speaking but of what Lloyd would say about it.

"I know. I recommended you."

"I'm not sure I can do this." The words came out shuddering, sounding like a scared child.

"Do you want me to get someone else?" he asked abruptly.

I stood there with my mouth gaping. I didn't want him to ask someone else.

"Okay, I'll do it." I felt unsure. I didn't have much confidence in myself.

"Good." He nodded as if to say *that's that*, and continued on his way down the stairs.

My heart pounded hard in my chest, excited, scared. I remembered when I was in Grade 3 and 4 winning trophies each year for oratorical speeches. But that was in front of the parent–teacher association, my mom, and all her friends. "My Summer Vacation" and "My Canadian Heritage" by Cathy Mulroy.

My arms were crossed tightly around me as if holding on to myself, and my head was down when I told Lloyd I was to speak in Toronto. He didn't share my excitement. He became agitated and told me I would have to find a babysitter. I wanted to ask why he couldn't babysit but feared he wouldn't let me go. I knew it was better to ask my mom.

This was my first time in a plane. Take-off was the best—the power of the plane going fast down the runway excited me.

The groups putting on the benefit were paying for everything. I forgot about my home life.

The night arrived. I was nervous. I didn't know anyone. My stomach turned and knotted. I was excited and scared, all at the same time.

I called Dave at the Royal York Hotel and asked if the bargaining committee was going to show up at this benefit. He said they would try if they got out of bargaining. I reminded him that he was the guy who put my name of that piece of paper, so he had better show.

I peeked from behind the velvet curtains that hung in the closed position of the stage. The front-row seats where the bargaining committee was supposed to sit were empty. I startled when one of the organizers tapped me on the shoulders, and I let out a "Fuck!" He was the MC—he apologized for scaring me and asked for a copy of my speech. I gulped, embarrassed and ashamed when I told him I hadn't written anything, hiding the fact that reading and writing were not my strong points. He looked worried when he asked me what I was going to talk about. I told him I was going to speak from the heart.

He shrugged his shoulders and walked away.

Music from a string band played to open the party. The audience cheered with excitement when Linda George Obonsawin, head of Wives Supporting the Strike, walked up to the lectern. Her red hair hung down to her shoulders and her bangs were cut straight across her forehead. Her skin was reddish in appearance. She was shy and very modest, yet when she began to speak all the shyness was gone. I grinned at how comfortable this small twenty-one-year-old was, as she told the 600 people what was happening to us in Sudbury.

"It's our strike too." Her voice was soft and relaxed, but her message was loud and clear. "Thank you for putting on this benefit. The money raised here will go to the children's Christmas party." The audience cheered and once again I peered through the curtains, observing their faces as their eyes were glued to Linda.

I glanced at the front row—still no bargaining committee.

My heart sank, my mouth went dry, my legs shook when I looked down at the borrowed high-heeled shoes I wore, not feeling very comfortable in them. I kicked them off, afraid of twisting an ankle crossing the stage.

Just as I did that, the audience roared, whistled, and yelled as Dave and members of the bargaining committee came down the aisle of the auditorium. The crowd was up on their feet, giving them a standing ovation. They waved like celebrities and took their spot in the front row. I couldn't have been happier.

The crowd settled down and Linda continued. "We are supporting our husbands. The company will not use us against our men like they did in 1958. We are part of this strike; it's our company too." The crowd howled with excitement. "We are here to fight to the end. If that contract would have been offered to us in September, it may have been accepted." Her voice raised a little. "But now they are asking us to give up things that our fathers, brothers, and uncles fought for years ago. The wives are trying to care for the material things on food vouchers for thirty dollars a week. We plan to spread the word about trade unionists too." Her voice was softer now. "It's fear that makes you want to go back to work. We are not afraid; we will survive. This is not going to be a repeat of 1958, when the company got the women to stage a massive rally to get the men back to work. They went back just before Christmas for a bad contract. The women got blamed. Not this time. We are going to stand beside our men." The crowd jumped to their feet. Goosebumps ran up and down my arms; my heart thumped hard.

The next woman to speak was Joan Kuyek, head of the Citizens Strike Support Committee and Women Helping Women in Sudbury.

Tall, slim, and very attractive, she stood straight and proud. One could tell she was sure of herself. Her voice was soft-spoken and to the point. I could tell by the words she used and how she said them that she was very well educated. I felt a lump in my throat, unsure of how I was going to sound and what I was going to say. She told the crowd that every citizen hated Inco and that she was there to help the strikers and their families. She told how the company had milked the city of Sudbury for almost 100 years. She said that from 1974 until 1977 Inco had hired about 100 women, but during the big layoffs only thirty were left. Sudbury was a company town and Inco was the major employer, but it had the lowest female participation rate in the Canadian work force. The crowd yelled and once again stood on their feet, their faces beaming.

It was my turn. A woman introduced me to the crowd. I heard my name: "Cathy Duhaime Mulroy, an Inco striker." My entire body shook as I walked to the lectern. "Hi, my name is Cathy Duhaime Mulroy, I am a striker and a member of the United

Steelworkers of America, LU 6500." The words rolled off my lips like I had been saying them for years.

The crowd applauded. I explained what it was like to be a woman at Inco, about the conditions at work regarding safety and health, and how important the grievance procedures were in this environment. I went on and talked about my job with molten metal and casting copper, about how Inco made the best copper in the world, and I said it with pride. The crowd booed and hissed. I wasn't expecting that, and I became very defensive.

"Wait a minute, wait a minute," I said, waving a finger in the air, then holding the palms of my hands out to calm the crowd. "Shh," I said. "Just give me a minute. It's true … Inco does make the best copper in the world. It's the purest, 99.999 percent, it's the softest, easiest to work with. But!" Again my finger went up. "In order to get the 99.999 percent, *we*, the *workers*"—I hit my chest—"work hard to produce such a metal. The company takes the credit, but it's *us* who do the work." Well, the crowd liked this—they went wild, clapped their hands, stomped their feet, stood up, and yelled out, "You go, girl!" I was stimulated by the power I felt at that moment, controlling the crowd. I continued to talk about the previous layoffs, which had wiped out almost all of the 100 women because of low seniority. This was the old story: women are the last hired and the first fired. At the end of my speech the crowd was once again on their feet.

Linda and Joan joined me at the lectern. The energy in that room was so powerful. Many union representatives lined up at the mics to give their greetings of solidarity and pledge financial support.

Dave got up to the mic. The crowd went silent.

"Hey, Cat," he called into the mic, "I know we're on strike, I know we are poor, I see you're not wearing any shoes. So here are mine." He threw his brown loafers up on the stage.

A little embarrassed, and without thinking, I walked over and slipped Dave's shoes onto my feet. The crowd hesitated, waiting. I raised my one finger in the air to tell the crowd *one minute* again and walked up to the lectern. "Thanks Dave. All I've got to say is … I can fit into your shoes anytime." The crowd was hysterical; I laughed so hard tears rolled down my cheeks. Linda and Joan's smiles radiated from their faces. Again, the crowd was up on their feet.

The MC calmed the audience and said there was one more person to hear from, and her name was Bea Stephenson. She had died several months prior but had written a poem called "Slag." Her daughter Sharon read it to the audience. It was about how Inco had raped the land in Sudbury. It was very moving.

That solidarity benefit in Toronto December 8, 1979 drew a crowd over 600 people and raised over $14,000 for the Christmas strike fund.

The new friends I had made would be with me for many years to come.

Chapter 35

Christmas 1978
Spotting the Split

It's true I had changed, or was at least changing. The old me was slowly being replaced by the new me. Like a phoenix, out of the ashes came the new, and my life as Cathy Duhaime slipped away.

A realization came that there was so much more to the world than Sudbury, Ontario. My best friend, my dog Cassiopeia, lay at my feet while I rubbed my toes through her thick collie coat, listening again to my favorite album: Murray Head's *Say It Ain't So*. I told the dog I couldn't make this marriage work anymore; in fact, I didn't *want* to make it work anymore. It was finished.

The newspaper lay open to a picture of Linda George Obomsawin, head of Wives Supporting the Strike, the woman who spoke with me in Toronto at that benefit. She was stating that the wives were looking for good used toys so the kids would have something under the tree this year. They needed several thousand more. They could be dropped off at the old Elgin Street Fire Hall.

A little reluctant, I would ask my kids to give up some of their toys. This could be tricky. The dog looked up at me with her gentle brown eyes as if she understood.

I stood at the door of the fire hall, bag of toys in hand. It was a beehive of action—women busy washing dolls and trucks, others putting the clean toys into brown bags and stapling them closed, writing the appropriate age and gender on the outside then placing them into the right pile. It was like walking into Santa Claus's workshop, and these women were the elves.

An older woman with greying blond hair and a big smile took my bags and thanked me.

I was off to the Steel Hall where Operation Turkey was taking off. Donations flooded in from other unions. The Retail, Wholesale and Department Store Union, Local 597, donated $6000 in certificates.

The response was overwhelming when Local 598 Mine Mill members gave two dollars a week from their cheques, especially with the history of Steelworkers raiding Mine Mill back in the '60s, but that's another story.

The Ontario Federation of Labour sent out letters to all its affiliations asking for help. Ordinary Sudburians dropped food and money at the hall.

Dave made a comment to the media that it may not have been the best Christmas, but it would be a Christmas the union can be proud of.

President Jean Claude Parrot of the Canadian Union of Postal Workers asked its 23,000 members to donate one dollar each to the turkey drive. We were getting donations from as far away as Louisiana.

Dave stated that thousands of tons of herring were on their way from British Columbia and would arrive in a week.

Something was changing at the hall too, or maybe I was never aware of it. There was a rift among some union brothers and sisters, rumours that some would like this strike to fail because all of this had made Dave look good. When I heard this, I made a washing-of-my-hands motion, then threw them up in the air as if to say, *I am not getting involved with politics*. As far as I was concerned, my job was to help out with Christmas and make sure people got their vouchers. Some people saw me as taking sides because I was a Dave Patterson supporter. I had no idea there were sides.

One day a man handed me a note. It had the names and phone numbers of thirty-six families in dire straits for food. He told me to call them, to have them come to the hall for four o'clock that day. There were potatoes, turnips, carrots, and onions in the basement and I was to bag them up. When I called them, they were pleased and said they would be at the hall by four. My excitement stopped abruptly when I got to the basement and found it bare, just like Old Mother Hubbard when she went to the cupboard to get her poor dog a bone. I sprinted up the stairs, taking two at a time, all the way to the second floor. Out of breath and half crying I told McDonald that the food in the basement was gone. He shrugged his shoulders gave me a quick glance as if to say, *so what*.

In a high-pitched cry, I said, "I promised thirty-six families groceries. There are no potatoes or onions or anything. Is there any food anywhere else?" Tears of dread welled up in my eyes.

"No," he said rather smugly, "there is no more food. I guess you'll have to call those families back and tell them that." I swear I saw a crafty smirk on his face as he picked up the phone with one hand and shooed me out of the office with the other.

Agitated and troubled by what just happened, I told one of my fellow workers. He said I had been deceived, that they wanted me to look bad.

"What the fuck!" The words came through my clenched teeth. I tried to shake off this negative emotion. What was I going to do? I sat at the desk, head resting in my hands, looking hopeless. My cockiness emerged. I had an idea and I was keeping it to myself. I took the phone book into the back room and called the Salvation Army. I spoke to a woman about my dilemma. She offered food and fifteen dollars per family. I told her I would be right there. The clock hit four just as I had finished bagging the last bit of food. The same man that had handed me the list of family names told me McDonald wanted to see me in his office. He should have said *Dave's* office. I got someone to watch the food, afraid it might disappear.

McDonald's lips quivered. He was irritated with me and demanded to know where I got the food.

"I got it covered," I sang in a theatrical kind of way.

"What do you mean you've got it covered?" He spit out the words contemptuously, crossing his arms on his chest, his eyes dark and cold.

"Not only did I get food, I got these too," I said, waving the thirty-six vouchers in the air like a Chinese fan. "Fifteen dollars for each family, I called the Salvation Army. They were happy to help."

Outraged, he stood up and slammed his fist on the desk. I thought his eyes were going to bulge out from their sockets. Hearing the commotion, the list man burst into the room. McDonald filled him in and both yelled at me about my behaviour. They said I had no business going outside the union. We would look after our own.

"Look after our own!" I shouted, standing my ground. "You knew there was no food left downstairs, yet you got me to call those families and arrange for them to come and get some food. You set me up!" I paused. "Well, it's done. These families will get this money." I shook the vouchers, "and the food too!" Tears filled my eyes. "Christmas is for giving and receiving, and at the moment we are on the receiving end. These families will be here in a few minutes and I am going to give them the food and these vouchers." I stomped out of the office as they were still screaming that I had no business going outside of the union. I turned, echoed McDonald's earlier shrug back at him, and, with a wave of my hand, I was gone to meet the families.

Without even trying, and not wanting to get involved with union politics, I had made enemies.

Chapter 36

The Real Meaning of Christmas

Negotiations in Toronto broke down. Dave was back in his desk. I stood at his office window, mesmerized by the winter storm brewing outside. My attention was held captive by the blowing snow as it swirled around cars while they slowly motored through the slippery intersection. I thought of going home before the storm got worse.

"Do you remember how we met?" Dave asked. "I'd met you before."

I had no recollection of this guy. I shook my head and shrugged my shoulders. "When?"

"I was called to the Copper Refinery to talk to you about not wearing a bra," he went on.

"Oh yeah, I remember that day. My job was to clean out the bottom of the bosh tank. Those tanks are usually filled with water to cool off the hot anodes after we take them off the casting wheel. I had drained the tank and the crane, brought over a steel box, and placed it inside." It was all coming back to me. "I climbed into the tank and began to shovel up the sludge left in the bottom of it from the anodes. There was a lot of precious metal in that sludge. My co-worker was in the other tank doing the same thing. It was a hot day; there was no cast running so it was safe to remove his long-sleeved work shirt. He was wearing a T-shirt. I thought that was a good idea, so I took my work shirt off too. I had a sunburn so I wasn't wearing a bra; my T-shirt was dark brown. It's not as if you could see anything.

"The tank was five feet deep and ten feet long. I didn't think anyone could see me. When I finished, I put my long-sleeved shirt back on and climbed out of the tank. No harm done. About an hour later I was called into the foreman's office. Someone had put in a complaint that I wasn't wearing a bra. So, you were the guy they called in to talk to me? Sorry I didn't recognize you," I said.

"Well, I didn't know what I was supposed to say to you. I was a little uncomfortable."

"It's not like I was walking around the plant showing off my boobs."

"The boss said you were being improper. Do you remember what you said?"

Memories of that day came floating back.

"Yes, I defended myself. I was not improper. What was improper were the fat men in the tank house standing on top of the tanks wearing white muscle T-shirts with their boobs hanging out, and some are bigger than mine. Maybe they should be wearing bras too!"

"Yes, that's what you said, and I told the boss you had a point," Dave said.

"That was as far as it went, but I never took my work shirt off again, even if I had a bra on."

We talked about the Wives and the great job they were doing on the children's Christmas party, their long hours of washing and bagging toys. I felt proud of them. The children would be happy just to get a gift under the tree.

Just then, a panelled truck caught my eye as it plowed through a snowbank that had just formed in the middle of the intersection. The driver laid on his horn and flashed the headlights on and off. I thought he had seen me at the window and was trying to get my attention. I told Dave to come over to the window and check it out. All he saw was the ass end of the truck disappear into the union parking lot. We looked at each other and our eyes widened with excitement.

Dave ran through the door like a child on Christmas day. The rest of us followed. Outside, the -35° air temperature took my breath away. A white five-ton panel truck, covered in dirty, salty, slushy ice idled in the parking lot. It had obviously had a long journey. We all shivered because none of us had grabbed a coat.

A man swung himself out of the cab, shouting, "Merry Christmas! I'm from St. Catharines. We heard you're in need of some toys and food. Well, here's a truckload." The ice crackled and broke off as he rolled the back door up. If the cold air didn't take our breath away, the contents of the truck did: thousands of new toys, hams, turkeys, vegetables jammed neatly into the back of the truck. We started laughing, crying, jumping up and down, everyone's face beaming, an indescribably, wonderful, emotional moment. I wrapped my arms around the man's neck, kissing him on his cheek, thanking him over and over. He said if he knew he was going to get this kind of reception he would have come sooner.

Just when we thought we couldn't get any happier, another dirty and icy white panel truck pulled up beside this one. A man swung out of the cab shouting Merry Christmas and disclosed that he too had thousands of treasures. Gordon Lambert, president of the United Automobile Workers and the St. Catherine's Labour Council, had stuck to his word when he said no child of an Inco striker would wake up on Christmas Day without a gift under the tree. He had kept his promise.

Large tears rolled down my face. I had to go back inside the hall so no one would see me cry. Besides, I didn't want the tears freezing to my face. If there is such a thing as a Christmas miracle, this would be it.

That night the volunteers unloaded the trucks. The Wives, Women Helping Women, and the LU 6500 Christmas committee worked all night, taking the used toys out of the brown bags and putting in the new ones. The toys that had been bagged earlier that were in really good shape were also given to the children.

The wives had made a colouring comic book for the children, called *What's a Strike?* The story depicted the bully in the schoolyard as Inco, and when the children stood together they were able to win against the bully and he backed down. Each child received a colouring book.

When one of the wives asked me to help distribute the toys, I was honoured. Every child, mother, father, and worker's eyes shone with pleasure. The Christmas party was a success.

A few nights later, a group of us were once again in Dave's office going over the day's events. A man whom we didn't recognize came to the office door to let us know there was a delivery truck in the parking lot. Dave was in a meeting with a few members, and someone went to get him. We grabbed our coats this time and headed out. This truck too was covered in the usual dirty winter slush, salt, and ice ... all the way from British Columbia. Memories of the trucks of toys and food flashed through my mind as we stood in the cold, eager to see what was in the truck. When the driver rolled up the back door, an awkward silence fell—we weren't sure what we were seeing. Large blocks of ice in cardboard boxes were piled on top of each other.

Dave took charge by thanking the driver, breaking the uncomfortable silence. Not wanting to look ungrateful, he climbed into the back of the trailer to figure out what to do next. He opened one of the boxes. Small fish, about thirteen inches long with blue-green backs and silver-white bellies, were tangled and twisted around each other, imprisoned in each block of ice, their heads and tails sticking out on all sides. What I was saying about feeding the people with fishes and loaves of bread? Well, be careful what you wish for.

Our eyes darted back and forth, and no one moved or said a word. Having trouble holding back my laughter, I ran into the hall to gather myself together. The driver informed Dave he had to keep the truck running to keep the freezer on. Dave told him not to worry; with it being $-35°$,

With a deep sigh, Dave said, "Let's get the chainsaw and safety glasses in here." He was always upbeat. The quiet night was broken by a buzz-saw racket as the chainsaws tried to cut through the ice blocks and cardboard boxes. Pieces of fish, cardboard, and ice flew everywhere. The expression on our faces suggested we didn't know what we were doing. The chainsaws were not working. All it was doing was dulling the chainsaw blades. Fish tails, fish heads, chunks of ice now covered the floor of the truck. The men holding the chainsaws lay down their arms in surrender, waiting to hear if anyone had a better idea. They were open to suggestions.

It was decided to fill a few pickup trucks with the blocks of fish and deliver them to where the members picked up their vouchers, and if anyone wanted them they were to come and get them.

Volunteers did their best distributing the ice blocks of fish by rolling them off the backs of the trucks and into the snow. The way this was done made many people angry; they asked if we thought they were animals. Dave tried to explain that this was the only way we could do it, and that dropping the fish into the snow would at least keep them frozen. Dave's phone rang constantly with angry people who didn't get any fish, accusing us of keeping all the good stuff for ourselves. This annoyed me. We were a handful of volunteers, running this strike for 11,700 members. You didn't see those complainers down at the hall volunteering their time.

Dave's phone rang again. He wasn't smiling when he hung up. He told us to stay calm, then smiled and told us there was another truckload of fish on its way. We delivered it in the same manner.

"I hope I never see another damn fish as long as I live," Dave said, gathering papers on his desk. The bargaining committee was heading back to Toronto the next day.

A little while later, I asked Tony, a car salesman who was renting a room from Dave, to let me into the house. I placed a fish bowl tied with a red ribbon on the table. The bowl held a large black bulgy-eyed goldfish. I left a Christmas card and some fish food. "Merry Christmas, Patterson. Enjoy your fish. Cat."

Chapter 37

Miguel Angel Albizures

MIGUEL ANGEL ALBIZURES

    I was at the union hall every day while the kids were in school. It was clear that not everyone at the hall was on the same page. Scheming and gossiping was going on behind closed doors. I didn't want any part of it, but I felt I was being dragged into it. Like a gale brewing over our blackened landscape, something was developing in the group. After the empty-vegetable-storage incident, I wasn't sure who I could trust.

    Ron Macdonald called me into Dave's office. He called me Cath in a friendly sort of way that made me uncomfortable. He told me there was a visitor on his way, a trade unionist from Guatemala named Miguel. He asked if I would put on a luncheon for him. Katrina, the cook at the union hall, would plan the food and I would sit with him and some reporters. Excited to meet someone from Guatemala, the vegetable incident left my mind. I knew Inco had moved into Guatemala and Indonesia to set up mining.

Sandwiches were being placed on the tables when two men walked in, Bob Carty the interpreter and Miguel. I stood and shook their hands. Miguel wasn't much bigger than me. Dark skin, jet-black wavy hair, a nice-looking man, he smiled at me through his thick black mustache. He wore one of our striker pins on his sweater, the one depicting Dave as a miner. Then a reporter and a man with a camera joined us. Every time Miguel said something, the interpreter repeated it in English. I was impressed. I had never met anyone who could do that.

Miguel and I hit it off as if we had known each other all our lives. This was another shifting moment in my life. Miguel told stories while the reporters were busy scratching it all down on their pads.

As his stories unfolded, he clasped and unclasped his hands many times. He told us about the peasants in Guatemala who were killed because they occupied their own land, land targeted for moderate capitalist development. It sounded similar to what the whites did to the First Nations people in Canada. Guatemala was hit by a development boom and the land value shot up, so the people were told to move. Canada's Inco Limited was one of the biggest developers currently operating, and they wanted more. A wave of horror had swept through Guatemala the previous summer. On May 29, the army opened fired on a crowd of people, killing 114 men, women, and children. Their bodies were piled into the back of a truck. I felt traumatized as I visualized what had happened to these people. The reporter asked, "What did the government do about this massacre?"

Miguel's eyes were transfixed as he relived this horror. "They sealed off the town to journalists and Red Cross representatives, denying them access to the area. The government said only forty-two people were killed and they had all been armed. The trade unions, the church groups, and student organizations all denounced the official version of the murders." He lowered his head.

While Inco was staking out its claims in Guatemala during the 1960s, it was also negotiating with the Indonesian government for the rights to exploit a deposit on the island of Sulawesi, which is potentially one of the world's principal sources of nickel. The Guatemalans knew that the game was fixed and the rules were rigged, and their government officials sat down with Inco management to bargain over the country's nickel. If Inco didn't like what was going on in Guatemala, they threatened to simply move to Brazil or Australia. When the nickel company came to their country, they had no idea that it had been playing for decades with the country's civil servants. They had little experience in plotting a course through the complexities of mining legislation. It was like dealing with political confusion and violence, and they had little hope of coming to a deal with these businessmen. It was the politics, not the technical work.

Inco managers literally rewrote the country's law to suit them. When the representatives read Guatemala's mining code, they decided it was not adequate to cover the activities of a modern mining company. An engineering company drafted a new code and it was ratified in Congress in 1965. At this time, his country's constitution was suspended because of a military coup. The military took over the country, all rights were gone, and it was only the military's laws that meant anything. Things got worse. The military regime didn't stop with financial favours to the company's dirty politicians. During the '60s, an increasing number of Guatemalans reacted to this harsh repression by joining or supporting the guerrilla movements. Many people were killed who were peasants, not guerrillas at all. Their leader was known as the Butcher of Zacapa. "A butcher?" I asked, "Do you mean"—I had a hard time saying it—"he ... he butchered people?"

"Yes," Miguel said softly. "Inco had many lending institutions when going into developing countries like Guatemala." When Inco and other North American companies operate in developing countries, like Guatemala, they can expect help from the World Bank, the Inter-American Development Bank or other regional banks. Any resources they use are considered "development," and as such are expected to be covered by loans at concessional interest rates. If Inco planned a similar project in Canada, it would have to depend on the generous but more limited subsidies Ottawa uses to tempt investors and would have no access to the World Bank or IADB coffers.

Miguel's life had been threatened by the Secret Anti-Communist Army (the *Ejército Secreto Anticomunista*, or ESA), a right-wing paramilitary group which published a hit list of thirty-eight popular leaders.

Miguel said, "Guatemala exploits and denigrates its workers. They had been hit by a new wave of repression designed to maintain the cheap labour conditions favourable to foreign investors like Inco. They want to destroy the movement by assassinating our leaders. The first person on the list to be killed was Oliverio Castañeda. He was a student leader who was shot down in broad daylight while several police cars patrolled the area."

My hands went to my mouth. "You mean they just shot him? They just shot him for standing up for his rights?" I felt scared; this was way out of my comfort zone.

"This terror is not confined to publicly named targets," he went on. "Every day, in both the cities and countryside, five or six bodies are found and tortured beyond recognition."

He told me he had spent Christmas here over the last few years and found it really cold. He had a wife and children but had to leave around Christmas because that's when the right wing in Guatemala would come after people. He had to leave for his family's sake. His family had to move hut to hut every few days.

That night a bunch of us met amid candlelight and whispers, like a cloak-and-dagger movie. Miguel was in danger and we had to keep his whereabouts a secret.

I asked him if he smoked grass and he nodded. We went outside and had a toke.

The poor interpreter couldn't keep up with us. We laughed even though we weren't sure what we were laughing at. We said our goodbyes. I knew I would never see him again, but I would never forget this man.

My children were spending the night at my parents'. I headed downstairs with my dog and filled her in on all I had learned.

VOL. V, NO. 7/8 $2.50
LAWG LETTER
Published by the Latin American Working Group

FROM BANANA TO RESOURCE REPUBLIC

INCO IN GUATEMALA

Chapter 38

The Bus Trip
January 1979

January 1979: one of the coldest winters on record in Ontario as the temperatures dropped to minus-forty and even minus-fifty. It was so cold Lake Superior froze over. Many families struggled without enough money to pay their heating bills. It was scary when banks threatened to foreclose on mortgages. Gas companies threatened to cut off gas and oil. More importantly, families couldn't afford their life-sustaining drugs like insulin or heart medication on thirty dollars a week, and the company knew that. It was hard on us volunteers as numerous phone calls came into the hall from families in desperate need of medication.

We needed to raise more money. How were we going to pull this off? These were the questions on volunteer's minds. The Ontario Federation of Labour and other unions across Ontario and Canada said they would help. We were pumped, so we said *let's do it*. Meetings were held at the union hall to organize bus trips to plants in Southern Ontario.

It was around 1:00 a.m. when forty-five of us gathered at the union hall. Looking around at the faces as we boarded the bus, I would have guessed the ages ranged from twenty to sixty-five years old. Our goal was to make it to Hamilton by 6:30 a.m. so we could get workers coming out of the plant from graveyard and the day shift workers going in.

I handed my small suitcase to the bus driver, who placed it in the hull of the bus next to dozens of five-gallon white pails.

The cold was unpleasant when I sat in my seat, so I cuddled in my down-filled steelworker's coat that was three sizes too big. When everyone was seated the guitars and banjoes came out and the passengers began to sing. *Oh, you can't scare me, I'm sticking to the union* ... This lifted our spirits.

The snow blew as we left the parking lot, resulting in low visibility. When we reached the highway, I couldn't make out anything on the side of the road. Through the front windshield it looked like the bus was going through a snow vortex. I was hypnotized by the droplets that ran down my window, reminding me of little rivers. I imagined they were like rivers; some would stop and just hang there while others joined another droplet to go in a different direction. Thoughts of home entered my mind: the fight with Lloyd about this trip, the kids playing with the new kitten I got them hoping that it would make them happy. I shook my head and joined in the singing.

Snow turned to rain the closer we got to Southern Ontario. It poured when we pulled into the motel parking lot. Hamilton 1005 Steelworkers were paying for our meals and lodging along with Oshawa, the Teamsters, and many more unions.

We dropped off our belongings and got back on the bus for our first plant gating. The cold rain pellets pounded my face when I was handed my five-gallon pail. I pulled the hood up, put my head down, and followed the gang. Our job was to stand at the gates of different plants with our buckets asking for donations. The workers in the plants were notified we were going to be there. We made it in time to catch the graveyard shift coming out and day shift going in, and when we went back for the afternoon shift it was still raining.

That night I hung my drenched coat in the bathroom of the motel room. It must have weighed an extra six pounds. I hoped it would dry by 4:00 a.m., the next time we were due on the bus. We were off to Oshawa, dropping off a few of our people at different plants and picking them up later. I was partnered up with Dave today; we did the graveyard and day shift and went back for afternoon shift. I felt like a drenched rat; my coat had no time to dry and it was still raining. I pulled the oversized hood tight and droplets dripped from the fake fur trim.

Dave met a few union representatives, a reporter named Peter Silverman, and a cameraman from the *Global Television Network*. They were to film us at the gates.

Workers began to file out of the plant around 6 p.m. They were very generous, dropping five dollars, ten dollars—even a twenty-dollar bill swam in the two inches of water on the bottom of my pail. The rain poured, my coat got heavier, the cold was in my bones and I couldn't feel my feet anymore.

More water pooled in my bucket. I tried to drain some out, but all I managed to do was get my mitts wet.

Peter Silverman was interviewing Dave while the camera rolled. They asked if it was okay to film the men dropping money in my bucket. The two men said yes and stood on each side of me, dropping money into my bucket. The cameraman finished and thanked us. The men didn't move, and they reeked of alcohol as they stumbled and laughed. They were coming out of work drunk. The man on my right had his left arm around my shoulders. He reached over with his right hand and grabbed my left breast.

My reaction was fast. The ninja inside me surfaced. I jumped back, causing the men to let go of my shoulders. My right foot went up, kicking the man with all my might right in his crotch. His eyes widened, a shocked look on his face. It turned white, drained of all its blood; he gasped and made puffing noises as if trying to get air. He fell to his knees clutching his manhood. I gave a startled gasp and covered my mouth with my wet mittens. My eyebrows shot up in surprise. *What have I done?* I felt a sickening wave of terror well up in my belly. Fear built up inside me. I looked around for help.

Silverman slapped the cameraman a few times on his shoulders. "Did you get that, did you get that?" he screamed. The cameraman shook his head, laughing. "Too bad, that would have been great," Silverman said.

Dave had faced me just as I kicked the man. He recoiled in horror and yelled out, "Cat! Cat! What are you doing? We are here to ask for money, not to beat up on other workers!" He ran towards me, dumbstruck. I just stood there, staring at the poor man on his knees. Thoughts of more men coming to beat us up for my actions was all I could think of.

Silverman and the cameraman laughed hysterically. Dave had a crazed look on his face. We both stood watching the other drunk trying to help his friend up off the ground.

"What were you thinking?" Dave yelled.

Traumatized by this emotional and disturbing experience, my body trembled.

Words came out in a stutter. "He ... he grabbed my boob, so I kicked him."

"Yes, I saw it all," Silverman added. "Too bad we didn't get it on camera."

"Okay, okay let me think, let me think," Dave said, rubbing his head to find the answer to this problem.

Panicked, I cried out, "We have got to get out of here right now! They are going to come back with other guys and beat us up. Please, please we have to get on the bus. Get the bus here!"

"Cat, just calm down," Dave said as we watched the injured man get to his feet. He couldn't stand straight as they wobbled to the lot.

"Why did you kick him again?" Dave asked.

"Because the bastard grabbed my boob." Tears rolled down my cheeks and my nose was running. The last thing I wanted was Dave to be mad at me. Dave's face changed to the compassionate man that he was. "He grabbed your boob?"

I nodded, my lip sulking, a pout on my face.

"With those boots?" He pointed to my feet. "Do they have steel toes?"

Another nod. "But I took the metatarsal guards off." It came out in a whine.

"Well, good for you. He deserved it."

All my anxiety flushed away at that very moment. This kind of action is what made Dave Patterson a truly great leader.

We got back on the bus and I sat quietly in my seat, watching my river droplets on the window, thinking of the poor man I had just injured: the image of him grabbing his privates, the look on his face, falling to his knees and then the gasping for air. My emotions were divided between knowing he deserved it and how sorry I felt.

Dave stood in the front and told everyone what had happened. I listened as he described the man falling to his knees. I wasn't proud of myself or ashamed. Everyone laughed and said he got what was coming to him.

"Cat will no longer be known as just Cat," Dave continued. "She will now be known as Bigfoot."

I called home when I got back to my room to tell Lloyd what had happened. Seven-year-old Peppy answer the phone and told me something was wrong with the kitten, that she wasn't walking right. When I asked him what had happened, he went silent.

Lloyd came on the phone and said, "I kicked the fucking thing because it keeps shitting under my side of the bed."

I told him to be nicer to her and she wouldn't do that anymore. He said I should get back to Sudbury, now, but I told him I couldn't but would be home in a few days, and asked him to please be nice to the cat.

Guilt filled me and I buried it; I would deal with this when I got back. I never told him about the guys at the plant.

The rest of the week went well. I spoke to a packed Local 1005 Steelworkers meeting and loved it. By the end of the week, the bus gang was very tired. I slept most of the way home, waking often with pains in my gut.

The kitten had something wrong with its hip and I was going to take it to the vet, but it disappeared a few days later.

The fights continued at home. "I want a divorce" was met with laughter and I was told I could never do it on my own, especially now because I was on strike, but I knew I wouldn't be on strike forever.

Chapter 39

Negotiation Talks Break Down Again

Dave told us we were asking for improvements in wages, pensions, sickness and disability benefits, and job security. The union wanted third-stage grievance procedures to be held in a common area, the Copper Cliff general office, where all the stewards could congregate so everyone knew what was happening at other plants and mines in case it was applicable at their location. The company wanted these stage-three procedures to be held in the individual plants and mines where the grievances occurred. The company wanted fewer union representatives in the grievance procedure.

We lost 1300 hourly rated jobs last year as part of a force reduction of 2800 jobs. The company said it would have to resolve the strike before making any decisions on rehiring laid-off workers or before making predictions about the future.

The company was lying, telling us the union had refused to continue talks, but it was the company who wasn't showing up. The union wanted us to know that the company's demands regarding the grievance procedures were an infringement on our rights.

On January 15, hundreds of striking steelworkers, wives, children, and supporters blocked Inco staff personnel from entering area plants. We told them that it was a holiday and that they should go home. This was in response to the company's chief negotiator, Bill Correll, breaking off the talks. He said they would not do anything regarding this march, but they were baffled at the union's attitude.

On Wednesday, January 18, a crowded Steel Hall heard details of the union stands and the reason for the breakdown in the contract negotiations. After Dave finished talking, the bargaining committee got a standing ovation and people shouted that they were behind them.

More bus trips were set up in the Maritime provinces, Winnipeg, Regina, Chicago, and Minnesota. Our members would be at plant gates, benefit concerts, and local unions. When we were in Hamilton area, we collected $20,000.

With only thirty dollars a week, a bunch of us decided to pool our food vouchers and a few families ate together.

At the end of January, my home life was like a war zone. I wanted to make a move but I was terrified, afraid to go out on my own, and second guessing whether or not I could do this.

Chapter 40

Cambrian College Strike and the Popcorn

Dave Patterson talking to a large police officer

Dave told us that the Ontario Public Service Employees Union had gone out on strike at Cambrian College. He said it was terrible people who were crossing the picket line and the students just didn't understand. A few of us went down to stand with them. We stopped cars for a few minutes and talked to the people about what it meant to cross a picket line, then we let them through.

Dave stood in front of a blue Camaro, the driver edging his car inch by inch, threating Dave. Dave wouldn't move, and we joined him. It wasn't long before some big, burly police officers showed up. They told us we had to move, but we didn't. One police officer came over and picked me right up off my feet by the extra material in the shoulders of my oversized coat and threw me in the snow bank. Lucky for me I didn't slide out of my coat. He did the same to another person. I got up and went right back in front of the vehicle, and again he picked me up by the shoulders and threw me into the snow bank.

"Stay where you are," Dave said to me, putting his hand up. Always the protector. I did as I was told, but I wasn't happy about it.

The Camaro inched towards Dave, pushing him out of the way. The next thing I saw was the mirror on the side of the Camaro dangling. I felt scared as the driver attempted to get out of the car. He was stopped by the police officer who yelled at him to stay put, and he rolled down his window complaining about the mirror. The officer told him to zip it. I watched the Camaro continue through the picket line, mirror dangling on the side. This was enough for me. I was cold and I wanted to go home.

It was on the news and in the newspaper. Lloyd knew I was there and told me I was stupid and that I was going to get in trouble. I should be at home with the children, not off on some picket line somewhere.

It was the weekend. I popped some popcorn, the children sat on the couch in their pajamas, and we got set to watch a movie. I was being yelled at by Lloyd for something. The children looked scared. He grabbed the bowl of popcorn and dumped it over my head. In front of the kids.

"You're an asshole!" I yelled. The look on his face scared even me. He grabbed me and pushed me to the floor. The kids ran upstairs. He began to choke me. I pretended to pass out. When he stopped and got off, I stood up.

"You're so dramatic," he said.

"I want a divorce." I was crying.

"Ha-ha!" he laughed. "You are on strike and you don't have any money and you'll never make it on your own." He got his coat and left. I picked up the popcorn and noticed little pieces of black fur clinging to the popcorn—the kitten's. I cried, then made more popcorn. My stomach ached. I tried talking to my mom; she said everything would turn out okay. I tried talking to Lloyd's mom; she didn't want to get involved. I didn't have any girlfriends, and if I called Bruce it would only make his wife upset. There was always my dog—she always listened to me.

The Steelworkers were back to negotiations with the provincial mediator Hector Pathe, and he said everyone was to refrain from talking to the media.

Chapter 41

Meeting the Wives: the Story of the Women of 1958

The Wives at the arena

Inside.

I stopped on the landing of the stairs in the Steelworkers Hall and gazed out into the parking lot. The cold February wind howled and blew snow around the parked cars. I shivered. I heard a man yelling in the lobby. I descended a few more stairs to get a better look. A man was shaking his finger at three women holding leaflets. They stood just outside the main hall where an information meeting was set up for our members. As men passed the shouting man, some took the women's leaflets and glanced down while others crinkled them into a ball and threw them in the garbage. One woman tried to explain they were putting on a bean supper for the strikers and their families on February 16. They also wanted other wives to join in supporting the strike. This caught my interest and I proceeded toward them. The man shook his finger harder, yelling that these girls had no business there, that this was a union meeting and they should be at home. He was so patronizing. "Remember what you wives did during 1958 strike." His eyes narrowed in contempt for these women.

"1958 ... I wasn't even born then," one woman said.

"What's the problem, why can't these wives be here?" I asked. He glared at me.

"They don't belong here, and they fucked up the strike in '58. We are not going to let them do that again; they should just go home!" he shouted. He was an older man with a purple nose and large bags under sunken eyes; from the looks of him I'd pegged him as a drinker.

"Of course they belong here, they are the other half of the striking husbands. Let them be." He held his hands up in surrender and went into the meeting.

This was just a taste of how many struggles the wives were going to face. A pregnant woman of about twenty-one approached me, thanked me, and handed me a leaflet, and asked if I would go to their meeting. I told her proudly I was a striker and not a wife. Surprised, she blinked and smiled. I placed the leaflet in my pocket and told her I would think about it.

A few days later I received a call asking me to come to the meeting. It was Joan Kuyek, leader of Women Helping Women in Sudbury and the woman who spoke with me at the Toronto benefit.

All eyes were on me when I entered the room. Some of the older women were knitting and glanced up at me, not sure if they liked me or not. The meeting was well run. Under "new business," I was asked if I wanted to join. I would be an honorary member but couldn't vote. My job was a liaison between the Steelworkers and the Wives, filling them in on the information about pensions, wages, rate of inflation, layoffs, unsafe working conditions, the grievance procedures, and anything else.

An information meeting was set up to explain what had happened in 1958, about why the men had such a negative attitude toward the wives.

Linda Obonsawin began the story. She was the other woman who had spoken at the Toronto benefit.

"In 1944, the first union at Inco was the Mine, Mill, and Smelter Workers." Mine Mill caught my attention—this was the group that donated their camp for the draft dodgers.

Linda went on. "The wives were involved right from the start; they were able to attend and speak at union meetings but couldn't vote, and they set up a ladies' auxiliary until 1958. In 1958 Inco was on strike. Sudbury civic officials and the provincial and federal governments coordinated their efforts to help the police in order to smash the union. The second week of December, the women's auxiliary called a meeting of the wives to support their striking husbands. Nine hundred women attended the meeting and agreed to support the union and to march on city hall. The mayor, realizing these women would give a great deal of weight to the union, wanted them stopped. He agreed to meet with the women at the Sudbury Arena. The wives did not want any part of these officials. The *Sudbury Star* headlines announced the meeting of the wives. The wives were confused: was the mayor going to their meeting or were they going to the mayor's meeting? Over two thousand women crowded into the arena. It was a circus. The broadcasting equipment was not working properly, and no one could understand what was being said, let alone vote on anything. It was complete chaos.

Some wives thought they were asked to come down onto the ice if they stood behind the union, so 150 of them did. Before they knew what was happening, the meeting was over and the headlines read: "Wives Vote to Settle Strike," forcing the men back to work. It was all propaganda. The union, in fear of being smashed, agreed to settle. As a result, the wives were blamed for the men accepting a bad contract and were branded as anti-unionist.

This was a lot of information for me to take in. I'd had no idea.

I decided to join the Wives because in the '70s, women's groups had been popping up everywhere since the woman's liberation movement. Women were helping women. The wives called themselves Wives Supporting the Strike. Most were homemakers and felt their main goal was to provide moral support and practical assistance to families of the strikers.

They wore black T-shirts with a yellow circle in the centre. Around the inside of the circle was yellow writing that said, "Wives Supporting Local 6500." Superimposed on the letters "USWA" in the middle was a woman in a little black dress. Mine was the same, except to the right of the circle in small yellow letters it said "I support" next to "Wives supporting LU 6500." This group was going to clear the false history of the women of 1958 and prove that they were a big asset to this strike.

Cathy's T-shirt.

Chapter 42

Wives Organize Festivities

Women were still having babies, so the Wives opened up a baby depot. Formula, diapers, and other baby accessories. They also started a clothing depot. They signed up for bus trips. Their goal was to create a sense of solidarity. They played two roles: first was peacekeepers and second was organizers. They had an elected steering committee that changed every three months. There was a chairperson, a secretary, a treasurer, and two spokespersons. One French, one English, and they had a liaison person: me. I kept the lines of communication open between the union executive board and the Wives.

I was scared, nervous, and proud all at the same time when they accepted me. Most of the women were from the home, inhabiting traditional roles. They began to communicate with other women's groups from around the country to help set up benefits.

Meanwhile, the newspaper indicated that the strike was going on longer because of the changes in the grievance procedure. They were trying to divide us.

To encourage greater awareness, the local union, in cooperation with districts six and the education department at the national office in Toronto, set up a strike education program. I attended the second one. I ended up on the front cover of the *Miners' Voice* magazine. I was thrilled.

The Wives' bean supper fed about four thousand people. Suppers were held at the Steel Hall, while other halls throughout the city donated their space to the Wives. Over 100 women served the suppers of beans, coleslaw, fresh bread, coffee, and refreshments. Registration was so high in the neighbouring valleys that the organizers had to hold three different settings in the Tenniel Arena. What a success. The Wives made a cookbook to be put out on Valentine's Day called the *Stretch Your Nickel Cookbook*. Their theme: "The company gets the gravy and the workers get the beans." Live music and entertainment filled the air in several of the fifteen halls. The Wives went through seven hundred heads of cabbage for coleslaw, five hundred pounds of carrots, seven hundred loaves of bread, nine hundred pounds of beans, and bottomless coffee and soft drinks. All the halls were donated, and Mine Mill was the major contributor. Some of the halls had already been booked for other celebrations, but the people gave up the halls so that the Wives could do their bean suppers. The community was behind us.

On February 21, 1979, the Wives organized an amateur night at the Steel Hall. You had to be nineteen years old, and admission was free. Great music, old-time fiddling, harmonica, square dancing. There were eight Carol Burnett and Sammy Davis Jr. lookalikes. Family and friends got together to boost their morale.

Central mortgage and officials were concerned over the length of the strike. So far there had not been any foreclosures, but concern was growing. Some people were four months in arrears. Steelworkers continue to dispatch delegations across Canada for more financial aid, travelling to Sault Ste. Marie and big fundraisers in Montréal, Nova Scotia, and British Columbia. Northern Ontario small towns Espanola and Elliot Lake raised another thousand dollars.

Chapter 43

The Filmmakers of The Wives' Tale

UNE HISTOIRE DE FEMMES

Prix de la critique québécoise 1981

A WIVES' TALE

Un film de
SOPHIE BISSONNETTE, MARTIN DUCKWORTH, JOYCE ROCK

Distribution CINEMA LIBRE

Sophie Bissonnette, Martin Duckworth, and Joyce Rock were a film crew from Montréal who came into our lives to make a documentary of the women's role and the Wives during the strike. I thought it only right for me to leave the meeting room in the basement of the Steelworker's Hall, since I wasn't a wife of a striker.

Linda came out to tell me I was part of their group and for me to stay while they were filming. I spoke at a few meetings about safety and what it was like to work with the men. We discussed bargaining and why the grievance procedures were so important.

This was another big moment in my life that changed me forever. These women were inspiring. I watched them blossom right in front of my eyes as I blossomed along with them.

I learned a lot from the film crew. They were the ones who taught me all about the Sudbury story. "What do you mean rocks aren't black? Of course they are, just look outside!" I had never realized that the rocks in Sudbury were not naturally black, but had been changed by the mining and smelting industry. Sophie enlightened me about this.

After the Sudbury crater was formed, the landscape healed itself over the next 1.8 billion years resulting in forests of red, white and jack pine on rolling hills, with hundreds of lakes full of fish. Wildlife was abundant through the thick forests.

When the railroad was built through Sudbury, all the large trees were cut and the hillsides became bare. They needed large amounts of logs for the rail ties and bridges. At this time, these trees never replaced.

In 1881 Sam Ritchie snapped up 15,000 acres of timber land in Southern Ontario that was rich in iron and nickel deposits. When he was in Northern Ontario visiting Sir William Van Horne at the Canadian Pacific Railway office, he spotted a sample chunk of ore sitting on the window ledge, which he pocketed, knowing it was valuable. He had it analyzed, then staked a claim on 97,000 acres before Van Horne heard about it. The land was considered worthless with muskeg and bush. All the trees had been cut and erosion had quickly followed. Instead of the value of the land being on surface, the value was now underground.

With this new knowledge, more mining companies came in to Sudbury and the remaining timber was claimed and cut for the construction of mine heads, shaft support, shelter, and the greatest sin of all— open roasting beds.

These roasting beds had timber piled two meters high and as wide and long as several football fields. The ore was then placed on top of these piles and the whole yard would be set ablaze and the ore would "roast" for 3 to 4 months. This roasting burned off the sulphur in the ore so that the metals could be more easily extracted. Huge clouds of black smoke filled with sulphur dioxide billowed from the beds of fire, as the ore roasted. The poisonous black smoke rose into the air. It was so thick animals could not be seen and if birds flew into it they would fall to their death.

The ore would sit for two months for cooling. Once cooled, large bulldozers removed the ore from the roasting bed and the ore was sent to the refinery.

The Copper Cliff Roast Yard operated from 1901 to 1915. Other roast yards operated in the Sudbury area until 1930, when the process was replaced by roasting in smelters. There were approximately, 80 roasting beds throughout the Sudbury area.

The sulphur dioxide in the smoke combined with atmospheric water vapour to produce sulphuric acid. This acid would fall as acid rain, acid fog and acid snow. This acid rain increase the acidity of the soil, lakes and rivers to a point where nothing could possibly grow or live, essentially poisoning the landscape.

This is how the Sudbury hills became barren and black, burnt from this poison smoke. Some 10,000 hectares had been reduced to desolation.

A feeling of unhappiness filled my whole being as I learned the history of my hometown. There it was again, sulphur, the devil's calling card. I recalled memories of climbing to the top of the blackened hill and watching the sun disappear over the black horizon. I recalled the red and purple reflection in the sky as the slag was dumped down the hills in Copper Cliff.

Slag is the by-product of smelting after all the desired metals have been taken out of it. I used to call it "dead rock".

The molten slag was transported in large pots by rail. The inside of the pots were painted with lime so the slag would not stick to them. They were then pulled by a locomotive out to the dump site area. The pots weighed 96 tons when empty and 151 tons when full. Molten slag temperature is 1800 degrees Fahrenheit. When the pots reach their destination, one by one they are poured down the hill. The result is a beautiful display that lights up the night sky. It was a beautiful place for young lovers to cuddle in their cars watching this spectacle.

The slag operation continued seven days a week, 24 hours a day— but not when we were on strike.

Martin, the cameraman, attended a Sudbury strike benefit in Ottawa on February 1979. He said he saw three women speaking from the Wives Supporting the Strike committee and he felt right then that there was a story to be told. "It's also important because this strike had taken on a life of its own," Martin said. "It was a rank-and-file strike. The workers voted to strike against the advice of the United Steelworkers. The USWA was one of the two biggest industrial unions in control of the Canadian Labour Congress, and the CLC had been losing contact with the rank and file over the last few years. By doing the film, a lot of misunderstanding about the wives forcing the men back to work for a bad contract in 1958 will be cleared up—the truth will be told."

Some people said the Wives brought a spark to the strike; in fact, I thought the Wives were more like a bonfire. They did so much during the strike. They assembled a choir and sang union songs with their children on the picket lines. They were always right there. I also believed that because the Wives were involved there wasn't much vandalism or fights on the picket lines.

Chapter 44

The Burning of the Effigy

Cathy at the burning of the effigy.

    I received a letter from Inco outlining the company's offer. I called Bruce and he told me that all the hourly-rate employees had received this letter. He told me to check the newspaper for a full-page ad that Inco put out with the same information. This was the company's dirty shadiness that they were trying to convince the public to buy. On March 9, 1979, over 700 people assembled at the Inco's Copper Cliff general office, at the smelter gate. It was minus 35°, and the cold wind blew in my face as I exited my car and pulled my hat over my ears. I knew Inco's attempt to make us look bad had backfired on them when I saw all the people.

    Big fluffy snowflakes fell as two men erected and secured a hangman's frame. We cheered, expressing our excitement, and the Wives sang union songs and everyone joined in. The same men carried an effigy, better known as a dummy, of Bill Correll, Inco's chief negotiator. They tied a noose around the dummy and strung it to the hangman's frame. Laughter and a sense of optimism filled the air along with the shouts and curse words to express our dislike of Bill Correll. A sign was attached to the dummy that read *INCO: may they burn in hell.* One by one we threw our letters under the hanging dummy. Thousands of letters made a large pile while Luke, one of the activists who was married to one of the Wives Supporting the Strike, poured a flammable solvent over them. We stood back when he lit them and watched the fire grow. More cheers, more singing while the dummy of Bill Correll caught fire and began to burn. I observed pensioners, laid-off workers, wives, children, strikers, and city support people joining in and enjoying the heat it gave off.

Once the fire was out, we began to march through Copper Cliff to Newman's house, who was the president of Inco's Ontario division in Sudbury. We sang while some locked arms as we trudged through the snow. Little fog puffs of air escaped from singers' mouths and rose into the air, symbolizing the rise we felt in our hearts. Some marchers carried signs that read *Pensioners are the backbone of INCO*, others read *Inco widows*, another *Inco's chairman 10.50 a month*.

Our large group stopped at Newman's home, a well-groomed house with large white pillars in front of it. The door opened: a woman in her 60s dressed in a housecoat came onto the porch. The singing stopped. Murmurs hummed among the crowd. "Who's that? Who's that woman?" people were asking each other. "That's Newman's wife," someone answered. By now, big fluffy snowflakes were falling. It was a sight to see.

"If you're looking for my husband, he is not at home," she said to the crowd.

I was shocked that he would send his wife out in the storm to face these 700 people. Out loud, I shouted, "She certainly is a brave person. She has a lot of balls to come out and face us. I have a lot of respect for her, but not for her cowardly husband." We had a good laugh, sang some more songs then left.

What a day. I sat in my car waiting for it to warm up so I could see through the frosted windshield. I felt proud of myself for how I was changing. I felt I was the frozen windshield, and now my pride was the heat thawing me out, giving me courage to make a move in my life.

The Wives continued to do a lot of plant gate collections at Falconbridge, the other mining company in Sudbury. Even though the Steelworkers had raided them in '69, they gave a lot to our cause.

Some of the Wives were busy working at the baby and clothing depot. Some older women were showing the younger women how to knit. I didn't want anything to do with knitting. Others had landed part-time jobs at the corner stores. Every woman seemed to be changing in some way, along with the rules we once lived by. One woman told us her husband would sleep until noon and this would start a fight. She told him her kids were his kids too, and that he should get up and look after them, and that while he was up, he could do the housework when she was out plant-gating. Another woman who had turned sixty years old told her husband that she had always stood behind him supporting him in his career, so now that he was retired she was going to start her career and she wanted the same support.

At one of the meetings, a woman explained she received a proxy in the mail for Inco's board of directors' elections. She read that the directors wanted us to strike, that it was a good strategic move to get rid of the stockpile. She went on to tell us that the directors had something to do with banks, and that they all held positions there. There it was again: *banks*. I remembered back to when I met Miguel from Guatemala and all the people who were killed. Banks had come up then, too.

The board of directors' elections were to be held on April 18, 1979. Most of the women couldn't go. The ones who stayed behind decided to put on a play, putting Inco on trial and holding the board of directors responsible for everything that had happened at Inco.

Chapter 45

The Mock Trial

The Wives' mock trial began the night before the Inco directors' election. The audience was the jury. We were to decide if they were fit to run the company. Among the participants were Nickel Belt MP John Rodriguez; he was the citizen's judge. He charged the company with the following: destruction of the environment, monopoly of work, failure to pay taxes, manipulation of the economy for workers here and abroad. Dave Patterson accused the company of bargaining in bad faith, attempting to smash the union, and pollution. The wives wore papier mâché masks and three-piece suits. They portrayed Inco's chairman J. Edwin Carter; President Charles Baird; and directors Arnold Heart, David Barr, Donald Willmott, and Alan Lambert. They sipped red wine in long-stemmed wine glasses being served by a woman in a maid's costume. They puffed on Cuban cigars and made smoke rings as they sat in the large arm chairs while the charges were being read out. One of the Wives charged the company with criminal negligence, for failure to notify families when workers were injured at work. Linda expressed her fear and anger, knowing the sacrifices families faced when there are shutdowns and strikes and no money. She knew the frustration of not being able to find a job to make things a little easier, because there were next to no jobs for women in Sudbury. Linda's voice sounded much stronger and she was more sure of herself than the first time I heard her speak.

Bruce McKiegan, our Steelworkers Occupational Safety and Health representative, talked about how many men were killed at Inco. He choked up a few times when relating the message of the man who was killed on the number-two fine-casting furnace. This was the story about the bar going through the man's throat and the company not stopping production, just washing the blood away and continuing the casting. That was the same casting wheel we used in the initial Right to Refuse Unsafe Work complaint. From 1966 until 1979 there were ninety deaths at Inco. Eighty of these men were married with children, so 240 children were now without fathers. He went on to tell the crowd that our local inquest committee had only been allowed full participation at inquest since 1970. Defense attorney Mouthy Lies-a-Lot was portrayed by Sudbury lawyer Don Kuyek, entering a token defense for the company's directors, saying, "We all know you the people have no right to judge these good men. They came here out of the goodness of their hearts. They know they can rest on their record and their company's record. The charges are unwarranted; it's inflammatory and just not nice. We all know the company has never discouraged the organization of unions. We all know the company has been considerate of unions and will always know the unions act responsibly. The company is the best judge, not the union. These men enjoy the community; they are important." The crowd booed and hissed.

Another Inco worker talked about the bad working conditions we worked in, the union busting, inadequate pensions, devastation of the environment, and manipulation of the economy. "There is no doubt that Inco has put profits ahead of people. I ask you to find the company guilty as charged," he said.

The crowd got to its feet, yelling and fisting the air. "Guilty! Guilty! Guilty! Off with their heads!"

A hooded figure appeared on stage carrying a large two-sided cardboard axe wrapped in tinfoil. He descended upon Inco's board of directors, executing them for their crimes against the community. The crowd roared with laughter and yelled, "Off with their heads!" Later that week, the media said we were too violent and that our behaviour was unacceptable because of the mock decapitations.

Chapter 46

Too Much Fighting

The fighting was getting worse at home. The children would hide up in their rooms as the yelling continued.

One day, Lloyd was standing on one side of the kitchen counter and I was on the other, spicing sausages. His arm went up in the air and swooped up six or seven of the freshly-spiced sausages and threw them against the wall. I felt terrified about what he might do next.

The sausages splattered, their insides mashed and stuck to the wall. Pieces fell into the rubber plant that was sitting below. I laughed nervously at the mashed artwork it left. He warned me not to laugh at him.

"I'm not laughing at you, I'm laughing at the sausages," I said.

"You're a liar, you're laughing at me." His eyes narrowed with contempt.

"No, I'm not," I yelled back, "and I am not a liar. Look at the plant, it's full of sausage."

He grabbed the plant, picked it up over his head, and threw it into the living room. The dirt spilled across the rug, and a piece of the plant broke off. I yelled at him to stop. He turned to me, still fuming, and started towards me. I backed up to the counter. Everything was in slow motion. A large butcher knife lay where the sausages used to be. A calm came over me. I picked up the knife and held it out toward him. "Don't come any closer," I warned.

He stopped, a strange look on his face. "How dare you pull a knife on me."

"Well, you pulled a rifle on me," I said. "I mean it, I have had enough. You might be stronger than me, but I tell you, you ever hit me like your dad hit your mom, don't ever fall asleep. I have a cast-iron frying pan." I pointed to the cupboard the pan was in.

"You're crazy!" he said, and headed toward the door. He stopped and picked up the full clothes hamper and threw it at me. I had time to jump into the living room, but the bottom of the hamper hit my back. It didn't hurt but I flew into a rage. I ran toward him, pushed him down a few stairs and out the door, and locked it. I ran and got two butter knives and jammed them in the frames of the front and back doors. I yelled at him to leave or I would call the police. He came back later that night; I could see the scratches I had left on his arms. This was the end. We had to separate or one of us was really going to get hurt, and in the frame of mind I was in after that night it wasn't going to be me. I knew if we stayed together something bad would happen. The relationship was like the molten metal I worked with: all it needed was to hit water.

After we separated, the children stayed with me in the house we had bought. I knew it wasn't going to be easy with thirty dollars a week on vouchers. I was now a single woman.

Chapter 47

The Smoke Detectors
May 8, 1979

A. P. Statham
Vice-President

INCO LIMITED
1 First Canadian Place, Toronto, Ontario M5X 1C4
(416) 361-7790

Alfred Statham's business card.

One of the filmmakers needed a place to stay, and I told her she could bunk with me. I told her she could sleep in the rec room. She was only twenty, with short black hair and a heavy French accent. She was the editor/producer of *The Wives' Tale* documentary. On May 1, the film crew and some of the Wives had a meeting at my place to discuss how we were going to raise money for the documentary.

Bruce and I were off to Toronto on May 8, 1979. I was to speak at a posh women's club. Knowing this might put Lloyd and Bruce's wife Madlyn's noses out of joint, I asked if I could bring my seven-year-old son Peppy with us.

In 1973, a Scottish-born Isabel Beveridge broke new ground by opening the 21 McGill Club. It was the first women's club that catered to the young and ever-expanding newer class of career women. I realized I was not in that class, but I always knew I had class—just a different kind. We never got a tour of the place but what I saw was extravagant. The club was breathtaking, especially when I went to the washroom and saw that the taps were gold-plated. They may not have been real gold, but they were very impressive. I had never seen anything like this.

We entered the main hall of the club. About eighty chairs faced a stage where a lone table and chair sat looking rather deserted. I decided to sit on the edge of the stage with my legs dangling over, closer to the audience.

I talked about what it was like to be a woman at Inco. I talked about safety and I mentioned the large four-legged rats as well as the two-legged ones. A man who was sitting in the back stood up to ask a question. He was slim and pale, wearing a light-grey suit. His hair was reddish blond and very thin; from my angle it looked like the hair you'd see on a store mannequin.

"Hello Cathy, my name is Alfred Statham, and I am the vice president of Inco Limited at First Canadian Place here in Toronto." No microphones were set up and it was hard to hear him, so we yelled back and forth.

"This is not working well," I said. "Why don't you come up and sit beside me." I patted the stage with my right hand and motioned him forward with my left. "You can be my right-hand man; I know you won't think of ever going left." I giggled at my joke. He didn't.

I talked about the film and how important it was to get the message out about what these women were doing. When I finished, he handed me his business card and I put it in my back pocket. It was a great evening and we raised a good amount of money.

Bruce, Peppy, Sophie, and I were late heading back to Sudbury because the film crew talked a lot. They didn't seem to have much sense of time. They gave us some money so we could stop and eat. We picked up Melanie at my mom's and headed to my place. The shit hit the fan when Madlyn and Lloyd got to talking. One had called the other, feeding off each other and what they thought was true—that Bruce and I were an item. Lloyd called, yelling at me that he knew that Bruce and I were sleeping together. I yelled back that I had told him many times that we were just friends. The reason I had taken Peppy was to reassure both Lloyd and Madlyn that nothing was going on. We were just good friends. I was so sick of hearing this. Whispers at the Steel Hall, whispers at work. Bruce was my best friend. I never thought of him as a lover.

The next day, a police officer came to my door. He said there had been a complaint that my dog wasn't being looked after properly. I let him in and we talked while he scribbled on his notepad. He asked if he could use the phone, and I pointed to it on the kitchen counter. I went back to cooking the pork chops that were in the oven. I opened the oven door, which always set off the smoke detector, then realized the officer was on the phone and shut the oven door really fast, not wanting to disturb him. I looked up to the smoke detector, expecting it to go off. It was gone—only wires hung from where it used to be. I stared at it, not understanding what it was I was seeing. The police officer was looking at what I'm sure was a look of terror on my face. I ran up to the kids' room: no smoke detectors. I ran down to the rec room; again, no smoke detector, only loose wires. All the smoke detectors in the house were gone. What was going on here? Why were they all gone, and who took them? The police officer was still by the phone when I got back, and when he hung up he asked what was wrong. I told him I had just separated from my husband, that I had just gone to Toronto, and that I thought my husband had come in and taken all the smoke detectors. He flipped the page of his note book and began writing.

The officer asked why I thought he would do such a thing. All I said was, "There is only one answer to that and it's a scary thought."

I was so thankful the officer was there, and the dog problem took a back burner. After the officer left, Sophie and Joyce showed up. We sat at the table and I told them what had happened. There was a loud banging on the front door; it was Lloyd. I opened it and he tried to come in, yelling that it was his house too.

"No, you're not coming in. And I know you took the smoke detectors and I know what you were planning on doing!" I yelled.

"You don't know anything!" he yelled back. I tried to close the door, but he blocked it with his foot and pushed hard to get in.

Joyce got up from the table. She stood about six feet tall and had no problem grasping the door above me and opening it wider. Lloyd had a surprised look on his face when he saw this tall woman dressed all in black with beautiful thick reddish-brown hair in curls that went everywhere. "Do you have a problem?" she said, flinging her long black scarf around her neck. "Maybe you should talk to me." Joyce could be very intimidating. I backed out from under her arm. She told him to leave or she would call the police. I got a peace bond to keep him away from me. The laws were really stupid in the '70s; he couldn't come in the house but he could enter the yard. Some days he sat in his truck in the driveway. I felt sorry for him, but he brought it on.

Chapter 48

The Contract is Turned Down Wives Get a Blast

Cathy at the Wives' meeting.

The strike put a lot of emotional strain on all of us. My marriage wasn't the only one that had split up. One of the Wives suggested that our marriages didn't break because of the strike, but because it all added to already rocky marriages.

Many of us were red-baited, some calling us communists or socialists. I didn't even know what that meant. I never did like labels, because not everyone has the same idea of what a label means. One man told me I was a communist sympathizer because he saw me talking to a woman who was a member of the Workers' Communist Party. She had become a good friend. To me that was just another political party, like the Liberals or the NDP. I didn't really care what anyone was. Red-baiting happened in the Wives' group too; people said they were too radical and that they should have been more of a ladies' auxiliary. Others called us feminists or women's libbers, as if that was a negative thing. Some people thought that if a woman was a libber, then she hated men. Being a libber to me was something I was doing for myself and other women; it had nothing to do with men.

Splits were happening within the union membership as well as the Wives. It was probably always there, but now that women were becoming more aware the split was more pronounced. One thing all the women agreed on was that the film crew was going to rewrite history from the women's point of view about what really happened in 1958. That kept us as one. We wanted the true story to be told about 1958, and the stigma and the blame put to rest.

Monday, May 7, 1979: the bargaining committee came back with a tentative agreement, recommending that the members accept the company's contract. The vote would be held one week later.

The Wives were on the phone calling a special meeting. As far as I was concerned, this was a shitty contract and I was going to turn it down. If we would have been offered this back in September it would have been okay, but now it sucked. Eight months had gone by and we deserved more.

I parked my car next to Dave's in the Sudbury Star parking lot. He looked exhausted when he exited his truck, black rings below his eyes.

"What the fuck is with the suit and tie, Patterson?" I shouldn't always say what's on my mind.

"What! I can't wear a suit?" he barked at me.

"Well, you haven't worn a suit during this strike in front of our members, why now? What do you think this says to the membership? You're a blue-jean, cowboy-boots kind of guy. Why now?" I snarled as I ran after him.

He stopped and turned toward me. "Look! Cat, I just drove all the way from Toronto and I haven't had time to change." He was upset.

I felt miserable giving him shit; that was all he needed: a little yappy dog at his ankles. "Well, I am telling you it doesn't look good, especially when you try and sell us that shitty contract." Again, I said this running after him.

He stopped. "Cat, it's all we could do. Please stop yelling at me," he begged.

I lowered my tone. "No. It's not all you can do. We believe you can do better." I was still on his heels.

He threw a hand up in the air as if to say this conversation was finished.

Over a thousand members packed the hall, murmuring about the contract. I stood in the back and watched Dave get up on the stage. Someone whispered to him to be careful, that he'd had death threats. He walked to the lectern, and I glanced down at the Steelworkers crest carved in the front of it. *Come on Patterson*, I thought to myself. *This is who we are; fuck the politics, we the people are the union.* He removed his suit coat and hung it on the back of a chair. Off came the tie and he undid his top button, rolled up the sleeves of his dress shirt, and waited for the yelling to subside.

"Now that's the Patterson I know!" I yelled out. I couldn't have been happier. A large six-foot-plus overweight guy, whose wife was in the Wives group, didn't agree with me. He hovered over me and called me a cunt, which is one name I really don't like. He stood there, hands on his hips, his eyes shooting daggers at me.

"What the fuck is your problem?" I yelled at him. I had no fear; my happiness was replaced by rage. A few men circled him while Bruce steered me away. "I hate that C-word, and no wonder his wife is such a bitch, being married to an asshole like him," I was yelling as Bruce put his arm around my shoulders to calm me down. He told me to let it go.

The bargaining committee sat at tables on the stage facing the crowd. Dave went to the mic; the grumbling, yelling, and name-calling didn't cease.

"Okay," Dave said, "if that's the way you want to play it." He didn't raise his voice. "I can wait until you're finished then we can start this meeting." It began to quiet down. "You have all read the contract …" The crowd roared in anger. Dave backed away from the mic; the crowd got the message and was again quiet. "This bargaining committee"—he gestured toward the men on stage—"has asked you to accept this agreement." The crowd became unruly, screaming obscenities at Dave. One man tried to get up on the stage to get at him but was stopped. Big burly miners guarded the stage after that.

"Well," Dave said softly, "we thought this was a good deal and we thought wrong."

At every meeting, the union hall was packed, and at every meeting the members stood strong and said, "No, it isn't enough; we demand the bargaining committee go back." We wanted thirty years of service to retire with a full pension, no matter how old you were. For me, starting at the age of nineteen years old, I would be eligible at forty-nine. The company would have to pay me full pension until I was sixty-five. That would be sixteen years. They didn't want that. At the age of sixty-five our pensions are reduced when the old age pension kicks in. We believed that because of the conditions we had to work in for thirty years we deserved a full pension.

It was obvious the bargaining committee was surprised to see the members so unified, so strong. This was not the message they were getting back in Toronto from the right wing of the Local. Go back and get more—the members had spoken.

I felt an intense excitement in those few days. Dave understood the power of the people. The bargaining committee would go back to Toronto if the contract was turned down. But sometimes people can say one thing and vote another. There was so much tension in the hall.

The Wives' meeting was just as intense, if not more so. They had read the contract and agreed it would have been okay back in September, but not now.

One of the Wives who was strong during the strike announced that she didn't know how her husband was going to vote, but that she thought it was a shitty contract. She said she would back him if he voted no, but if he voted yes, she would not tell him how to vote but would let him know that she thought this was a bad contract.

Another woman, one who wanted us to be an auxiliary group, said that her husband had thirty years of service and there was a lot at stake, and that she would go along with whatever her husband decided.

Another woman said, "We've been in this together, we've had a voice to a certain extent, why shouldn't we be allowed to turn around and tell our husbands, or anybody, that we don't agree with this contract and hope that the members turn it down?"

Another woman: "The Wives had to live down the lie from 1958 because they took a stand. We had to get the men's confidence and we've done a damn good job up until now. I believe it's up to the men to do their share and vote this contract down, and only after that will we make a stand." She hit her book hard with every word.

Another woman said, "My husband and I are both against the contract, and I'm supporting him. But if he was for it, I'd still be against it because I think it's a shitty contract."

And another: "If the men say yes to this contract and in a few months see it's bad, who will get the brunt of the anger? Us. I say we tell them our opinion so we cannot be blamed. I'm not saying we should do anything right now. Maybe it can wait till after the vote, but I still don't see where we are wrong in saying we don't like it."

Another woman yelled out, "We've been quiet much too long and look where it's gotten us!"

The woman who didn't want the Wives to make a stand began to back down, and said, "Okay, I'm not eliminating making a public statement, but I want to hear exactly what is going to be said. As far as taking any action that could backfire in our faces or influence the men in their decision, remember it's up to them, it's up to them to make a decision. If we add our input, it infringes on their rights. They have to make that decision on their own, and whatever that decision is I am supporting it, and if they don't know that by now, I don't know what the hell we're doing here."

I couldn't stay quiet. I may not have been able to vote but I could put in my two cents. "If your husband changed his view about the strike and he decided to accept the contract and you disagreed deep down in your heart, would you still stand behind him? Would you stay quiet?" A few women nodded and said yes. "Why? Why would you not say something?"

The woman running the meeting stepped in, rambling and not making much sense. She and I had locked horns a few times and it was her husband that had called me the C-word at the union meeting. I spoke over her. "You feel this strike, you feel the tightness at home, and you feel bad you only have bologna on the table instead of steak. Deep down you're struggling because you believe that this strike means a lot, and if your husband—not *your* husband, but *a* husband—said he changed his mind and was going to accept the contract, but you don't like the contract and feel that the strike is still worth continuing, why would you change your mind?" I began raising my voice.

"I am not going to tell him to stay out on strike!" she yelled. "I am not going to tell him how to vote, to stay out on strike if he doesn't feel that he wants to do this any longer. Maybe he wants to get back to work and get his family back on the ground, and I'm not going to tell him how to vote on this contract."

"I'm not telling you to tell him *how* to vote, all I am saying is have your own input. I'm not telling you that he should go back to work, all I'm saying is don't change your mind just because he did, if your mind is still for this strike." I was trying to make her understand.

She cut me off. "I'm not for this strike, Cathy, I am for my husband, and if my husband decides what's best for him is to go back to work, then fuck the strike, that's how I feel." Some of the older auxiliary women clapped.

Now I was mad. "This is not just your fight anymore!" I yelled back, my finger pointing and shaking at her. "It's everybody's strike and that's what you have to get through your head. If we lose this strike, all the other places in Canada that are looking to us are going to say, 'If they couldn't do it, nobody can.' This is history in the making."

She yelled that she didn't care about others in Canada.

Another woman cut in. "This is getting too personal; we should decide what the Wives are going to do."

Another woman said that she had come out to make a stand no matter which way her husband was going to vote, that she didn't like the contract and wanted to say so. She added that her husband was supporting her and hoped that the committee wouldn't try to stop her.

Everyone in the room had their say. A motion was on the table: we felt that there was still confidence in the LU 6500 bargaining committee, that they were not trying to sell us out, and that they could go back and get a better offer, so we needed to know all those who were in favour of sending this to the media. Everyone except the chairperson, the woman who was fighting with me, put up their hands. One opposed.

A press release issued by Wives Supporting the Strike was put out before the vote, stating that they felt that the contract offered to LU 6500 members was not worth an eight-and-a-half-month strike. A group spokesperson said that they supported the bargaining committee, who they strongly believed could achieve a better contract if given the mandate by the membership to return to the bargaining table, but that they would, however, support the decision of the members if there was a major vote to accept the contract.

Needless to say, the union executives were not happy with the Wives' committee. Dave called Arja, one of the Wives. "Dave, just listen to me. We don't think that this is a good enough contract," she said as a bunch of us stood in the kitchen, listening to the one-sided conversation, wondering what Dave was saying on the other end. She went on to say that it wasn't just her, that the committee felt they had to make a stand. "We've been so active supporting the strike, supporting our men and women, and all of the women last night disagreed with the contract. Our husbands disagree with the contract too. So, don't we have a right to our opinion?" She added, "You guys came back and said this was a total union victory. It would have been a total union victory eight months ago but not now. Now that Inco wants us back to work, we make them wait another month. We support the bargaining committee to go back and get more." She was firm.

"They want us to follow their rules," she said as she hung up the phone.

"Well, if it gets done according to their rules," another woman said, "we won't get much done."

Another WWS meeting was called. Ronald McDonald and Dave were both there. Dave sat in a chair that leaned against the wall with his head down. Ron was going to chastise us women.

One of the women said, "We've never had to get permission for press releases before. Does this mean we have to do it in the future?"

Ron stated, "We're are all in this strike together. There wouldn't be any Wives Supporting the Strike if there was no strike." We all looked at each other and shook our heads at this stupid statement. I curled my lip. He continued, "The strike was determined by the membership. They rejected the contract proposal back in September. We all have a big job to do. We all have to do it together, but if you want the animosity of the executive board regarding your efforts, that is not going to help anything. That's how the board feels right now. You have to support the bargaining committee, their recommendations, or keep out of it." He paused and pointed to Dave slumped over in his chair, looking at the floor. "Dave could say, 'I'm not asking you, I'm telling you not to have any more press releases.' Get them approved by him or whoever he designates. If it's okay with the Local, then you should go that route and it's better for everybody concerned. But if you're going to go and say that this is the way you feel and you think we should be doing these things, then you are dividing us. We're going in different directions and that's all he's trying to say to you. Solidarity is working together. This is the first time we've really had a rift, because of this press release, and it's obvious that there's not solidarity here because people have different opinions *and that's what we don't want.*"

To me, that last statement said it all.

After that meeting, a few women went down to the arena where the women back in '58 had gathered. One woman said she thought we were back to being a ladies' auxiliary. "We are not the women of 1958, and we will tell the men we are strong and we can negotiate. No man is going to tell us what we can or can't do. We have changed; we are not the same women we were eight months ago. We are not an auxiliary buttering sandwiches. We are thinkers, and our men know it but don't want to accept it. They may not want to accept this now that we're independent people. We are different and we have minds of our own. Yes, we made the press release; yes, we made a decision, and we made up our own minds on how we were going to do it. It just shows we can make up our minds and we don't need men or committees to tell us what to think. We can make up our own minds and I think it's scaring them a lot."

Fifty-seven percent of strikers rejected the settlement. Rejecting this offer was the real victory, a triumph over the international union that wanted us back to work. A triumph over the company who thought we would crawl to their demands. A triumph over the unsuspecting bargaining committee who had told us we should accept the offer. All the work, all the hardship, all the worry paid off when the contract was rejected.

We all headed downstairs to the union bar. Cameras were rolling, people were smiling, and the Wives were singing. This was the win. We the people had spoken. Not too many people in this world would ever get to feel this kind of victory. I felt privileged to be a part of it.

> PRESS RELEASE ISSUED BY WSS:
>
> "Wives Supporting the Strike feel that the contract offered to local 6500 members is not worth 8 months of strike."

> A group spokesperson said:
> "We support the bargaining committee. We strongly believe that they can achieve a better contract, if given the mandate by the membership, to return to the bargaining table. We will however support the decision of the members if there is a majority vote to accept the contract."

MY VIEW FROM THE BLACKENED ROCKS

Cathy in the early years.

Sudbury's blackened rocks.

The Smelter.

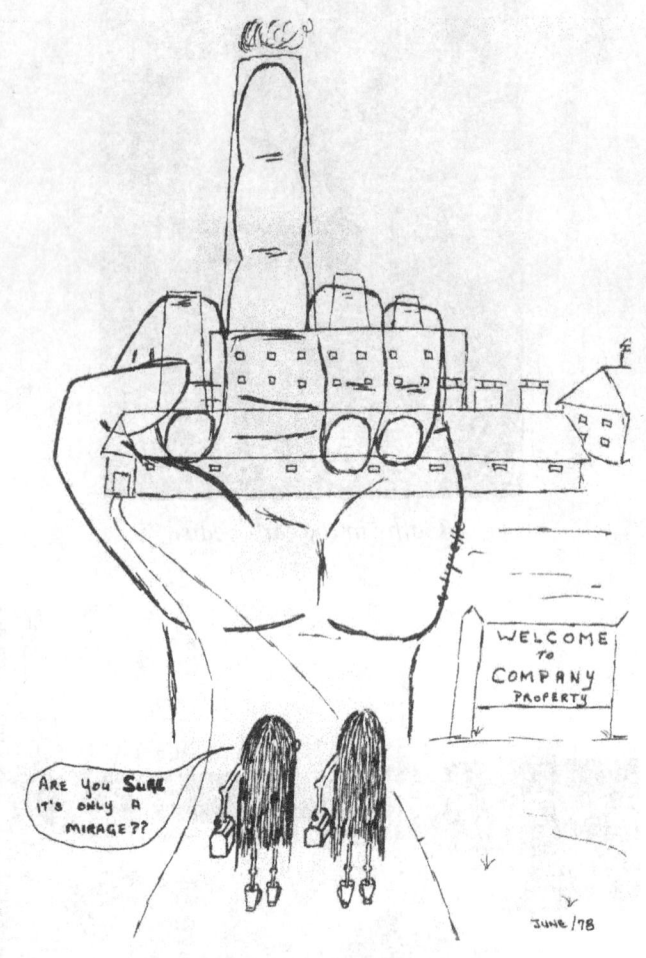

The stacks by Noris Valiquette

Corn Roast.

Corn Roast.

OFL Convention with Dave Patterson.

Labelling of the cans for Queen's Park.

Children's Christmas party.

Cathy helping at children's Christmas party

Bean supper.

Bean supper.

The Wives meetings.

The Wives meetings.

The Wives meetings.

The burning of the effigy.

The burning of the effigy

Marching.

Newman's wife facing the marchers.

The mock trial.

The mock trial – off with their heads!

Singing in the park. Patty's Patriots.

Singing in the park. The Wives and Cathy.

The contract is turned down.

The contract is turned down. The Wives singing.

International Women's Day, Toronto. The Wives

Women in slag.

Cathy in the Anode.

Melanie, Peppy, Cathy, and Cassi.

Peppy, Melanie and Cathy.

Chapter 49

Back to Work After the Strike June 3, 1979

Cathy back to work.

Wire bar being poured.

A few weeks later, the bargaining committee came back and informed us that Inco had agreed to the thirty years of service for full retirement and a few extras.

Almost nine months on strike and I was back on the job. I thought of it like a pregnancy. The first trimester was the vote to strike and going on strike. In the second trimester, like a fetus, I began to grow and became very active. In the third trimester I became stronger, used different parts of my brain. Then a new person was born.

All of this had taken its toll on my health, which was deteriorating. Anger was always on the surface. I was getting more attacks. The strike had covered up the feelings of the rape, but every once in a while that too surfaced and I fought hard to keep it buried. I still blamed myself for going for that coffee.

The doctor told me I had a hiatal hernia that had to be fixed. The top of my stomach was ripping away. The pressure of being a single mother working three shifts and all the responsibility slipped into my reality and only made it worse. It wouldn't have been so bad if I didn't have to put up with the horrible harassment from some of the men. All I wanted to do was do my job and for them to leave me alone.

Melanie was four and Peppy seven. It was an early morning when I walked through the wire bar and into fine casting on this particular day. The familiar stench of acid from the tank house invaded and burned the inside of my nostrils and throat; I curled my lip, having never gotten used to that odour. Even though I hated to be there, I felt comfort from the plant, like an old friend. It was a love–hate relationship.

After jumping through many hoops, the film crew finally got permission from management to film me back on the job for the conclusion to A *Wives' Tale*.

What happened after the strike? After it was over, I was summoned to the general foreman's office, the man with the beer belly that hung over his pants and the buttons on his white shirt that were so tight they hung for dear life in the buttonholes. His trusty snake man stood beside him, puffed up with self-importance. They reminded me of cartoon characters.

I was told I was no longer allowed to leave the department unless I had to use the washroom. I was no longer allowed to go over and talk to Bruce in the wire bar and he was no longer allowed to come over and talk to me. I reacted by blowing out a loud puffing noise from my lips and asking if that was all ... then I left. Three workers hovered outside the office as I walked past, reminding me of a small wolf pack in stalking mode. I could feel their hostility towards me. I glanced over and gave them a smirk. One turned away and the other two were stone-faced. That split in the union during the strike, the left and the right—well, they were on the right and I was on the left. Now I had to put up with union politics too.

Bruce and I stood in the doorway that connected the wire bar and the fine casting areas, each of us in our own department. We could still talk to each other.

The next day I was called into the fat-bellied general foreman's office again. I asked if I needed a steward and was told no. The snake and tight-shirt guy were at their usual positions. They told me they received a call from Toronto from the vice president of Inco, Alfred Statham—he wanted to talk to me. The memory of the red-headed mannequin at the posh women's club pictured in my mind. I asked what he wanted and was told the company was flying me to Toronto, and that they would pay me for the day. I asked if they would pay my sitter too, but they said no.

"Okay, I'll go and see what Al wants," I said, waving a hand in the air as if it was nothing that the vice president of Inco wanted to talk with me. Their mouths gaped when I got up to leave. I am sure they wanted to know what this was all about.

Linda, head of the Wives, called me to say she too was invited to Toronto. They wanted to talk to us about the documentary. I was suspicious.

On June 8, 1979, we boarded a plane and were picked up in a large shiny black car that drove us to First Canadian Place in the financial district of Toronto, on the northwest corner of King Street. It's Toronto's operational head office of the Bank of Montréal. Linda and I stood outside the tall structure, eyeing the height of the seventy-two-floor building. A security guard ushered us into the building and told us to wait in the lobby. It was like we had walked into another world. The walls, the floors—everything was made of marble. I touched its cool surface and wished I had a piece of it. Linda began to sing. *The walls are made of marble ...* My eyes widened, and I wondered what the heck she was doing. She said it was a union song for the farmers and for the miners in Italy who worked in the marble mines. She continued to sing.

But the walls are made of marble

With a guard at every door

And the vaults are stuffed with silver

That the farmer sweated for.

I saw the seaman standing

Idly by the shore

I heard the bosses saying ...

I didn't know the words, so I hummed along.

The guard returned and we were told to follow him into the elevator. It was padded, and I made a joke that the people who worked there must be under a lot of pressure to need a padded elevator. Linda laughed; the guard didn't.

We exited the elevator and stood in front of two beautiful wooden doors. When they opened, I was expecting a glamorous office but was disappointed by the bland furnishings. It was almost barren. Alfred the mannequin man sat behind a table-type desk. He pointed to the two chairs and told us to have a seat. His desk was bare except for a yellow magazine: *The Latin American Working Group*.

"Hey, I have a copy of that magazine too; do you subscribe to it?" My innocence and ignorance showed through.

He didn't smile. "I see your picture is in this magazine. How did it get in there?" My gut tightened, giving me a warning alarm.

As a smart ass, I said, "Someone used a camera and put it in there." He opened the magazine to a picture of me and Miguel. He tapped his finger on Miguel's picture and said that he wanted to know how and what I knew about this man. By his tone it was clear it was more of a demand than a question. I told him he lived in Guatemala and was trying to organize a union.

He raised his voice, wanting to know what else I knew. I felt uncomfortable, unsafe. The stories I had read in the magazine about all the people killed for their land played in my head, along with the pictures of the dead bodies of women, children, and men piled in the back of trucks, heaped on one another like bales of hay. I felt I was in danger.

Again, he said he wanted to know what I knew about Guatemala and this man. He pounded his finger on the picture of me and Miguel.

I stared at the mannequin man as the night of the secret meeting played in my head. Miguel telling us about his family and that they had to hide for their lives. That there was a death list and his name was on it. I smiled when I thought about sharing a joint with Miguel. Alfred's voice was thick with insinuation. He wanted to know how I picked my friends.

My anger surfaced. Who did this mannequin man think he was? "I don't pick my friends because of their status, or who they are. He's a nice person and we got along just fine. I was asked to meet him for lunch and that's what I did." My teeth clenched. "I don't even know where Guatemala is." I waved my hand in the air as if I was shooing him off. It wasn't a lie. I really didn't know exactly where Guatemala was. I knew it was somewhere in South America but not exactly where. He stared at my face, maybe trying to read if I was lying. "Is this why you called us to Toronto?"

There was a calm and then he changed the subject, wanting to know about the documentary and how it was going. There was no more talk about Miguel and Guatemala. Flying home, I wondered how dangerous that meeting could have been. What kind of people were they?

The smelters back up and running in Sudbury.

Chapter 50

Applying to be a Steward

On June 13, 1979, I applied to be a steward for United Steelworkers of America, LU 6500. It wasn't hard to get the forty-two signatures that were required. I was so excited. Maybe if I was a steward I wouldn't get in so much trouble.

Bruce told me there was writing on the walls down on the loading dock—*Cathy is a slut, Cathy is a cunt, she can suck my cock*. Big black Magic Marker was used. I was surprised and shocked then hurt. Why would someone do this? Was it from my union brothers, the ones who were always hovering and glaring every time I walked by?

I went to the foreman; he just shrugged his shoulders and asked what he was supposed to do about it. He told me that if I wanted to work in this environment to suck it up and get used to it. I went to get Bruce and we had a meeting with the boss. Again, he said he couldn't do anything about it, until Bruce asked him why he would let someone deface company property. You could see the wheels turning, and he said he would get it painted over but it didn't matter much because I was being sent back to the anode. With a smug look on his face, he told me there was no room for another member on the OHSA committee in the anode, and no room for another steward.

Fucked again.

My stress was getting worse; my gut hurt. My doctor said I was too stubborn to have a nervous breakdown but one day my body would give out on me. I had healed okay from the gallbladder operation, but I was still getting the attacks. The muscles were still locking in my esophagus. The stress between work and home was taking its toll on me. I was not going to quit; I was not going to give up. I would go back to the anode and do my time.

My anger grew. I was always sick and now I was diagnosed with irritable bowel syndrome. Good thing there was finally a woman's washroom in the anode.

My temper was always near the surface, sitting just below the explosion line. My stomach was filled with a lot of acid, like the tank house. It began to destroy my mental and physical health. I fought with the foreman about why I was back in the anode. He reassured me it wasn't personal. Like fuck it wasn't personal.

Unfortunately, my kids got a lot of my anger. I couldn't get a break.

Days later, my doctor told me I had to do something about the hiatal hernia. The attacks were happening more and more. Both my mental and physical states were deteriorating. I was a human pressure cooker, exploding at everyone and everything. Being back in the anode brought memories of the rape. I didn't sleep well. I buried the incident as deeply as I could, but sometimes it crept into my dreams. There were men laughing at me, pointing to the black writing on the wall: *Cathy is a pig*.

I don't know what happen to the rapist but he wasn't on my shift. I don't think he was even in the anode. I never asked.

Back on those ridiculous shifts: four afternoon shifts, three graveyards, then two days off, sleeping most of the first day. Then three afternoons and four graveyards. Two days off, sleeping one of them. Then finally day shift. Monday and Friday off. Then start that circle all over again. After weeks of this I finally had two day shifts off together. It was going to be hard to get a babysitter. If Lloyd would have taken his kids every second weekend like he had agreed to it would have made it easier. There was no chance of that happening, and the law said it couldn't make him live up to what he had agreed to. What the fuck?

Not only did I get separated from my husband, but the rest of his family wouldn't talk to me or the kids. I had no money in the bank and my ex wanted the house sold. He took the lawnmower when he moved to his apartment, now I had to fight to get it back. Exhausted and depressed, I had frequent rages, outbursts; my poor children got the worst of it and the men at work thought I was nothing but a bitch.

Chapter 51

Back in the Anode Summer 1979

I wouldn't be able to pull off the same trick of using my real name to get out of the anode again. The strike and my action made the name Mulroy recognizable.

Dirty and sweaty, I was crammed into the anode lunchroom with forty men who are also dirty and sweaty. Some of us smoked, so that just added to the ambience. A man opened his aluminum lunch pail and I noticed the stamp on the end of it that read, "May"; almost all the lunch pails were stamped. A man named Leo May from Sudbury made a sturdy pail. This was so workers could use them as a seat as well as a lunch box. It made me smile.

The sound of John yelling snapped me out of my daze. He was another wheel man. He was cursing—someone had washed out his blue plastic tea cup, the kind that screws onto the end of a Thermos. Many men just rinse their cups, leaving the tea or coffee stains to coat the inside so it doesn't have a plastic taste. A greasy-haired man who was known to cause trouble giggled, revealing his yellow teeth. I curled my lip and wondered why he didn't clean them, especially since we had dental coverage. An argument between the two men started. John marched over to the greasy-haired man when he told him he had to use comet in order to get the stains out. I didn't want to stay in the lunchroom listening to the men fight, so I headed down to the casting area, climbed up on the wheel stand, and watched the furnace crew poling. The roar of the furnace and the hissing of the gas blowers were like old friends. I pulled out a small black notepad and pen from my shirt pocket and began to write.

Memories of the eight-and-a-half-month strike played in my head. The Wives, the places, the people, the unions, and all the things we did. Now I was back in the anode as a type of punishment. Not only was I sick, I had fallen into a deep depression. *We mean nothing to this company. We are just numbers*, I thought to myself. I remembered the time I changed my name to get out of the anode away from the rapist. I said to the cigar-toting little shit, "35554, that's me, that is my identity. First, last, middle name—doesn't matter, it's all the same." So, I wrote this poem:

We Are Just a Number

35554
That's me.
That is my
Identity

First, last,
And middle name,
Doesn't matter,
It's all the same.

Just a number
Written on your hat,
Not Mike or June
Or Ralph or Pat.

They pick you up,
1, 2, 3, 4,
If not enough
They'll add on more.

Coming or going,
It's all the same.
Pick a number,
Lose your name.

23 and
54,
Move them up
Another floor.

62 and 78,
Left the plant,
Gone through the gate.

> Give the new man
> 77,
> The other one
> Has gone to heaven.

– Cathy Mulroy, 1979, 25 years old

I watched Ray push the end of the pole into the furnace and take a sample. His finger went up, indicating another pole. I relaxed back in the seat. Then more inspiration came, and I wrote another poem.

The Strike of '78/'79

> 15th of September,
> 1978,
> No more workers
> Crossed the gates.
>
> The votes were cast,
> Majority ruled,
> There would be a strike,
> We were nobody's fool.
>
> Layoffs and shutdowns
> Were Inco's course,
> Offering us nothing
> With no remorse.
>
> Told us they had stockpiles
> Miles high,
> Asked us to sell ourselves;
> They were ready to buy.
>
> 4 cents
> Is all you'll get
> For your hard work,
> Your lives, your sweat.

Unions had gathered
From all around;
They supported us workers
Surface and underground.

The wives got together
And stood by their men.
They were there at the beginning,
They were there at the end.

8 months out,
A proposal came in,
Our leaders came back
To say it's a win.

But our members said NO,
It wasn't enough,
We want more
And we're hanging tough.

The tension built up
As the ballots came in,
The doors were shut
And the counting begins.

The wait wasn't long
And the answer came out:
"NO" was what
The members did shout.

We're not going back
For pennies, we cried.
We took a big breath
And let out a sigh.

They've taken the resources
Out of our land
And put back nothing
To give us a hand.

The profits they made
Were more than enough;
They're in other countries
Where it isn't so rough.

For the people there
Have no say;
25 cents an hour
Is their pay.

But the union here
was strong and tight,
And we were ready
To put up a fight.

With Dave Patterson the leader
Of 6500
And all of the members
11,700.

We're standing together
Through thick and thin;
We knew the only outcome
was to win.

Off to Toronto
Our team did go
To tell Mother INCO
The members said NO.

They say it's no good
And they want more:
30 and out
And part of the score.

Back they came
In a very short time
With 30 and out
And much more than a dime.

June 3rd,
1979,
Ballots were cast
For the very last time.

Take it, take it,
INCO cried,
Don't you know?
We're on your side.

We want you back to work,
We've had enough,
Money's getting low
And we need that profit.

67 percent
Accepted this deal,
The strike was over
But it didn't seem real.

The first rejection
Was the real victory
We beat Mother INCO
And made history.

So off to work
Our members did go;
Back to their job's
At the company INCO.

And what we learned
We shan't forget,
The places and the
People that we met.

For the people are united
For evermore,
From North to South
And shore to shore.

– Cathy Mulroy, 1979, 25 years old

Chapter 52

The Current 1979

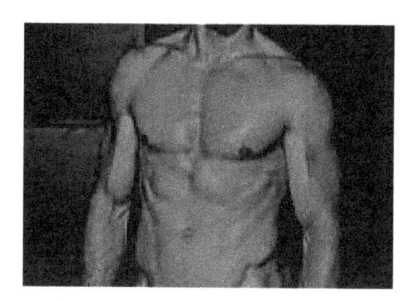

I hated being back in the anode. It wasn't the work, it was the shifts that were killing me. I believed it was punishment for my action during the strike.

It was graveyard shift—11:30 p.m. to 7:30 a.m. Forty men and I sat in the lunchroom waiting for the furnace to be ready to cast. We finished casting the other furnace and rushed through the clean-up. Clean-up was bull work: it's hard, it's hot, and it's filthy. The other furnace wouldn't be ready until 6:00 a.m., and it was only 3:30 a.m.

I sat on a very old wooden bench at one of seven stacking tables in the anode lunchroom. At a guess, the size of the room was seventeen by seventeen feet made of sixteen- by eight-inch concrete foundation blocks. The flaking paint revealed the many colours used over the last 100 years, making the wall look like it had psoriasis. I cradled my head in my hands, both elbows resting on the filthy table. I felt trapped. Often, tormented memories of the rape found their way to the surface of my mind and caused painful physical reactions when the muscles locked in my esophagus. The best thing to do was bury the incident deeper, along with the guilt always accompanying it.

Only my eyes moved as I scanned the room. Then, focusing on the dark brown vinyl tabletop, I curled my lips at how disgusting the lunch table was: old food stuck on it and spilled coffee mixed in with dried cement. I wondered how long it had been since someone had wiped that table off—probably never. My stomach churned at the sickening combination mixed with the odour of copper dust, sweaty men, and a room full of cigarette smoke. Just about everyone smoked. "Grungy" was the attitude in the anode. I wondered if we were a product of our environment or the cause of it. All I knew was that it was acceptable, and no one ever said a word. Nothing had changed in a hundred years. Same wheels, same furnaces, same production, same dreary lunchroom that looked like a dungeon.

I rolled my eyes up the wall to the only window in the place; it was so filthy you would have needed a putty knife to scrape away the dirt. If you could see through it, you would only get the view of the pig storage and the narrow-gauge trains. I observed an old weathered tomato sitting on the window sill. Someone had thrown it there and it had been there for months, maybe before the eight-and-a-half-month strike. It was now a grey powder, joined by a dried-up shrunken tea bag. It was common for a tea bag to pole-vault across the room from someone's spoon. Sometimes it hit someone and sometimes it ended up on the windowsill ... forever. Why would someone do that? Why is it still there? A *pffft* came from my lips and I shrugged my shoulders. I didn't know. I didn't care. I didn't put it there and I'm wasn't taking it down. My anode attitude was back. I rolled my eyes downward to the hole in the floor. One would think they would put a drain cover over it, especially after two rats had gotten into the lunchroom. A man tried to corner them with a broom and one rat had bared its teeth and jumped towards the man's face. He hit it away with the broomstick and another man held the door open as the rats ran out. They scooted under the cement floor into the pig storage. It reminded me of the time someone put a dead rat in Mike's lunch pail. Mike was a little simple, so he was bullied a lot.

Some men tried to get a few winks, resting their heads on folded arms. It wasn't a good idea to fall asleep—someone might start a fire under your chair using paper towels. I remember one man falling asleep once, and another man tied his bootlaces to the legs of the chair and then lit a fire underneath. Someone yelled, "Fire!" The man jumped to his feet and he tipped his chair back, unable to run. Some men laughed. I didn't think it was funny. This is what happens when men got restless in the anode. You'd never catch me falling asleep in the lunchroom.

I wanted a coffee but was disappointed when I opened my lunch pail to find I had left my Thermos in my car after I had it filled at Country Style Donuts.

A large jar of instant coffee and whitener sat on the counter beside the sink of the lunchroom; it was supplied by the company. I picked up the jar and read "For Institutions Only" in big black block letters.

"What does 'For Institutions Only' mean?" I threw the question out to whomever would answer me.

A man with long, black, greasy hair snarled at me. "It don't mean nothing. It's free, just drink it."

A younger man who I knew went to university piped up. "It's meant for prisoners, people in jail. It has saltpeter in it, potassium nitrate. It takes away your sex drive so more energy can be used for work." He smiled. I half smiled back, not sure if I believed him.

I'll drink it, I thought to myself. I don't need my sex drive anyway. I asked if anyone had milk. Ray told me to look in the fridge.

When I opened the fridge door, a centerfold of a naked woman rolled out. Someone had taped it there. Some men roared with laughter, others didn't say a word. I ignored them. The milk carton was empty, no surprise. One of these fine men put it back in the fridge empty.

Men made comments about the woman's breast and her vagina. I put on a poker face, not wanting them to know how this offended me. I took a spoonful of whitener, plunked it into my coffee, and curled my lip—I hate whitener. I watched as it mixed with the coffee. It didn't look good, and it smelled even worse. I wasn't looking forward to the taste.

I sat back down on the bench with my back against the wall and began stirring the mixture, watching it make a swirl. The faster I stirred the more pronounced the swirl became, looking more like a current. It reminded me of the currents in the Ottawa River at my grandparents' camp, a place I felt safe as a child. It hypnotized me, drawing me into my cup and away from reality, away from the anode—far, far away. I felt good. I felt safe.

I was woken from my trance by men hooting and hollering. I looked around but didn't know what was going on. That tall, bony, greasy-haired man had entered the lunchroom and was shaking a pry bar above his head. He stuck the pry bar into the hinges of a cupboard belonging to another shift. The men egged him on with their hollering. "Go Johnny, go go go!" His name wasn't even Johnny. One pry and the door ripped off its hinges. "Johnny" threw the pry bar onto the floor, got down on one knee in front of the damaged cupboard, and began unloading magazines. Men stood on the benches, reaching over other men to get their hands on a magazine. Magazines flew through the air as the men acted like sharks in a feeding frenzy. I was still not sure what was going on.

"Here Cathy," the bony man laughed. "You want to read something?" He threw a magazine at me. It fell at my feet and opened, revealing a disgusting hardcore pornography picture of a naked woman. I felt painfully uncomfortable; my dignity shattered. Never had I seen a magazine like this. Some men made comments about what sex acts they would like done to these women. I kicked the magazine away from my feet.

"What's the matter, little girl, you don't read?" the bony man probed, waiting for a response. I didn't answer. I couldn't answer, I was embarrassed, and I held back my tears. I wanted to run out of the lunchroom, but there was nowhere to go. Anger built inside me, along with pain in my gut as my intestines wrenched. I turned back to my coffee and began stirring it vigorously; I went back into my current. *Maybe this saltpeter stuff will start working on the men, that should take the fun out of reading those magazines. Take me away, current, take me somewhere safe.* I no longer heard the men. This is where I would go when the going got tough. There were many years ahead of me, so I had to learn to survive.

Days turned into weeks. Back on graveyard shift again, the sleazy Hustler magazines regularly made their appearance. Disgusted, I got up and left the lunchroom, walked past the roaring furnaces and watched the flames as they squeezed through the cracks around the doors. They looked like flaming arms reaching and stretching to get out. It reminded me of the religious pictures of hell that Roman Catholic nuns showed us in grade school. In my opinion they weren't far off.

The large doors at the end of the railroad tracks were opened—the hot car was on its way from the smelter. I peered through the grimy window of the foreman's office; he was reading a newspaper. I walked in, sat down beside him. He didn't lower the paper.

"I want to talk to you about those magazines the men are reading in the lunchroom. I don't like them. I feel uncomfortable sitting with the men when they make comments about the women." My voice sounded insecure.

The foreman lowered his newspaper and glared at me over his glasses. "Look, Cathy." His voice was patronizing, annoyed I had interrupted him with this trivial complaint. "This is a man's environment. You knew that when you were hired. If you don't like it, go work somewhere else. I'm not going to tell my men what they can and can't read. This is the culture here." He shook his finger at me. He was rigid and uncompromising.

"Well ... do they have to read them in the lunchroom? Can't they read them somewhere else?" I could hear a lack of self-confidence in my whining.

"Hey, it's their lunchroom." He gave me one of those alligator smiles and flapped open the newspaper as if to say he was going back to reading. More anger boiled up inside me. He couldn't hear my stomping feet on the cement floor, but he did react to the slam of his office door when the plexiglass rattled. With a last look through the grimy window, I could tell he was yelling at me but the words were drowned out by the roar of the furnaces. I muttered to myself, "How can this be right? Why is this acceptable behavior?" I kicked the lunchroom door open and threw my hardhat and glasses on the shelf, making a loud clanking noise.

Some men looked my way; the greasy-haired man chuckled. "What's the matter, little girl, is it that time of the month?"

That was the last straw. I lost my temper.

I was inches from his face. I spat out the words, "Why don't you just go fuck yourself? I wish you were dead! Don't fuck with me!" I was surprised at myself but fearless as quiet fell over the lunchroom. All eyes were upon us. Mr. Greasy Hair flinched, just for a split second. He continued to laugh, but with a slight nervousness. I took note.

The next night was worse. I walked into the lunchroom and the place was wallpapered with pornographic pictures of naked women. I couldn't look anywhere without seeing a filthy picture and wondered how they could even be legal. The greasy-haired man jumped on the end of the bench I sat on. "So, you want us to get rid of our Hustler magazines, eh, little girl?" he sang as he jumped around making ape motions. "If you can't handle it, quit!" he barked. It's obvious he had talked to the foreman. I poured a coffee from my thermos and waited for the current. There it was, and there I went.

The men in the room disappeared as I travelled down into my safe haven. I began to ask myself, *What are you doing here? Maybe you should be at home with your kids. Maybe you don't belong here.*

A second little voice joined in: *What do you mean you don't belong here? This is your job, you need this job, and this is your chance to change your life and your children's lives. With this job you can support your children the same way the men support theirs. You don't need a man to look after you.* I argued back and forth with myself. I felt sick and was glad when the shift was over so I could go home and talk to my dog.

Over the next month the pictures of the naked women were still on the walls of the lunchroom. They kept them up on day shift too, and management never said anything.

On my day off, my mom asked me to drive her to the second-hand bookstore. I watched as she disappeared into the romance section. I'm not interested in books—the letters were always backwards or moving around the page—so I looked through the magazines. A stack of them sat on the floor. I bent down to investigate.

I felt my heart leap to my throat as I flipped through the pages. Adrenalin coursed through my veins in pleasurable anticipation of what I had just found. These were similar to the magazines that the men were looking at, but instead of pictures of naked women they were filled with pictures of naked men, and I mean naked. Not a stitch on, all the men were at the ready position, tools as long as eight to ten inches. The magazine was called Playgirl. Never had I seen magazines like these. The wheels in my head began to turn. I felt empowered. If I couldn't beat them, I figured I might as well join them.

I counted the magazines: eighteen, nineteen … twenty-four in all. "Bend your knees, Cat," I said to myself as I picked up the pile. "Wouldn't want to hurt your back." I giggled at my own joke as I slammed the pile of magazines on the counter. My mom cradled a few romance novels and asked me what I was up to when she looked at the pile of magazines. Her eyes widened when she saw the shirtless blond male beauty on the front cover.

I couldn't get the smile off of my face. "Oh, just some magazines for work, Mom," I answered nonchalantly.

"Cathy … what are you doing? What are you up to?" I've heard that tone many times over the years.

"I'm bringing these magazines to work, Mom," I said with as much confidence as I could muster.

"No, you're going to get yourself into trouble!" She was scared for me.

"It's okay, Mom," I reassured her. "Everyone at work reads these kinds of magazines. The foreman says it's okay; he says it's part of the culture." My smile grew as I paid the lady and carried the magazines to the car.

"You might be pushing this a little too far." She shook her head and got into the passenger side.

"Are you saying I'm a little cocky, Mommy?" I laughed. "Get it? A little cocky? Or should I say big cocky?" I laughed some more.

"Oh, I give up," she said. "I never know what to do with you."

The next day I was a soldier armed with Playgirl magazines and rolls of Scotch tape. Before the men came into the lunchroom, I taped a few pictures of my naked men on the walls, then waited for the reactions.

As the men entered, some took a second and even third look before they figured out something was different.

"What the hell? Who put these up?" I didn't admit to it yet, I just sipped on my coffee. The next chance I got I taped them to the window, the door, the windows in the cranes, and all over the walls. I watched with anticipation when Greasy Hair opened the fridge door and a picture of a naked man unrolled out in front of him, the model displaying a very large and erect penis.

"What the fuck?" he shouted, his teeth clenched together. He grabbed the picture, ripped it into pieces, and threw them toward me. They landed on the floor. I was beaming, laughing so hard tears rolled down my face. I had waited for that moment for a long time.

"What's the matter, Dicky?" I said. "Is it that time of the month for you?"

Another man glared at me. Some were not pleased with my choice of magazines. They ripped them off the walls, leaving the pictures of the naked women. I kept putting more up. It aggravated some when I sang, *Dum dum dum dum dum, I feel good, dum dum da dum.*

I had to keep my magazines safe. If the men got hold of them, they would throw them all in the furnace. I couldn't keep them in my locker in the women's dry because management had keys to our lockers. An idea hit me one day in the washroom of the pig storage when I looked to the ceiling tiles. *Bingo!* Ceiling tiles—another smile on my face. I climbed up on the toilet then onto the sink and moved a tile away. "This will be your new home," I said as I placed all the magazines and tape up there. I climbed back down, wiped my footprints off the sink and toilet, and went back to work. Every chance I got I visited the bathroom, gathered a few pictures and tape, hid them in my coat and continued to tape them up. As fast as the men tore them down, I put them back up. I began to tear their pictures into little pieces and throw them in the garbage. Some men began to grumble, not happy with me.

"You know, Cathy, we are going to keep tearing down your pictures," one man said.

"Go right ahead." I shrugged my shoulders in defiance. "I have a lot. But notice, I've been tearing down your women pictures too."

"Ooh, brave, are we?" he continued.

"You want war?" I stood up, yelling. "You've got war!" My heart pounded hard in my chest. "You don't scare me." But I *was* scared. "The war is on." I sat back down and sipped my coffee.

Needless to say, this caused quite a stir. The men ripped down my pictures and I ripped down theirs. It wasn't long before I got called into the foreman's office.

"Cathy ... I have to have a talk with you." He looked uncomfortable when he forced a smile. "Sit," he said, and pointed to the unoccupied chair. I plunked myself hard on the chair, showing my rebellious side. He rotated in his chair to face me. This was much different than the last time, I thought to myself. "Cathy," he began as if I were a child, "we don't like your attitude. You have to stop bringing these magazines in and putting up these pictures. The men are not happy with you."

I raised my eyebrows. "Oh, really? They're not happy with me?" The words came out in a sarcastic laugh. "Well, like you said, *boss*"—I put a lot of emphasis on the "boss"—"if they don't like it, maybe they should go work somewhere else. Boss, you're the one who told me that it was okay, that this was the culture here. Boss, you're the one who told me it was okay to read these kinds of magazines; you said you could not tell anyone what they can and can't read. So, boss, I'm just trying to fit in. If the men can bring in pictures of naked women and stick them on the walls, then I can bring in pictures of naked men and do the same."

"This is not going to work." He tried to take control by raising his voice to intimidate me. "Cathy, the men are very unhappy with you."

I smiled. "Well what is good for the goose is good for the gander. If you are going to let the men put up their pictures but I can't put up mine, that's discrimination and I will have to put in a grievance." His face drain of colour. "I'll make a deal with you: the men keep their naked women magazines out of the lunchroom and off the walls, and I'll do the same with my naked men. If they continue, the war is still on." There was a long pause. I don't think he was ready to negotiate.

"Okay, okay, I'll see what we can do." He shook his head.

Still smiling, I got up to leave, then said, "Just like the guy who landed on the moon, boss." He looked confused. "One small step for woman, one giant leap for womankind." I smiled; he didn't.

The pictures came down, the magazines were no longer allowed in the lunchroom. This was the beginning of awareness.

It was never easy swimming against the current, but it definitely made me a very strong swimmer.

Chapter 53

Dating Ray
August 1979

I was invited to a wedding. I had never been on a date, so I wasn't sure what the rules were. I decided to ask Ray, our head furnace man. Being my friend from my Donovan days, I felt comfortable asking him. His mother and my mother volunteered at church functions. He said yes, and after our date we continued to see each other. Lloyd was not happy that I was seeing someone and asked the children if Ray ever stayed over. I never asked Ray to stay over when the kids were home. I didn't want them to get too close to Ray in case this didn't work out.

It was a lot of fun dating Ray. He took me fishing with the guys and asked if I wanted to go hunting in September. He said that Cambrian College had a good hunting course I should take. A guy on our shift we called Porky sold me a beautiful twenty-gauge shotgun made in Russia. Ray and I got along great. It was a good relationship and it seemed some of the men treated me a little better when they heard we were dating. Most people liked Ray.

I was wondering how other women at Inco were doing. As it happened, I found out from the newspaper that Inco had given two women training jobs in the smelter after they put in a grievance to work in the Cottrells, huge vessels in the smelter that accumulate dust and other gases and control emissions from the furnaces to the Superstack. It's too bad I had to learn about other women at Inco through the newspapers.

I was getting sicker and had been scheduled for a hiatal hernia operation. I asked the doctor to tie my tubes while he was in there. Having two kids already and being a single mom with a full-time shift-working job, I was sure I didn't want any more kids. The operation was so painful: they cut me open from the chest bone down to the bellybutton. My ribs had to be expanded. It was the worst pain I had ever felt; I wanted to die. A few men from my shift and a woman from the tank house came to visit me while I was in there. I was hooked up to so many tubes it was hard to talk. I could hear Ray calling my name. I opened my eyes and saw a shoe box above my head. Another man pulled out a live lobster and dangled it above my face. "This is for you when you're feeling better." The legs of the lobster wiggled as it hovered above me and the visitors laughed. One man said he should put it under my blanket so I could use it like a live teddy bear. All I could do was shake my head no, but inside I was laughing.

Lois, the woman from the tank house, brought a small book entitled *Crafty Things to Do in the Hospital*. She unwrapped a long white eight-inch dildo, batteries included. She placed it on my table and turned it on. *RRRrrRRRRR*—the dildo vibrated across the table. Everyone laughed, including me. She had heard a story of my ignorance in the anode: one day I had read an article in the newspaper that said a man had been charged with buggery using a dildo. I thought it should have read a man was charged with "burglary using heavy equipment." An old Italian man put his arm around my shoulders an explained to me what the article really meant. I was a little embarrassed, but enlightened once again.

My visitors left, leaving the white plastic Superstack dildo standing straight on the table. When the nurse came in to change my IV, she was surprised to see the toy at attention on the table.

"What's this?" she laughed.

"My friends from work," I moaned.

Six weeks later I was back in the anode and on the wheel, which meant I needed to make a ladle. In order to do that, I had to mix cement by hand in a trough using a hoe. Ray saw that I was having trouble and came down to the pit to give me a hand. It wasn't long before someone ran to the foreman and I was called in the office. He told me if I couldn't do all of the jobs required then I wouldn't be a wheel *man*. I told him that I only needed help until I got my strength back. He said once I could mix cement, I could have the wheel job back. I couldn't understand why they wouldn't buy a cement mixer. Even the safety guy said the motto was "if there is a need, help is available." I guess that wasn't for me. Back on the cast.

On March 8, 1980, International Women's Day, some of the women from LU 6500 USWA attended a rally in Hamilton: "Women Back Women into Stelco." A committee had been set up that was supported by the United Steelworkers of America, Local 1005. Five women filed a discrimination complaint with the Ontario Human Rights Commission and conducted a major public campaign to make the Steel Company of Canada hire women for production jobs at Helton works in Hamilton, Ontario. The five women won a favourable verdict from the provincial Human Rights Commission and Stelco began hiring women.

Back at Inco, another woman, Sally Matthews, came into the anode, and of course they put her on a different shift. So now Sue was graveyard shift, I was dayshift, and Sally was afternoons.

Chapter 54

Sally's Death

Sally S. Matthews

Why didn't anyone check to see if the staging was bolted to the forks of the charge crane? Eight children are now without a mother. Who was to blame? In my view, everyone involved.

This made the sixth death at Inco this year.

I tossed and turned; it was a restless sleep. I was woken by someone banging on my back door at 1:30 a.m. I rubbed my eyes and tried to focus on who it was. It was Ray. What was he doing here at this time? I grabbed my housecoat and let him in.

"What's up?" I said, my voice raspy. He asked to come in. His eyes had a wounded look, bloodshot from crying. He sat on the couch and cradled his face in his hands. I put on the coffee. His voice quivered. "Sally Matthews was killed at work today."

"What happened?" I was shaking.

He took a drink to clear the lump in his throat and told me the story.

Sally and her co-worker were working on a raised platform about six to ten feet off the floor, depending on which nuts and bolts on the furnace they were working on.

The work platform was approximately four by ten feet with guard rails around it. The rails were made of one-and-a-half-inch tubing and sat about forty-two inches high. There were pockets under the platform which would enable it to be bolted to the forks on the charge cranes. This was the same charge crane that Ray used when he was charging the furnace with the copper skulls.

Bolting the platform to the forks would make it safe to work from the platform. A large rivet gun had been attached to the guard rail. Their job was to either loosen or tighten the bolts on the furnace. The charge crane was always very jerky with each of its movements. Sally was working afternoon shift from 3:30 p.m. until 11:30 p.m. The platform was already in place when the two of them climbed in. Neither Sally nor her coworkers checked to see if the platform was bolted down. The day-shift foreman didn't tell the afternoon-shift foreman that the maintenance crew had not bolted the platform down. The afternoon-shift foreman didn't check. The charge-crane operator didn't check. No one checked, so no one knew the danger that lay ahead. As Sally and her co-worker used the rivet gun, it caused vibration and the platform, along with the jerky charge crane, began to move, and no one noticed it was slowly working its way off the forks. The platform slid off and fell, and Sally and her co-worker fell out of the platform. The large rivet gun landed on her head, killing her instantly.

After he explained the accident, Ray moaned, his eyes filling with tears.

The bad news struck me like a hammer blow. The pain tugged at my heart.

"You know Sally's a single mother," I said. "She has eight kids ranging from twelve to twenty years old. She's only thirty-nine." I began to tear up. "She was laid off in 1978; I think she came back in September. What about the other man?"

"I think he broke a few ribs and will be released from the hospital today." Ray finished his coffee and I walked him to the door. I went back to bed but never fell asleep. Memories of Sally played in my mind. She pushed really hard to get a woman's washroom in the anode pig storage. I cried, but a few minutes later the sadness was replaced by anger.

The next day at work, I was back in that dream-like state with no sense of reality as I descended the stairs from the women's dry. A foreman waited at the bottom of the stairs and told me to go into the wire bar lunchroom. The place was packed with wall-to-wall men and the two women who worked in that department.

No chairs were available, so I hopped up onto the counter beside the sink and began chewing on my lip. Some men watched me, maybe waiting for some kind of reaction. Everyone knew what had happened to Sally.

The superintendent stood in the front facing all of us. He started by saying, "I am sure you heard about the fatality in the anode." The word "fatality" hit a nerve in me and I lost my temper, jumping off the counter.

"Fatality!" I yelled. "How can you be so cold? Her name was Sally, Sally Mathews, she is not just a fucking fatality. You're heartless." I started shrieking. "She's not just a statistic, okay? She is not just a number!" Tears rolled down my face. I didn't care if the men saw me cry. "She was part of us, not just a fucking fatality!" I kicked the fridge door as hard as I could and put a large dent in it. I ran out of the lunchroom and hid in one of the train's box cars. I came out later and the foreman told me not to do any work today. I got out my little black notepad and wrote this poem:

Sally

June 24, 1980
At 5 p.m.
Sally's life
Came to an end.

She worked for Inco
In a company town
When almost a ton
Came tumbling down.

She had nowhere to go;
It was the end.
She called for Elaine,
Her very best friend.

The drill she was using
Fell on her head
And shortly the doctor
Pronounced her dead.

> The cage she was in
> Wasn't bolted down.
> Looks to me like
> Communication breakdown.
>
> A single mother of eight
> Ranging from 12 to 20,
> She's the 6th fatality;
> Now that's too many.
>
> 1980
> We will never forget,
> And the people who screwed up
> will always regret.
>
> – Cathy Mulroy, 1980, 26 years old

Five of us from the anode shift went to Sally's funeral after our foreman denied us a few hours off work to attend. The foreman was furious with us and we all got a counselling slip, a step 1. I didn't care.

So many accidents happened at Inco it was lucky more of us weren't killed. Like the time the furnace blew up …

The hot car arrived. The head furnaceman said there was too much cold charge and it should not be dumped yet. The foreman crooked his finger at me, ordering me to dump it. I said I would go with what the head furnaceman said and wait. Red-faced and scowling, the foreman was not happy with me and said he was taking me off the water job if I wouldn't dump it. I shook my head no, and said, "Take me off it."

He asked Robbie, who got up and grabbed his hard hat, headed down towards the hot car and hooked it up. Meanwhile, number-three furnace was being rebuilt. Only the frame was there. Men were busy inside laying the floor. The tapper was no longer at the tap hole but down in the ladle pit. I looked down at my T-shirt, tried to rub off the dried cement, and thought I would go put a clean shirt on. No matter how dirty I got, in all the years I had worked there I had never changed my clothes during a shift.

I remember seeing Robbie start the engine to pull the hot car down the tracks. Did I make the right move, now that Robbie has my job? I would be on the cast the rest of the shift. Oh well, if he wants to dump it that's his business.

I reached inside my locker, took out a clean T-shirt, and pulled it over my head. I heard and felt a loud rumble that shook the foundation. I grabbed my work shirt, slammed my locker door, and ran down the stairs toward the anode. Something was definitely wrong.

I slowly slid the barn door for the anode open. I couldn't believe what was happening. The place was full of smoke and dust. It was hard to see anything. Alarms were going off and I could see red flashing lights. I wondered if anyone was hurt as I made my way to the lunchroom. The furnace had blown when the hot car was dumped. Robbie was off to the hospital with injuries to his ankles because he had jumped off of the hot car to the floor, maybe thirty feet. We were told to stay in the lunchroom in case there were more explosions. When the dust and smoke settled, we could see a large hole in the top of the furnace. The side of the furnace was also blown away. The furnace crew said a flame had blasted through the hole as if a dragon had discharged all its fire at once into the furnace under repair. It travelled to where the men were working. The gods of the anode must have been working overtime, because everyone who would have been in the line of fire had decided to take a coffee break. It had passed right through the empty walkway. Everyone including myself was in a safe area, and the only injuries were Robbie's.

There was another time the furnace blew, when liberator acid anodes were charged into the furnace. Liberator circuits are critical in copper refinery to control the impurity level in the electrolyte. Often these circuits were plagued with inefficiency, such as the quality of copper cathode, acid mist, hazardous arsenic generation, low-grade copper sludge, and so on.

During the electrowinning (see glossary) stage of copper production, a series of impure copper anodes and thin starter sheet cathodes (such as thin copper foil) are suspended in a tank in electrolyte solution, which produces an aqueous solution of copper ions. Sometimes they were charged back into our furnace. From what I remember, the acid-drenched anodes were supposed to be suspended over the molten metal to dry before being put in. Well, this day it had just been put into the bath and *BOOM!* There went the side of the furnace again, and again no one was hurt. Just another day in the anode.

Chapter 55

The Artist Comes to the Anode

Artist rendition of the anode by RD Wilson.

The foreman entered the lunchroom, clipboard in one hand, pen in the other. A whiff of a fried egg sandwich filled my nostrils when one of the men unfolded it from a tinfoil wrap. Everyone was either stirring coffee or digging something out of their lunch pails. A bite to eat before work.

I was told I would be wheel man that day; I nodded in reply. He finished the lineup and lowered the clipboard.

"Just to let you know, an artist will be here today drawing pictures of what goes on in the anode. He's going to all the mines and plants. If anyone has a problem with this, let him know." Most men shrugged their shoulders, indifferent to it. Others didn't respond.

I was totally excited about this. The cast wouldn't be ready for a few hours so there was bull work to do. The other wheel man and I needed to install two ladles, so I asked the crane man if we could do it as soon as possible. Everyone wants the cranes on day shift.

I got comfortable in my chair and casting began. About an hour into it, I felt a hand tap me on my shoulder. The man said the foreman wanted to talk to me, pointing to the foreman standing on the tracks. The man took over my job and the foreman motioned me with his curled finger to come with him. We walked down the tracks and passed the artist coming the other way. The foreman stopped and said he would be with him in a moment. The foreman kept walking, but I stopped. He motioned me again with the curled finger. I didn't move. He told me he was taking me off the wheel, and gave me another job in the maintenance pit beside the pile of poles. In other words: hidden from sight.

The fight began. "You're taking me off my job, the job I hold, because the artist is here."

The foreman was facing me and couldn't see that the artist was still close by. "You will do as I say!" the foreman yelled. "You go down in the pit or go home."

"This is so fucking unfair, and by the way, the artist is still standing behind you." The foreman was a little red-faced but still pointed for me to go down in the pit.

"I will not cry, I will not cry," I murmured to myself. It was obvious the foreman took great pleasure in sending me away while the artist did his drawing. Every once in a while, I peeked down to see the artist on the track drawing the casting crew. I leaned on my broom, wishing I was there. The foreman came back in half an hour and told me I could go back on the wheel—the artist was finished.

I climbed the stairs to the wheel man's chair, defeated and sad. I poured the next anode and felt another tap on my shoulder. It was the artist. He said how sorry he was that this had happened. I shrugged my shoulders—nothing new here. Then he showed me the picture and pointed to the wheelman. It was me, with my plaid jacket on. I smiled at him and gave him a thumbs-up. I was forever memorialized. He smiled back. "Thank you," I mouthed over the roar of the furnace, then smiled and went back to pouring.

Chapter 56

Norm Takes a Puck in the Face for Me
January 1981

Finally, I was able to transfer out of the anode once more. I was working down on the loading docks where wire bars are loaded into transport trucks. It was still three shifts but weekends off.

One day in January at 7:30 a.m., the crew waited for the foreman to give us our line-up. I didn't notice the little brown mouse poking her pointed snout out of a hole in a green garbage bag that sat just outside the lunchroom. The hole wasn't much bigger than a quarter. She fanned her ears listening for danger and was off. She travelled at a high rate of speed, staying close to the wall. A man yelled out. "Cathy! Behind you, watch out!" The mouse stopped dead in her tracks, startled from the yell. It all happened so fast, yet I saw it in slow motion. My right foot went up, smashing the little brown mouse against the wall with my steel-toed boot, killing her instantly. She lay there with her tongue hanging out of her mouth, blood trickling down her nose. I showed no facial expression as I turned back to the foreman waiting for my instructions. He pointed to the loading docks. I chuckled and casually walked away, passing men whose jaws were hanging open. *I could never do that again if I tried. What is it about me and kicking?*

Norm was the leader of the loading dock, an hourly-rate man, really nice. We finished loading two trucks and waited for another that was late because of the snowstorm. Norm kicked a wooden disk the size of a puck across the floor and went after it to retrieve it. We all began to kick the wooden puck. "You can kill a mouse with one kick; let's see how good you can kick this puck," Norm said, kicking it towards me. I gave it all I had, and the wooden puck soared into the air. Norm grabbed his mouth in pain and looked down at his hand, now full of blood. He needed to go to the first aid room. There was no getting around it—all injuries have to be reported. I froze, terrified. I knew I was in trouble. I could lose my job for horseplay. Panic set in while Norm was off to the first aid room. He came back with two band aid strips on his lip, the kind that is used instead of stitches. He told me the foreman was coming down to investigate. It felt like my heart skipped a few beats, then started pounding hard. The boss wanted to know how this happened.

Norm said he was in the box car strapping some cathodes when the steel strap broke off and flung toward him, cutting his lip. He said he was alone in the boxcar.

At coffee break, another Bible reader said the strap had hit Norm because it was possessed by a black witch. He wasn't far off. He shook a little white Bible in the air. "The pearl and the swine," he announced. He was talking to me.

"What does that mean?" I asked.

"This is the pearl," he said, pointing to the little white Bible, "and you are the swine."

I walked right up to his face.

"Are you calling me a pig?"

"Never mind him, he's always going on about the Bible. Just let it go," Bruce said. I curled my lip at the Bible thumper, a curl starting to look like a snarl. It matched the feeling behind it.

Chapter 57

First Aid Competitions 1981

Cathy and the First Aid team

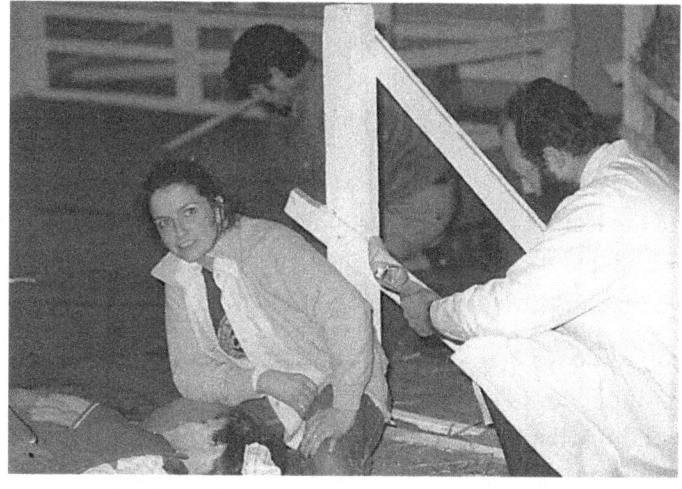

Cathy and competition judge Bob Sallows.

A few days later, my boss came down to the loading dock with the yard foreman. Remember the man who I first worked with, the one who I said had worn out the seat of his pants? The dark-skinned Diefenbaker. My boss smiled as he approached, my body stiffened, my guard went up. I felt like a cat reacting to an approaching dog.

"How would you like to be on a first aid team representing the copper refinery?" he asked.

"Just tell her she is on the team," the yard foreman grumbled with a heavy French accent. I curled up my lip, wrinkled my nose, took a long drag of my cigarette, and blew it his way. I think he got the drift.

My boss held up his hand to silence him and said, "I'll handle this."

I smirked at their performance of good cop, bad cop. He told me they were putting a first aid team together and would like me to be on it. I had no idea what a first aid team was. The selling point was I would be on steady days for a few months. He went on to say that Inco put on competitions called the Finlayson between all surface plants every year. There were competitions amongst the mines too, called the Moots. The winners of the Finlayson and the Moots compete against each other for the Parker Shield. The winners go to Toronto to the Ontario competition. This was Inco's forty-fourth year of first aid competitions, starting back in 1937. He told me that a man from the yard crew named Donny would come and talk to me if I was interested. He would be the team captain.

"If I say yes and don't like it, can I quit?" I asked.

"Yes, yes, of course," he said. The yard foreman grunted, shook his head. It was obvious he wanted my boss to tell me I had to do it. I shot him a hard glare that said *don't fuck with me.*

It's been seven years since I worked for him. I was not that little girl anymore.

"Okay, I'll give it a try. What's the next move?"

I was told to be at the Copper Cliff Copper Refinery (CCCR) general office at 7:30. The dark Diefenbaker would meet me there. "Don't be late!" he snorted. I tilted my head back, blew out a long line of smoke into the air, and headed to the next transport truck.

Always on time or early, I headed to the basement of the CCCR general office where I met the rest of the team. I was told I was going to be second captain. Donny gave me a first aid book and told me that this was the new bible, and to learn it inside and out. There were two captains, two bandage people, and a runner.

One afternoon while we were studying, I got a whiff of chicken noodle soup cooking and went out of the room to find out where it was coming from. There was a kitchen in the office building that had a handful of Italian women making homemade soup. I stood in line to get some, money in hand. The lineup of people were definitely not hourly-rate employees. The men were in suits and the women were in dresses and high heels. They stared at me as I took my place in the line wearing my tight blue jeans and sweatshirt. One woman whispered to another, her hand covering her mouth while she looked right at me. I smiled and nodded my head hello. She stopped talking and removed her hand from her mouth. It was like she was troubled that I was in their line to buy the soup. I felt uncomfortable, but I wanted a bowl of hot soup and my money was just as good as theirs. I carried the bowl of soup back to the room we were working in. I could feel many eyes on my back. My dad always told me, "Don't let people intimidate you; we all look the same sitting on the toilet. Even the Queen has to do that herself." Every time soup was on, I was in line.

Over the next month our team worked and studied hard. We used volunteers as our casualties. We used Scotch tape marked with a red Magic Marker as cuts. The coach would let us know the severity of the blood flow so we would bandage it appropriately. Broken legs, broken arms, unconsciousness, poisons, and so on. If the casualty had an open fracture, the coach would just say so and we would make a donut bandage to protect the bone. I studied until I knew that book by heart. Donny had told us not to look at the audience when we were out on the competition floor, to just look after our casualty.

The competitions were held at the Inco Club downtown, the hospital I had gone to when I was a kid, the same building I went to when I was hired. I was so nervous when it was our turn to run out onto the floor where a simulated accident would be. Donny told me to take the first casualty and he ran to the next. I did, and I could hear people laughing and a lot of commotion. I never took my eyes off of my casualty. We didn't win, but we had a great time and learned a lot. Donny asked what I thought of the bull that got loose, the one that had to have a runner chase it back into the corral. All I could say was, "What bull?"

I was asked to be a casualty for the other team from the CCCR from the electrowinning department. I jumped at the chance to learn more and there were two women on the team, one of them from the tank house. It was Lois, the woman who had come to the hospital with the dildo.

I couldn't have been happier. Now the teams were getting ready for the Parker Shield. Over three hundred people packed the Inco building. Our team was up against the Levack Mine team. This was the first year in Inco's history women were on first aid teams and we were very proud. The Levack team won, and it was such a great learning experience. Funny how ships pass in the night. I would get to know the coach of the Levack team many years later—it was Merv.

Chapter 58

Insubordination
April 1981

The god-voice news report said Inco was fined $10,000 for the death of Sally Matthews. What a slap in the face! $10,000 to Inco is like a few pennies in our pocket. Her eldest son wanted criminal charges laid. He felt the charges were inadequate. He was right.

I pulled into the copper refinery parking lot and my van let me know it was out of gas. "Shit, shit, shit, how could I be so stupid?" I knew Ray had a gas can in his truck. I would just go over to the anode and ask for his help.

I went down to the loading dock, told Norm my dilemma, and asked permission to go to the anode to talk to Ray. Ray and I had split up—we had just changed but were still good friends. The bosses were always watching me, and I'd been told not to go anywhere without permission. I told Norm I would do it on my coffee break. He said it was okay. Ray was poling the furnace, so I waited patiently while he pushed the pole in all the way. He said he would meet me in the parking lot after work and he would fill up the can. I started back to the wire bar and saw my foreman walking toward me on a mission.

"You do not have permission to be here!" he yelled over the roar of the furnace.

"Yes, I do. I asked Norm," I yelled back. "Is that why you're here, you came to get me?" My blood began to boil.

"I am going to have to give you a step for not having permission," he yelled, looking over at the anode foreman who was watching us through that grimy window of his office.

"For fuck sakes, I ran out of gas. This is fucking stupid!" I was now screaming over the roar. I headed to the foreman hiding in the office. My foreman followed.

"What the fuck is the matter with you? I am not bothering anyone. Why do you guys have to be like this?"

"I don't want you in my department." His face was full of resentment.

"What the fuck are you talking about, your department? You don't own this department. You guys can go fuck yourselves." I was livid.

I was sent to see the general foreman, the one who thought my coveralls were too tight. The one with the screaming buttons on his shirt. He sat behind his desk, his gut even bigger than before. His hair was so greasy I could make out the comb lines. He told me to sit. I said, "No thanks." He handed me a slip of paper, a step 2 for insubordination. I was furious—a step 2 meant that this would be on my record for at least two years, and they could add onto it. This was so unfair.

The next day I found Bruce and once again I watched him fill out the grievance forms: I, *Cathy Mulroy, have a grievance under the CBA* blah blah blah. He asked if I used the word fuck and I said yes, a number of times.

In my love life, I had begun dating Val Patrick. He was a wonderful man who loved kids, he held a job, and he loved the union as I did. The only thing was, he lived in Hamilton. We talked every night on the phone, and I filled him in on what happened. He told me there was a similar case about the word "fuck" and they had won. The word "fuck" was now industrial language. He sent me a list of ways it could be used.

My case went to arbitration. A woman lawyer from Toronto was hired by the company. She wore a purple tweed suit that was buttoned tight. My foreman was up first, then the superintendent (who wasn't at the scene). Both of them testified that I had used the F-word. When I was on the stand, the tweed-clad woman asked if I had used the F-word.

"All the time, and so does everyone else in the plant, including the bosses." This included the FEW. I pulled out the paper Val had sent me and began to read it. This came from a steward in Hamilton who won the case that determined "fuck" to be industrial language. I began:

Fuck You.

Perhaps one of the most interesting and colourful words in the English language today is the word *fuck*. It is the one magical word which just by its sound can describe pain, pleasure, hate, and love. *Fuck* falls into many grammatical categories. It can be used as a verb, both transitive (John *fucked* Mary) and intransitive (Mary was *fucked* by John). It can be an active verb (John really gives a *fuck*) or a passive verb (Mary really doesn't give a *fuck*), an adverb (Mary is *fucking* interested in John) and a noun (Mary is a fine *fuck*). It can be used as an adjective (Mary is *fucking* beautiful). It should be obvious now that there are not many words as versatile as *fuck*. Besides its sexual connotation, this lovely word can be used to describe many situations:

Fraud: *I got fucked by my insurance agent.*

Dismay: *Oh, fuck it!*

Trouble: *I guess I'm fucked now.*

Aggression: *Fuck you.*

Passive: *Fuck me.*

Confusion: *What the fuck?*

Difficulty: *I can't understand this fucking business.*

Despair: *Fucked again.*

Philosophical: *Who gives a fuck?*

Religious: *Holy fuck.*

Incompetence: *He's all fucked up.*

Laziness: *He just fucks about.*

Displeasure: *What the fuck is going on?*

Rebellion: *Fuck off.*

It can be used in descriptive anatomy: *He's a fucking asshole.*

It can be used to tell time: *It's five fucking thirty.*

It can be used in business: *How did I get this fucking job?*

It can be a prediction: *Oh, will I get fucked.*

It can have maternal connotations: *as in "mother fucker."*

The mind fairly boggles at the many creative uses. How could anyone be offended when you say *fuck?* Use in your daily speech to add to your prestige. Today, tell someone: *Fuck you.*

Everyone had a surprised look on their face, even Bruce. The purple-tweed lawyer chatted with the bosses and asked for a fifteen-minute break. When they came back, the lawyer said I had called my boss a cocksucker. I was still on the stand. "That's a lie. I never called you that."

She said that three people signed a paper saying I called him that. "Are you saying, Miss Mulroy, that all three of these men are liars?"

"Yes. Yes, they are all lying." I pointed at the snake-like man. "He wasn't even there, and that guy"—I pointed to the anode boss—"was in his office. Do I look like a stupid person? If I were to call a boss a cocksucker, do you think I would do it in front of witnesses?" She didn't answer. They found me guilty of insubordination, but we did win the right to say "fuck," because now it was industrial language at Inco.

Chapter 59

Patterson's Campaign May 1981

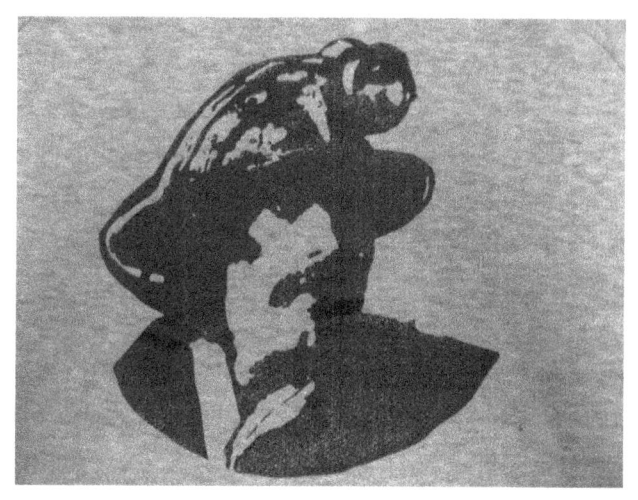

Dave Patterson's image on a sweatshirt.

Our hard work paid off, or so we thought. This was to be the modern-day battle of David and Goliath, or should I say David and Stew.

Dating Val Patrick was great; we were always on the same page. He and I worked on Dave Patterson's campaign for District 6. Members of the Steelworkers were broken up into districts. Ontario was District 6 with about 90,000 members. Patterson was running against Stew Cooke, the person who held the job, the same person who told us not to strike after our elective Local executives told us to turn down that one-year contract.

I climbed into my black GMC van wearing my grey sweatshirt embossed with a picture of Dave Patterson's head wearing a miner's hard hat. All the people on his team wore one. I threw a bag of buttons and pamphlets into the back and got comfortable for the long ride to Southern Ontario, but first I had to stop at the union hall to pick up Jim, a man who was coming with me. We taped posters on the side of my van with grey duct tape that read: "Dave Patterson for District 6."

I was to drive and Jim would be the navigator, mapping out what places had unionized Steelworkers in District 6.

Our job was to inform the workers that Dave Patterson was running and that we needed their support. We were so naive, thinking we could fight the Steelworker establishment, the people who held the power. We wanted to build a grassroots campaign made up of ordinary workers in ordinary jobs who opposed the Steelworkers leadership. The same brave people who had fought hard during the strike were the same people working on this campaign.

We felt if we could take Inco on and win, we could win against the Steelworkers too. We were idealist dreamers, ready to take on the world. We would obtain all the goals we had set out for ourselves, with our high standards and principles of what was right and what was wrong. We were the warriors who were going to rid the kingdom of all evil; we were the knights of our own round table. We were going to win.

People in Southern Ontario opened their homes for us to spend the nights. By day we went to as many plants as we could. Up at 3:00 a.m. and back on the road. Sometimes we had to do graveyard shifts, catching the workers coming into work.

Jim told me to make a left. This took us through a graveyard. I drove slowly, feeling uneasy as we passed all the headstones. He said there were ten Steelworkers somewhere in this vicinity. I joked that these guys couldn't vote. We drove to the end of the graveyard and spotted a warehouse in the distance. "Bingo! There's the ten!" I smiled.

We drove in through the back and didn't see any guards, so I drove right up to the shipping dock. I jumped out with a handful of leaflets and pins. Two workers stood beside a forklift truck with blank looks on their faces, not sure what to make of us.

"Hi," I said, greeting them with a wide smile. "My name is Cathy, and this is Jim. We're from Sudbury." I extended my hand; the men automatically extended theirs, shaking ours with a puzzled look on their faces.

"We are campaigning for Dave Patterson," I continued, still smiling. "He's running against Stew Cooke for District 6." Their facial expression didn't change. "Do you know … what I'm talking about? You guys are Steelworkers, right?"

Dumbfounded, they nodded. "We pay union dues, if that's what you mean," one of the men said with a raspy chuckle. "I've been here for thirty years and this is the first time I have ever seen anyone from the Steelworkers." Proudly, I told them we were there because we cared.

We filled them in on who Stew and Dave were, and told them we wanted Dave as our leader. Our conversation was cut short when a man wearing a white hard hat approached us, looking like he was on a mission. "This has to be your foreman, right?" I spoke out the side of my mouth, and the men nodded.

"Who are you, and what do you want here?" The boss's voice was loud and deep, displaying that he was the authority around here.

Still smiling, I introduced myself and handed him a leaflet.

"You are trespassing," he said, his chest puffed up with self-importance.

"Sorry, I didn't see any signs saying we couldn't come on the property."

"Well, if you would have come in the front gate instead of coming through the graveyard you would have seen the signs." His eyes narrowed in contempt. Now all ten members were standing on the shipping platform. I quickly passed out some more leaflets and we were off. I held my hand down on the horn as we drove towards the graveyard, waving my other one out the window. I could see all the men waving back in my rear-view mirror. This was a good day.

We hit as many plants as we could through the rest of the week.

On May 28, 1981, Stew Cooke's career as the incumbent director of Ontario came to an end. I was happy to hear that a record number of workers turned out to vote. Dave Patterson won with 9000 votes. This was a shock to the bureaucrats in Pittsburgh. Val called to say the Steelworkers Hall in Hamilton had put up a sign that read, "Under New Management."

We were on top of the world. Dave told the media that he wanted a separate Canadian Constitution for the Canadian section of the Steelworkers union. Val wanted to start unionizing 10,000 people at Dofasco, the other steel company in Hamilton. Meanwhile, Stew Cooke called us a bunch of communists and said we were out to destroy the union.

At the victory party, Patterson paid homage to all of us. "Well," he said, "we neutralized Cooke in the south, we won with an overwhelming majority here in the north—Sault Ste. Marie, Elliot Lake, Sudbury, and Hamilton. Look what we can do when we organize!" We got all ten votes out of the shipping area we went to.

We hoped this victory would greatly fuel the growing movement to Canadianize the American trade unions. Some of the organizers wore T-shirts that read "Stew Who?"

We knew that Patterson was in deep. The Steelworkers bureaucracy would try to isolate him, stifle him. He would have to make decisions without the help or advice from the international union who did not want the control of the unions in the hands of the Canadian workers.

The Northern Life newspaper and its editorial staff in Sudbury determine who or what was the top story of the year. Dave Patterson was selected as Northern Life's Local Newsmaker for 1981. Patterson had accomplished what many had thought was impossible: defeating Stewart Cooke. Dave became the first local union president in District 6 history to be elected director. He would be responsible for 450 unions across Ontario, close to 90,000 workers. He had many firsts in his life. First being elected president of LU 6500 in 1976 at the young age of twenty-eight, the youngest in history. He led us through a strike in '78 and '79 that received national attention, the longest strike in Canadian history. He was re-elected president again after the strike and was now the District 6 leader.

But this was bittersweet; we had made a mistake. We had bitten off more than we could chew. There were sad days ahead for us and for Dave.

While Dave was in Pittsburgh, someone had raided the District 6 office, taking all the records. The secretaries had been transferred out. There was no one to help him run the office. Keys were broken off in the locks of the drawers and cabinets. The rest is not my story to tell. Maybe one day Dave will tell it all.

Chapter 60

Goodbye Little Person
June 1981

"It's your fault!" my family doctor yelled at me. "You agreed to let this doctor do a tubulisation back in February when he repaired your hiatus hernia. He was not a gynecologist."

I couldn't believe what my doctor was saying. "How was I to know he wasn't qualified? Then why did he do it if he wasn't qualified?"

It was nearly midnight when I boarded the overnight train to Toronto. I was both sad and mad, and unsure which feeling was worse. I was off to the McMaster University Medical Centre in Hamilton—a gynecology training hospital. I sobbed into my pillow, remembering what the ticket man said before I boarded: "Oh, you have a berth," as he checked my ticket.

"Yeah, I guess you could say that." I laid in the berth car. I was alone, totally alone. Why did this happen to me? I took responsibility. I had my tubes tied so I would not bring any more children into this world. I had to make this horrible decision to abort the baby I was carrying. It wasn't my fault. The doctor that did the tubulisation did not tell me he wasn't qualified to do it. He screwed up and I was paying for it. Now my case had to go in front of a panel of *men*. They would determine if I qualified to terminate this pregnancy. I didn't sleep much.

Tears rolled down my face as the nurses handed me a hospital gown. A woman doctor in green scrubs wearing a surgical mask asked me if I was okay. I nodded. She wanted to know why I was crying. I told her I just felt sorry for myself. She placed her hand gently on my shoulder and told me I had a right to feel that way.

I boarded the train back to Sudbury and cried most of the way back. That was one of the hardest things I ever had to do in my life. I was so alone.

Holding back my anger of what had happened to me and the doctor's fuck-up, I decided to bury it along with the rape.

My eyes teared up. I tried hard to supress all these feelings. I threw cold water on my face a few times and headed to the loading dock.

I sat on the forklift truck, puffing away on a cigarette and trying desperately to stop the horrible feeling I had. A jolt into my side woke me as an overweight Italian man motioned for me to get off his truck. A group of students, there for a summer job, toured the area of the wire bar. A young girl about nineteen hurried to catch up to the crowd. I waved at her and she smiled and waved back. The fat forklift truck driver poked my shoulders. "Did you see how beefy her hips and legs are? She is really fat." He bellowed out a laugh. "A small waist and those big hips; she's like a pear."

I curled my lip, the emotions that I thought were intact surfaced. "You're one to talk." I reached up and patted his blubbery fat belly. "What about this and your beefy double chin? You're no Romeo yourself."

His nasty smile disappeared, replaced by a crazed look. Roger, the other forklift truck driver, doubled over with laughter and slapped his hand against his thigh. "She told you, and it looks like you may deliver soon!"

"Deliver" wasn't a word I needed to hear at that moment. Tears began to fill my eyes. "I have to go to the washroom," I said, and headed back to the dry. I could hear the fat truckers yell that the transport truck had arrived, but I pretended I didn't hear. I looked into the mirror. *Just forget about it.*

The trip to Pittsburgh for Dave Patterson's inauguration would take my mind off of what happened.

Groggy individuals placed their suitcases in the hall of the bus. We found our seat and headed out on the long bus trip to Pittsburgh. Dave did a head count, the banjos and guitars came out, and we were off. The side of the bus was plastered with pictures of Patterson, the new director of District 6. Motivated by this historical win, a sea of smiling faces sang as we departed.

Once on the highway, people began to pull out their drink of choice. I didn't drink so I pulled out my grass and began to puff away.

Dave made his way toward me and told me I had to get rid of the stuff before we hit the border, as there may be sniffing dogs. He knew I didn't drink and was apologetic for having to do it, but he couldn't put everyone in jeopardy. I agreed, wondering how I was going to handle it. We stopped at a Chinese restaurant so everyone could get a snack before we crossed the border. A large fish tank with a man-made pond in front of it caught my eye. It was surrounded with rocks and plastic flowers. I lifted one of the rocks and placed my small bag of grass under it, then placed the rock back over top. I told Dave it was done, but that we had better stop here on the way back so I could pick it up. Dave nodded. I took that as a yes.

The inauguration was held at Lindon Hall. It was a beautiful mansion on 785 acres of rolling hills and a golf course. I just couldn't wait to see the inside. I was dressed in a borrowed little black dress with black sequins all over the top and a pair of high heels. I had changed in the bathroom of the bus. The blazing sun was blinding when I exited. Dave rounded us up to tell us we would not be going inside the hall, because the inauguration was in the field where a stage had been set up. The bus was locked and the driver was gone. I had no choice but to wear what I had on. The longer the day went on, the hotter it got. I was sweating in that black polyester dress; there was not a tree around because it was a golf course. Every time I moved, black sparkles detached themselves from the dress and latched onto my arms by the hundreds. I looked like I had some kind of black measles. I tried to brush them off, but it was like I was a magnet—they wouldn't move off my arm. Val laughed. The inauguration began and everyone moved toward the stage like a herd of cattle. A large woman began to sing the national anthem. Val leaned over and said, "Name that tune." It was funny.

I was glad to get on the cool bus. When I cooled down, little black sparkles littered the seat and the floor. I reminded Dave that we had to stop at the Chinese restaurant. He said he didn't think that was a good idea. I began to protest, and he flung his hands in the air and told the bus driver to stop at the restaurant. The restaurant was full: a Chinese wedding. All eyes were on me as I went to the washroom, and on the way back I pretended to smell the plastic flowers, then lifted my rock and retrieved my small bag. I was happy.

Chapter 61

Jennifer Penny is Writing a Book: Hard Earned Wages October 1981

I received a call from a woman named Jennifer Penny, an author writing a book about women in the workforce—and not your average women, but ones who worked in jobs that are not usually held by females. The book was to be called *Hard Earned Wages*. She wanted to interview me.

She talked with management and they gave her permission to talk to me on the job and take pictures. I was down on the loading dock when she came in with her group. She was accompanied by an industrial relations woman, dressed very nicely in a skirt and high heels. We were off to the anode.

The foreman from the anode would not hear of this and refused us entry. She had to call upper management, who had already given her the okay. This was the same foreman who had lied and said I called my boss a cocksucker, and now because of him I had a step 2 on my record.

As context for this story, I had been in Montréal and had gone to the hairdressers to get a perm. I said "afro" instead, and ended up with a very big bushy head of hair, so much so that I couldn't get my hair under my hard hat and it pushed it up every few minutes.

Anyway, after a while we got the okay, but the foreman refused to let me lift an anode off the wheel for the pictures, even though I had done it for the previous seven years and I was good at it. He was very adamant and warned me that I had better not pick one up. They took a picture of me beside the wheel holding the hoist. The foreman gave us five minutes—not enough time to scrunch my puffy hair into my hard hat. That's why my hair is down in this wonderful picture they took—I would never leave my hair down when working around machinery or molten metal. We went back to the loading dock and got a great picture of me and Roger. That night they came to my place, took more pictures, and interviewed me. I was very excited to be put in a book. As a matter of fact, I ended up on the front cover with my tight coveralls, puffy hair, and cat-like safety glasses the company bought for the women. Some fashion statements.

Val, my live-in babysitter Joy-Ann, and I sat at the kitchen table playing Risk, a strategic board game. The object of the game is to conquer the world and eliminate all the other players. The board depicts a political map of the Earth divided into forty-two territories, which are grouped into six continents.

Val loved the game. He was ahead when the phone rang. It was Dave Patterson.

"Hi Cat, I have some bad news and I want you to hear it from me. Miguel has been arrested by the secret police in Guatemala." My heart sank. The board game took on a reality. I asked if there was anything we could do to help him.

"No," he said. "I'll let you know what comes out of it." A few weeks had passed when I heard back from Dave that the secret police had let Miguel go, but he couldn't stay in Guatemala and he had to go to Argentina. He said his family was safe. It's funny how souls cross in your life. I hoped he would be safe.

Chapter 62

Susan and Christmas 1981

Before Dave left for Toronto, he told me that Inco would be hiring 100 people. I called a good friend, Susan Kennedy, and she was hired.

Susan was a great leader for the women's movement and for the labour movement. She voiced her concerns for women's security, equal pay, and maternity benefits, and against sexual discrimination. She said all of this must be addressed in the contract. She said we didn't want any special privileges, all we wanted were the rights that would ensure equality in the work force.

There were many firsts for women that year. I heard a woman became the first female conductor for CP Rail. Another woman became a manager of the Royal Bank, and in '78 the first female captain on a scheduled airline. Women were trying to get into the trades. Susan said, "A 1975 national survey showed that three-quarters of Canadians believe that women should stay at home full time with pre-school children. That is a bunch of BS. Who would feed their children then? Who would pay the rent if they were not married? And let us not forget about the fathers who don't pay their child support. Another woman was going back to school after sixteen years of being at home to become a mechanic!" I loved Susan's rants.

Val had been on strike that summer against Steelco in Hamilton. The slogan was: "Fun in the Sun in '81."

Over the next few months he came up to Sudbury often and invited me and the kids to spend Christmas with his kids in Hamilton.

There were rumours about a workforce adjustment at Inco. Workforce adjustment is a situation that occurs when a deputy head decides that the services of one or more indeterminate employees will no longer be required beyond a specified date. Susan Kennedy told me that on September 4, two jobs in the roaster area were cut. That's where she worked. More layoffs were coming. Inco was trying to turn worker against worker by making up stories that the cuts were coming because employees were sleeping on the job. Back in August, Susan discussed contract demands which directly pertained to women. We talked about four main areas: investigation, education, information, and mobilization. We needed to know if women were faced with discrimination in their work areas. We needed to educate women on the union by putting information in *The Searcher*, a newspaper put out by the LU 6500 that was getting women more active in the union. Our next meeting was held on October 13. Susan was so right for this kind of stuff. She was well educated and could hold her own. More rumours were flying about layoffs.

Chapter 63

The Spirits of Christmas 1981

It wasn't an easy decision to go to Hamilton for Christmas. Lloyd was not happy I was taking the kids. I told him I would drive back Christmas Day so he could be with them. In my opinion, he didn't care about the other 364 days; he never took them every second weekend like he was supposed to. I just shook my head.

We had a great time, and Christmas Day we were headed back home. Val motioned to Peppy to go in his car and Melanie and I would go in the little yellow Datsun. When we got to Barrie, big snowflakes began to fall. The wind picked up and it was getting dark. Val and Peppy had disappeared far ahead of us. Melanie and I sang to the songs on the eight-tracks. The snow became heavier; a storm was brewing. The snow covered the highway and it was hard to tell where the road was. My anxiety began to build. There was nothing open. It was Christmas Day en route to Northern Ontario.

Then everything went dark—I suddenly had no headlights. "Holy fuck!" I glanced over at Mel and smiled, telling her all was okay. But of course it wasn't. The storm got worse. I could feel the wind blowing against the little car as it trudged through the heavy snow. I was mad that Val and Peppy didn't wait for us. The little yellow Datsun trudged along the highway, giving us all it had. More snow was falling, and I couldn't see the road very well. I had to stay calm or I would frighten my six-year-old. I checked the gas gauge—I was good for gas. I could just make out that a snowplow had come by earlier, and there was a small ridge on the side of the road. I would use that as my guide.

All my senses were at the ready when I drove over the ridge of snow, remembering to go through all the what-ifs. I maneuvered the little car's tires so the left side of the car would be on one side of the ridge and the right ones would be on the right. I put on my four-way flashers and puttered on, using the snow ridge as my guide. Melanie began to cry. I told her the only thing we had left to do was pray, and if Christmas gave miracles then this would be a good time to pass one out. I felt like a hypocrite, because I'm not sure what I believe in when it comes to religion, but I do believe in the power of prayer. The Datsun's four-way flashing lights blinked on and off, reflecting off the small snowbank as we moved slowly along. I prayed some more by myself. I hadn't seen a car in over an hour. Then car lights appeared, coming over the hill in the other lane. "Please help us," I said as the car passed us, and my heart sank. Then I saw the red brake lights. The car was turning around. Afraid of who it might be, I was on my guard. It was a station wagon, a family. They pulled up beside us and a man got out. The problem was that one of the fuses had blown and I didn't have a spare. The man took some tinfoil and wrapped it around the fuse, then took the one from the radio and heater out and placed the other one in for the lights. They came on. I thanked the man and we were off.

The next day Lloyd's dad passed away. I was sad; he was a part of my life too for eleven years. Maybe it was his spirit that helped us out on the highway that night.

Chapter 64

More Layoffs
January 1982

Marching in downtown Sudbury

First aid competitions came around again in January, and the company has asked me to be on the team. I was named second captain again. I loved being back in the book, reading, practising, learning. I would rather do this than be in the plant anytime; it was steady days with weekends off. It made life at home a lot easier.

There were hints of layoffs once again. I hoped I wouldn't lose my job. More stress in my life. My anger came on quite quickly, more like rage, explosive outbursts were my norm, destructive to myself and my kids. If only Lloyd would take them every second weekend, I could have some time to myself. I dropped them off at my mother's. That just added guilt to my already overwhelmed mind. Then Lloyd would criticize me, saying I wasn't raising the kids, my mother was. He said I should stay home with them, that I wasn't a good mother. This would just make me angrier. This coming from a father who wouldn't be a father.

The winter was starting off cold. A winter blast nearly brought Sudbury to a standstill. It was an indication of what the year ahead was going to be like.

On January 4, the women's committee of LU 6500 encouraged women to play a bigger part in the union world. I would have loved to, but I had too much on my hands being a single mother at this time.

On January 5, the company announced that 850 people would be laid off. The company and union were working out ways of reducing the impact. Anyone with four and a half years seniority or less would be laid off, and we were also going into negotiations.

Dave Patterson, now leader in District 6, said there didn't have to be layoffs. He said the company always did this before every set of negotiations. Every time management found itself in a tailspin, it always came back to Sudbury, Thompson, Port Colborne—we always got the cuts.

On January 20th, the Steelworkers protested the layoffs at Inco. We raised our signs as the guests arrived at the Sheridan Casswell Hotel, chanting "scotch and whisky for you, unemployment for us." One of the guests was Larry Grossman, a politician in Ontario who served in the Legislative Assembly as a Progressive Conservative and the Minister of Industry and Tourism.

He confirmed the establishment of a $19 million resource machinery development center in Sudbury. Nothing about the 850 workers being laid off. We were not allowed in the hotel where Grossman was to speak.

There was a picture on the front page of the Sudbury Star. Jim Giroux, a member of the LU 6500 bargaining team, stood in front of Grossman as he held an impromptu meeting with the group. Giroux towered over Grossman by a good seven inches, and he shook his large miner's finger in Grossman's face and demanded a full-scale investigation into Inco's announcement of the layoffs. Giroux also voiced that the workforce reduction constituted a company move to influence our Steelworkers negotiation.

The pint-sized Grossman eyed the strong, bearded, long-haired miner through his owlish oversized glasses. He was expressionless and said he would report the demands to Ontario Labour Minister Bob Elgie.

Floyd Laughren, our New Democratic member of the Legislative Assembly of Ontario representing the Northern Ontario riding of Nickel Belt, stated Grossman had a lot of nerve coming in there in the middle of the layoffs to say that he had jobs for fifteen scientists from somewhere else other than Sudbury. He said he was tired of hearing local politicians defending Inco when layoffs occurred. This statement was echoed by Giroux in his rant.

Early retirement had been proposed by Inco as a way of reducing the impact of the layoffs, and anyone wishing to accept the company's proposal had until midnight that night to decide.

By January 25, as many as 600 Sudbury area workers would be facing layoffs in the near future. 250 senior employees had indicated the desire to retire under the early retirement incentive package.

On January 28, Sudbury Regional Council had jumped on the bandwagon to support the Steelworkers campaign to end the layoffs. A motion was set by the counselors to participate in the fight in the form of a telegram to Inco's head office.

I guess they were afraid of the negative effect on Sudbury, because more jobs were being eliminated. One suggestion was that Inco employees might benefit from a work-sharing program. We could collect unemployment benefit funds used to extend vacation time.

We did not get any support from Queens Park. They stated it was because of the vast layoffs throughout the country.

Sudburarins wondered why we had to suffer because of the company's bad investments.

Mike Mizuik, owner and manager of Mizuik Jewellers and a long-time resident of Sudbury, said, "Merchants don't know what to expect in this city anymore. Inco is playing their games again; they should be stopped from taking advantage of our city."

Gloria Bradford, Executive Director of the New Sudbury Community Service Centre, said, "We're looking at family problems, marital problems, and health problems. That's not even looking at the financial effect that will happen. It's demoralizing what Inco is doing."

Inco wouldn't listen to any alternative possibilities, and our jobs kept floating away. It wasn't just us: for every job lost in our industry, two or three jobs in the service sector would be affected.

The Local Steelworkers were seeking to avert the layoffs through increased emphasis on trades training, extended holidays to share the workload, and retirement. 416 workers took advantage of the retirement incentives. If Inco would have offered the hourly rate workers the same package they had offered staff, the company would have had to bar the door to prevent too many workers from leaving.

Keith Lovely, Recording Secretary of LU 6500, told the Sudbury Regional Council, "The only way to save jobs is to put pressure on Inco." He noted that when a report on acid rain was released late the previous year, members of counsel had said that if its recommendations were implemented, the community would be losing jobs. Inco was still pumping out 1900 tons of SO_2 into the atmosphere every day, and we were still losing jobs. The silence was deafening on the part of our local politicians.

I was scared. What was going to happen when all our young employees were laid off? What was really sad about all this was most of these workers were the same ones who were displaced in 1978, young families who came back after the '78 layoffs, a whole generation of young people. The union even asked if the company would relocate workers to Thompson, Manitoba, where Inco had a mine and a mill. One of the fights behind the scene was that 120 apprentices were to be laid off. The union wanted help from Canada Manpower, the Ministry of Labour, and colleges and universities to get these people into community colleges to upgrade their education. No help.

Over the last few years, 8000 jobs had been lost and it hurt our community. There are no words to describe how people felt about getting laid off for the second time in four years. The retirement package for hourly rated employees was a hundred dollars per year of service. That was an insult when they offered staff $1000 per year. Really?

Chapter 65

The Protest 1982

Cathy and Peppy on the front page of The Sudbury Star.

Peppy, Melanie, and I sat around the kitchen table making posters to carry in the march. We coloured and drew as I explained why we were doing this. I told them many people were going to lose their jobs, and if we could save any by fighting the company then it would be worth it. We were protesting because families and friends would be uprooted once again, lose their homes, and have to move out of the city.

On February 1 at 4:30 p.m., a group gathered at the Steelworkers Hall. We marched to downtown Sudbury, to Inco's offices on Cedar St., chanting "Stop the layoffs!"

Inco sent out 434 layoff notices that day and told the workers that their last day would be March 29, 1982. This was only part of the 850. The company said it would revoke the layoffs if enough senior employees indicated they would opt for an early retirement. There we went again: worker fighting against worker. Inco also said it would stretch the offer to employees that were fifty-five years old with twenty years' service. They had until February 12 to decide.

My feet were freezing as we stood outside Inco's offices. The cold winter wind blew in my face and I tightened the hood of my oversized steelworker's coat. The company had ordered the elevators in the building to be shut down. I looked over at Peppy; I wanted him to understand that nothing in life is given to you, that mostly you have to fight for everything. It was a good, peaceful protest; we had our say and I felt proud that my son was by my side.

Not everyone felt the same when Peppy and I were on the front page of the Sudbury Star with our protest signs in hand. When I picked the kids up at Lloyd's mom's, she slammed the newspaper on the kitchen table. I hadn't seen it yet and was quite pleased to see Peppy and myself on the front. She told me I looked really stupid, pounding her finger on the picture. Her calling me stupid lit a flame in me—that's where her son gets it from.

"I believe I am doing the right thing," I defended myself, ushering the kids out the door with their coats half on.

"*Maudit!* You took the kids away from their father, you could have worked out the problems." The real truth of her anger surfaced. It was me separating from her son that was the real issue, not the protest.

"Work it out!" I shouted back. "I will not live a life I am not happy in. You may have done that …" My finger shook in her face. "Just because you stayed with a drunken wife beater. *Worked it out* … ha!" My fingers made quotation marks in the air. "I don't want a life like that; I will not live like that." The mean words poured out of my mouth like a tap without a washer. I didn't mean to hurt her; I lost control of my emotions but stood my ground. "How many times did I call you asking for help, to talk with your son, and you would say you couldn't get involved. Well, I did something about it!" I steered the kids outside and slammed the door. Everyone was ready to blame me. Well, this was my life and I will live it the way I want to.

On February 13, 1982, I decided to go to the CCCR curling tournament. I watched as a drunken superintendent climbed on a chair then up on the table. The pressed pleats in his grey dress pants made me wonder if his wife had ironed them or if a dry cleaner had. The two top buttons on his shirt were unbuttoned and his necktie hung like a small noose draped around his neck. Pinkish-red lipstick smeared his collar. I curled my lip, thinking, *He acts as if he is so much better than us hourly-rated people on the job; look at his disgusting behaviour now.* I shook my head and smirked. *I'll bet that lipstick isn't his wife's.* No morals, no dignity, phony to the core. I could draw strength from his actions and these memories.

The company announced that they would be closing a portion of Garson Mine. 540 maintenance workers would be forced to be adjusted into production jobs. Yes, it would take away my job and I would be sent back to the anode.

They said they would be extending the four-week summer shutdown.

I felt frightened, exhausted, powerless, and worried about the layoffs, a pending strike, a shutdown, and the little money that would be coming in. I hadn't gotten back on my feet from the eight-and-a-half-month strike in '78–'79. The kids' father wasn't spending any time with them, so I decided to get Peppy a big brother. Lloyd was not happy. It didn't matter what I did to make life easier, it was never the right thing. *Well, then you should do your fatherly duties.*

Inco said there was some relief when they announced that only 253 workers would be laid off.

Yeah, but no relief for the 253 workers. I gritted my teeth when we heard J. Edwin Carter, who was president of Inco in 1979 and 1980, would receive $134,000 a year pension.

Chapter 66

Trying to Stop the Layoffs 1982

"Is it hot in here, or is it just me? I stood up removed my green work shirt, the bright red T-shirt, one size too small, was not an accident on my part. It was more than snug, it was tight. My intentions were to get a reaction from a certain general foreman at the second stage grievance meeting, and this I accomplished. He was a white-haired, upper-class person who never even said hello to me.

My push-up, push-together bra only enhanced my already large boobs.

Ron and I were there because we had received a step back in '81 when we were working in fine casting. It had been a slow day, everything was happening at a snail's pace, and most workers were on broom. Ron and I were partners for the day, sweeping at the end of the building.

"Have you ever been to the roof?" Ron asked, leaning on his broom.

"No, what's up there?" I asked.

"Nothing, it's a roof, but you can see all around the plant. Come on," he said, hiding the broom behind a beam. I did the same and followed him up the stairs. Ron pushed on a big door and the October sun shone bright. It was breathtaking up there, like another world. Ron sat on the black-tarred roof, resting his back up against a wall. I could see all of the copper refinery. I walked around the large roof. It was amazing. I could see all the way to Copper Cliff, the town.

We sat and let the warm sun wash away any worries. Except for the worry about getting caught up there.

"Not to worry," Ron said, "it's still our department."

I began to feel anxious, fearful of what would happen if we got caught up on the roof. We had been gone for forty-five minutes and it was time to go back down. We made it down the stairs without anyone seeing us, until the foreman came walking towards us, arms swinging, his legs in a march. He was on a mission. My heart pounded as I thought about what were we going to say.

"Let me do the talking," Ron said.

"Where have you been?" the foreman commanded an answer.

"Nowhere," Ron said.

Nowhere. That's your answer, Ron? I thought to myself. I forced a smile.

"Nowhere!" the foreman yelled.

"Not my fault you didn't see us. We were nowhere but in this department." He walked past the foreman.

"What do you have to say?" the foreman yelled at me.

"Nothing," my voice strained.

Ron and I received a step for not being at our posts. At stage one of the grievance, the foreman said we deserved it because we wouldn't say where we were. The second-stage hearing was booked for the new year. Another boss who hated me, who had never talked to me, heard the second stage. It was my reputation that was growing, growing bigger than me. February 1982: I knew we would lose in the second stage because we would not tell them we were on the roof. So, I was going to have fun at the meeting. I headed to a print T-shirt place. I wore a medium but bought a small in bright red, and I had the front printed in big black bold letters that read: "Stop the Layoffs," and on the back: "Inco slave."

The general foreman glanced up from his desk and motioned me to sit beside Ron. "You are going to tell me what you two were up to that day, or this will stay on your record." The threat was real, but it would be worse if they knew we were on the roof. The general foreman called Ron a liar when Ron said again that we were in the department.

"No, I am not lying," Ron said softly.

"Is it hot in here, or is it just me?"

"Wow!" Ron said, staring at my large rounded breasts with the bold lettering branded across them. I stood up and turned around, revealing the back of my T-shirt. Ron went into hysterics, laughing uncontrollably, slapping his hand across his knees. I sat back down. The general foreman's face was flushed, his eyes bulging from their sockets. He slammed his fist down on his desk and papers fluttered.

"Get the hell out of my office," he bellowed, spit flying from his mouth. Ron and I scrambled like mice, giggling as we bolted through the door and into the plant. I put my work shirt back on as Ron mocked the general foreman. *"Get the hell out of my office."* We met up with Bruce and put in another grievance because the general foreman refused to hear our second-stage grievance.

The next day I was off to practice first aid. I was walking in between the piles of wire bar. They were piled about twelve feet high, and the rows were about thirty feet long. The general foreman came from the far end towards me. He blocked me. I moved to the side to let him by and he shoved me against the bars.

"What the fuck?" I was startled.

He pulled on my shirt.

"Take your fucking hands off me or I will start kicking. I have been known to take a man down," I warned him.

"You better watch yourself," he said.

"Get the fuck out of my face." I jerked loose, then smiled as I went to practice.

Chapter 67

The Maintenance Men from Garson Mine March 1982

The company announced they would be closing down a portion of the Garson Mine, which would impact 540 employees. These workers would be moved to other areas in the Sudbury operation. They would have their salary cut and would have to travel a further distance to work. They would be transferred to an area that had vacancies. This meant surface plants like the copper refinery that had a seven-day swing shift—four afternoon and three graveyard in the same week. The union was hoping that the company would take employees who were short on qualifications out of production and give them extra training, and this would create job opportunities for others. This did not happen, because the company said it would cost them too much. The men that came to the copper refinery were maintenance workers and they were not happy with the force adjustment.

The Garson maintenance men arrived at the refinery. I had to go back to the anode after the first aid competitions had finished. I walked through the wire bar. Twenty newbies, brand new to working in the refinery, leaned against the brick wall. I glanced over, not recognizing any of them.

"Hey!" A man yelled at me to come over using that curled finger, the same way the bosses did. I walked over to see what he wanted.

"I knew I could make you come with one finger." He laughed and other men snickered, waiting for my response.

I got up into his face. "Go fuck yourself, you pig. You don't want to cross me. I will chew you up and spit you out."

"Oooh, you're scaring me," he laughed.

"Your nothing but a loudmouth piece of shit. You want trouble, you'll get it, just ask around. You don't want to fuck with me. That goes for anyone else too." I made sure I eyed all the men.

I stormed into the boss's office. "You had better straighten out those men from underground before I do."

"Yeah, yeah I'll talk to them," he responded.

It was like someone opened the asshole floodgates. A guy they called Crazy Vic approached me. He had two hard hats under his T-shirt, making it look like he had big boobs. He grabbed my wrist. I was terrified and wrenched it free.

"Don't you ever fucking touch me again!"

"I thought all the angels were in heaven." His voice was creepy and his eyes were glazed over, like he was on something. I reported it. The boss said Vic was harmless, and just to leave it alone.

"This is not funny. You keep him away from me, or I will go to human rights, or maybe I will go right to the police. Think about it." My anger was now my norm and it worked. This became the way I handled most things. It was taking its toll on my health.

Chapter 68

Continued Harassment on the Job 1982

On April 3, Val and I split up. I knew we loved each other, but I couldn't commit to a relationship. He was a great boyfriend and a positive person in my life. I just wasn't in the right frame of mind.

Susan got laid off, so did some of the other women. I was back at the bottom of the seniority list—this sucked. At least I wasn't getting laid off. I didn't know what I wanted in life. Most of the time I couldn't even think clearly. I thought I might have been having a nervous breakdown, but talked my way out of it in the mirror.

Our team did not win the first aid competitions. One of the men on my shift tormented me, saying cruel things, calling us a bunch of losers. I told him we didn't lose, we just didn't win. I had learned a lot being on the team and wouldn't change it for anything. He said he was in the audience and all he could see was my fat ass as I bent down to examine the casualty.

I lost it. "You're one to talk. You're a fat pig, look at yourself. You're fat and fucking ugly; you have a face like a bulldog, with all that flab under your chin." I was as cruel as he was. He got up and left the lunchroom. I was in trouble now because he was the guy who weighed the anodes before they went to the tank house. He would be lying about the weight of my load every time I was on the wheel. I would get shit from the boss: "You're too heavy, you're too light," and the ugly guy would laugh in his corner. The boss told me I had to do better or I would be taken off of the wheel man's job. I told the boss that this guy was out to get me, but he just shrugged it off. "If your weights don't improve you may lose your wheel job."

I confronted the guy in the lunchroom and he laughed. He stood up and raised his hand over his head—he was holding a banana peeling. He slapped it hard against my lap. It stung. He hit me again, and it stung. Ray told him to stop. He made a nasty comment about our relationship. I went to the washroom and saw that there were two large welts across my leg. I wanted to tell the foreman, but he would just tell me to suck it up. I thought the man was over it, but one day when I was pouring my coffee, he grabbed my wrist and gave me an Indian burn—that's when you grab a wrist and twist your hand in opposite directions and it leaves red marks. Ray said he would talk to him in private. The man backed off. Ray said he thought the man liked me and I wasn't paying him any attention, so he was getting back at me. I thought, *Is that what a man does when he likes you?* I wondered what he would do if he hated me.

My frustration and anger were so out of control. I felt powerless to change my situation. I couldn't even get out of the anode and stay out.

Chapter 69

The Strike and Me as a Ladle Tender May 1982

Some of the Garson miners ended up in the anode. They irritated me, invading my space and coming with a *we are better than surface workers* attitude. I hoped they would keep their testosterone in check. It wouldn't have taken much to provoke me at this point. They must have been spoken to because they were fine.

It was good to be back working with Ray. We will always be friends. One day we were down in the ladle pit, cleaning up. I was in charge of the water hose. I squirted a little on Ray and he gave me a warning look. I couldn't resist. I pointed it straight at him and he was drenched. I dropped the hose and ran. The lunchroom was crammed with day shift and the miners. Ray stood by the sink, his hard hat in his hand. He had removed the liner and was filling it with water. Payback time. He held the brim of the hat; it was full of water. He wore a grin that said *I'm going to get you*. Without even thinking about it, I kicked the hard hat—the same foot I kicked the man in the parking lot during the strike, the same foot that killed the mouse, the same foot that made the puck hit Norm. Water soared into the air, landing all over Ray. The men in the room went into hysterics. "You little shit," Ray shouted out. I laughed so hard I was crying. Ray laughed too. "I'll get you back," he warned, and I knew he would.

The foreman entered the lunchroom and the laughter subsided. He looked at Ray's wet clothes and the dripping hard hat. He wanted to know what was going on. There was no response from anyone.

"Cathy, you are ladle tender." I had never been ladle tender and had no wish to be.

"I don't think I will be very good at ladle tender," I said. "I'm too short."

"You're on it." Maybe he wanted to embarrass me in front of the miners. Ray said he would show me as he wiped out the inside of his hard hat. The ladle tender's safety equipment hung on a hook by the wheel. I put on the aluminum spats, tying them around my leg. They ran over and past my size-four work boots. I shook my head; I could trip on this. Then Ray helped me with the aluminum coat that was supposed to cover you to just below the knees—it went down to my ankles. The sleeves were six inches too long. I tried to fold them and make a cuff, but the material didn't have any give. I dropped my arms to my side; the shoulders of the coat went down my arms. Ray helped me with a pair of tapper's mitts. They had places for your thumb and your pointing finger. The rest of your hand filled the mitt. From the mitt part, the sleeve was eighteen inches. They were so big my fingers barely reached the part of the mitt. Ray pulled the mitts over the sleeves of the coat. They covered my elbows, and I couldn't bend my arms. I couldn't grasp the bar with my mitts. He took off my hard hat and attached a shield, then pointed me in the direction of the ladles. Just a reminder, the molten copper came down a V-shaped launder. There are two ladles pouring into the molds. I lifted the pry bar, but I didn't have a good grip. I placed it in the back of the ladle and was supposed to pry the back of the skull (see glossary) that had formed in the back of the ladle. I struggled to put the bar under the skull, but I was too short to get any leverage. Molten copper poured out the back of the ladle and onto the floor when the warning horn from the wheel operator told me he was going to pour the next mold. I stepped back—the heat from the copper was *hot*. The wheel moved to the next mold and I went back in to try and pry the skull. My shield was melting and had become so lumpy I couldn't see what I was doing.

My anger reared its ugly head. "Fuck this!" I yelled, but no one could hear me. I wobbled back to the foreman and Ray, throwing down the pry bar.

"Get me out of this!" My voiced was muffled by the shield under the roar of the furnace and the gas blowers.

"This is stupid. It's unsafe. If you want me to do this job, then you get me equipment that fits. Maybe the ministry will be interested in what you're doing." I felt helpless, standing there like a robot, my arms unable to bend, the aluminum coat almost to my feet. They couldn't get any equipment like that to fit, and I was never asked to be a ladle tender again.

On one Sunday afternoon shift, I sat with forty men in the lunchroom. All the bull work was done, and the furnace was not ready to cast. Everyone was agitated, worried about what was going to happen, what with talk of a strike and a shutdown.

Ray came bursting into the lunchroom and karate-kicked the tiles in the ceiling. He did this a lot. He was carrying a roll of copper wire.

"It's time I paid you back." He held out the copper wire. He grabbed my arm and hurled me onto the bench. I couldn't fight him, and the men in the room sat astonished at his actions. Somehow, he wrapped the copper wire around me, tying me to the bench. My arms were crossed in front of me and I was pinned. He sat down just as the foreman walked into the lunchroom. All the laughing stopped. Someone had squealed on him. The foreman demanded to know what was going on. No one said a word. If it would have been anyone else but Ray, I would have been mad. He was just paying me back. The foreman told someone to untie me, and one by one he brought the men into his office. No one said anything to him; it was the way he asked the men as each one went into his office: "I want you to tell me who tied her to the bench and what happened."

One of the men then told me the foreman thought something was going on in there. He used that sexual undertone I heard on a day-to-day basis. "The foreman said he thinks we were hiding something, implying that there is more to this story that meets the eye."

My anger grew. It was my turn. Before I went to the office, I walked over to Bruce, who was sitting against the wall, his nose in a book. The first two buttons of his shirt were open, revealing some chest hair.

"This will only hurt a little," I said as I pulled four hairs out. The look on his face said that it did indeed hurt. I forced the small hairs between my front teeth. This would give the foreman something to think about. I sat in the chair and faced the foreman with the biggest Colgate smile I could give. He wanted to know what happened in the lunchroom. I told him I didn't know who did it. I watched him stare at the little hairs caught in my teeth. He told me to get out of the office. I continued to smile as I nodded and went back to the lunchroom. I thought that if he was going to think that way about me anyway, I might as well give him something to think about.

Chapter 70

Maxie McGann
1982

Maxie McGann

"Why do the men keep reminding you you're black? It's obvious: your skin is the colour of coal," I said, pointing my bologna sandwich at his enormous arms, the size of my thighs. Maxie smiled, displaying a few missing teeth. "You know you're black; you look in the mirror every morning. It annoys me when they talk to you or about you and always bring up the fact that you're black." My bologna sandwich swished back and forth. I took a bite and covered my mouth so he wouldn't see the chewed-up sandwich.

He chuckled, amused at my observation.

"Just let it go, girl, don't give them another thought," he said with a heavy Jamaican accent, shaking his head back and forth. "That's just how they are."

"You know Inco doesn't hire many black or First Nations people, or women," I went on.

"You know, girl, I did notice that." He laughed a hearty laugh. "Now you eat that sandwich before it lands on the floor."

After work I got into my yellow Datsun. Maxie was waiting for the bus, and he asked if I could give him a ride home. "Sure, get in."

He looked doubtful at my fifty-five-inch high and sixty-one-inch wide car as he leaned on the roof, making my car look like a dinky toy. I pulled the seat back as far as it would go. Maxie squeezed his massive body into the passenger's seat. It reminded me of a jack-in-the-box. His knees were up by his chin, and he wrapped his large arms around them.

"Can you breathe?" I laughed. "I'll close the door." He looked like a caterpillar in a cocoon. It was so funny that tears rolled down my face.

"I don't think this is going to work." His voice was muffled. "I think I will get on the bus." I opened the door and watched him unravel himself like a butterfly getting out of its cocoon, shaking his hands and feet to get back his circulation. We smiled at each other, and I watched him get on the bus.

Chapter 71

Talks Collapse and the Strike Deadline Nears 1982

I didn't want another strike; I was still in the hole from the last one. I could lose my house. My van was not working, and I wasn't sure how long the little Datsun would last.

Sudbury Star, May 26, 1982: 170 stewards rejected Inco's offer; this was unanimous. The company offered a three-year agreement, no improvement in wages or vacations, and the company will not roll in the cost of living. "We want the same increase as Thompson Manitoba!" a man yelled out at the meeting. They got between $7.50 and $8 over a three-year period; all Inco was offering us was $3.50. The bargaining committee read the report: wage increase: 0, vacation: 0, vacation pay: 0, cost-of-living allowance roll-in: 0, shift premiums: 0, Sunday premium: 0, dental: 0, life insurance: 0, and disability pension: 0. We were on strike by Monday.

My gut was in turmoil; I was sick most of the time. My body couldn't take much more stress.

Again, I watched as staff workers rolled barbeques off a truck along with supplies for getting ready for a strike.

On June 1, Inco workers walked off the job. We were once again on strike. A few friends decided to go to the Colson Hotel and dance off the stress. I remember dancing with a woman friend on the dance floor, eyes closed, when I felt someone tap me on the shoulder. When I opened my eyes, I came face to face with the CTGF.

"Don't you ever touch me again," I yelled over the loud band music. I could feel anger building up inside me. Memories flooded my brain. The pain he had caused me, this man who said women would never work in his department. The man who said I committed fraud when I used my maiden name to bid on a job to get out of the anode away from the rapist. There he was, wiggling his pathetic, round body in front of me and wearing a stupid grin. How dare he touch me. My anger intensified; rage began to build. I snarled, baring my teeth.

"You listen to me, you little piece of shit. You're in my territory now; take your friends and leave." My body trembled with the amount of adrenaline that pumped through me.

He said they were not going anywhere, and he brushed the sleeve of his shirt as if to brush me away. The new boyfriend, not a real nice guy, stood beside the bouncer: a large muscular man in a black T-shirt with his arms crossed over his chest, large tattoos on his upper arm. He was watching the discussion on the floor, and just as the bouncer looked away I hip-checked the toter, sending him against the wall. The bouncer uncrossed his arms and headed toward us. I hoped he didn't see what I did. He asked if there was any trouble and I told him that this man and his friends were just leaving. I gave CTGF a queen's wave as the bouncer walked with him and his friends out the door.

Meanwhile, our picketers were not letting people cross the lines, so Inco had resorted to using a large and costly helicopter to airlift rotating staff and to move supplies. From what we heard, they were feeding the staff very well with barbequed steaks and roasts.

The wives were ready too. They were organized; it was a little easier this time. It didn't take them long. The union made pins in the shape of a nickel with a beaver on it that read: "Put our nickel to work for us." Val came to town and gave the Local a check for $2000 from his Local in Hamilton. It was great to see him again. I don't think he liked my new boyfriend—most of my friends didn't either.

On June 24, Inco announced the shutdown would last from July until October 3.

The strike had been going on for thirty-two days when the union came back, asking us to accept the offer. We got a modest improvement, and 82 percent accepted the deal, 7345 out of the 10,000 who voted. Port Colborne voted to accept it too, 4–1. We got a continuation of the cost of living payments, but a compounding or roll-in provision contained in the expired agreement had been removed. Thirty-year workers who retire would get $750 a month.

Now I had to register for unemployment insurance benefits. When the first check came in, it wasn't very much. I was still behind from the last strike and some of my bills were still not paid. There was a silver lining: the con man I was dating introduced me to a wholesaler from a restaurant. We were able to order boxes of chicken and bacon and sell them. We didn't make much, but enough to get our own boxes of meat. I got a licence to salvage and this was all legal. Sometimes food would come in that was labelled wrong, like it said it was hot capicola when it was really mild. It would cost the company more to repack than to sell it to us for cost. Another time, buffalo burgers were coming from the West and the restaurant decided they didn't want them. So, we set up a table at the flea market, plugged in an electric frying pan so people could taste the burgers, and made enough to have my own box of burgers. He showed me how to get a licence to do this and I had my own little company. I never made any money, but I did have food on the table.

In October, Lloyd wanted the house sold. It was hard for me to understand why he was so mean to us. It wasn't as if he had put any money into it. I know his mother had lent us $5000 for a down payment, and I was determined once I got back on my feet to give that back to her. Nothing like kicking you while you're down: the strike and then another strike and now a long shutdown. He threatened to split the kids up by taking our son and leaving our daughter. That was not going to happen. Like the Incredible Hulk, I transformed into a green rage. I had a meeting with Lloyd and asked him to think about the children, but he wanted the house sold. My dad asked me to leave the room so he could talk to Lloyd in private. I don't know what was said, but my guess is that my dad paid him off.

I received a letter from the bank. I was afraid to open it, but to my surprise it was positive. Back in 1974 when I started at Inco, I had taken out a certificate for $1000 dollars; it was now $1500. The gods were smiling down at me again. This would help at Christmas time.

Chapter 72

Every Miner Had a Mother
1983

The original logo with men only.   *Our new and improved logo.*

    Throughout the winter of the shutdown I sold meat. One babysitter would move out while another one would move in. I really didn't need anyone while I was on shutdown. By April 4, the shutdown had ended and I was back to work, singing "Back on the Chain Gang" as I hooked up a lift of scrap anodes. I loved working with this crane man, Austin. He was one of the best crane operators in the refinery.

    Norm, the man who got the wooden hockey puck in the face, the man who covered for me, died of brain cancer. I felt so empty and depressed. Why is it that the good ones die young?

    In 1982, the city of Sudbury announced plans to celebrate the centennial year. Our municipal and local historic society, the Centennial Foundation, unveiled the city's official centennial logo. It featured only images of men and they described it as recognizing the "price and dedication of the people who help build the community." The reaction from the women's community was swift. What about the women of Sudbury? The Sudbury Women's committee sent a letter to the representative of the City of Sudbury. They were the planners of the centennial year celebration.

The reply was that the women might sponsor their own centennial event during the year. They were not going to change the logo, even though it ignored our history and the work our mothers and grandmothers had played in building the community.

With a little creativity and a sense of humour, some women came up with an idea that would highlight the role women played while poking fun at the committee's oversight. They decided that the city fathers needed to be reminded that "every miner had a mother." We claimed Mother's Day as the logical date for the event. We gathered information highlighting the historical contributions of women's work to attract as many people as possible to the event. A traditional tea was served to recognize our mothers and grandmothers, complete with pink and green triangle sandwiches. But our tea made a political statement: that every miner had a mother. A new logo was made by artist Brenda Fuhrman and featured two women: an older woman with flowers on her hat and a younger woman with a miner's hard hat. The latter image reflected the move of women into production at Inco's Sudbury operation in the early '70s and the women during the war years. Many phone calls were made to friends and relatives and their neighbours and coworkers to gather pictures of women's work. Many pictures were collected: French, English, Finnish, and Ukrainian, along with taped interviews. The interviews depicted how women had taken on the physical and emotional needs for their husbands and children throughout history. They were caregivers and service workers, mothers and housewives, underpaid and undervalued. The women played a major role in this city, building and maintaining the labour force.

We set out to reclaim our women's past, what their roles were with the major mining companies, Inco and Falconbridge. What the women did during WWII. Their labour history activism that dates back to the early 20th century. Community experience during the strikes in the '50s, '60s, '70s, and '80s.

And the rival between Mine Mill and Steelworkers. (The Steelworkers had once raided Mine Mill.) Inco workers became Steelworkers. In history, all these events that shaped our culture and political landscape were remembered as men's struggles. Women were invisible.

I am so thankful for the documentary. A *Wives' Tale*, which told the story of what the wives did during the strike in '78/'79. It also crushed the lies that the women forced the men back to work for a bad contract in '58. There has been little information on the role women played in building Sudbury.

What began as a spoof on city hall became a politicizing experience as we gathered photographs and heard stories about what women had done in our community. My hat went off to the organizers Jennifer Keck, Mercedes Steedman, and Susan Kennedy. It was a great celebration.

Another babysitter moved in, with her two-year-old daughter. I didn't have to worry about my kids when I was at work. She was the little girl who had moved in with us when her mom and dad died when she was six years old. She stayed a while then moved in with her boyfriend, and I got another sitter to move in.

A copy of Cathy's suggestion.

Inco had an employee suggestion plan. This was a proposal to improve a problematic situation by means of a specific solution which would result in savings or other real benefits in any part of our operations. It had to be an original idea, or a new application of an old idea. It had to be submitted and signed on the official suggestion form. All hourly-rated employees were eligible to participate. The award could go up to $10,000. Ray had won the company's highest award, "Employee Suggestion," and had received

$10,000. He had suggested that we use a different kind of release agent called Barite, rather than bone ash to paint the mold and ladles. I was so proud of him.

I too put in a suggestion. When I was dating Val, he took me for a tour of Stelco Steel in Hamilton.

A worker had a shield on his hard hat that unclipped so only the shield was discarded. At Inco, we threw out the whole harness. My suggestion was to invest in these shields and save the company that money.

On September 29, 1983, I took my idea to the employee relations office and filled them in on my suggestion. About four months later the new harnesses arrived. I grabbed my copy of the suggestion and rushed down. A tall balding man and a blond woman were standing behind a desk when I entered the room.

"Well, I see the shields came in." I was trying to catch my breath because I had hurried down. I placed my copy of my suggestion on the desk. "How much will I get?"

"Well … Cathy, ahhh …" The man didn't look at me as he nervously shuffled the papers on his desk. "We can't give you this suggestion, because we had already thought of this before you put it in."

I recoiled in horror. I couldn't believe what he was saying.

"You're kidding me. This is a joke, right?" I could feel a rush of adrenalin course through my veins.

"No, no," he repeated. "I am not joking. We thought of this before you."

The reality of what they were doing hit me. Anger appeared.

"You're lying. Who thought of it? You stole my suggestion!" I yelled.

"How dare you call us liars and thieves! Get out of my office or I will call security." He slammed the papers down as if to intimidate me.

"Show me the proof; show me you thought of this before I put in my suggestion in September." Spit was flying from my mouth.

"I don't have to show you anything," he said, a sly cunning smile on his face.

"You're a fucking liar and a thief." I wanted to cry so badly, but I didn't. I could feel the tears welling up in my eyes. What a slap in the face. I threw my shield and harness on the floor. He said that if I kept it up he would charge me with defacing company property.

Chapter 73

Whitewater Rafting and Merv
January 1984

First aid competitions were once again on their way. Donny and I were the only team members from the previous year. The men we were to be working with were great.

We were low on equipment, bandages, splints, etc. A supervisor from the first aid and security department dropped off a large box of supplies. Inco had its own first aid and security coverage in all plants and mines. I recognized him as one of the team members from Levack, the group who had won the Parker Shield back in '79.

I also saw him a few times in the first aid room when I went down there for a coffee. He told me I reminded him of his sister, who also had long dark hair. She was twenty-nine when she passed away.

His name was Merv, and he was now a supervisor. He drilled us with questions, then took Donny and his bandage man to another room. When he returned, he fell to the floor and pretended to have an epileptic seizure. At first, I was not sure what was happening.

Donny came back in and said that this was my casualty. I sprang into action and went through the spiel.

"Is there any danger here to me or my team? Is this person breathing? What is the rate of breathing?" Donny answered my questions. The supervisor flipped around on the floor like a fish out of water. I loosened his tie and the first three buttons on his shirt. A mass of black curly hair popped up as if the pressed dress shirt had been holding them all down. The sight of all that hair made me lose my train of thought. I had never seen so much hair on a man; the thought that he had hair like a gorilla came to mind. I began to stammer. It had been a long time since I had been with a man and this took my breath away.

My teammates recognized my reaction, and everyone started laughing, including me. The supervisor sat up and buttoned his shirt. I watched as the forest of hair was tucked back under the ironed shirt. He too was laughing, and commented that I was not very good at taking care of an epileptic casualty. I threw a triangular bandage in the air. They had got me good. They would never let me forget this incident.

During the February competitions, they simulated a thunderstorm with heavy rain causing a motorcycle accident with a hydro pole down. We thought we had done a great job and were hopeful to win, but we didn't.

In March, all the teams went to the Parker Shield competition as spectators. It was my daughter Melanie's birthday, so I took nine little girls to the competition. It was a circus accident and a gorilla had escaped from its cage. After it was over, the man in the gorilla suit came over to see the girls. When he took the head of the costume off, it turned out to be Merv, the supervisor who had taken the pretend seizure. He said his hellos to me and the girls. The girls thought it was great. I commented to him that he didn't need the costume, as he was hairy enough.

In July, a friend and I decided to go whitewater rafting down the Ottawa River. Memories of my grandparents' camp filled my head as we climbed into the raft. When I saw the first set of rapids up ahead, the whitewater churning in all directions, I changed my mind, but there was nothing to do but paddle. The thrill invigorated me. I felt alive, and free from all the stress in my life. Two days of this and I was a new woman, ready to take on the world again.

It was late August or early September. I had just turned thirty and was feeling very depressed. Not about my age, but about my life. It was a slow day at work, so I went down to the first aid room to have a coffee with whomever was the attendant that day.

Merv was visiting our first aid room. He was one of two supervisors who managed all the first aid attendance at Inco. We got to talking and I asked him if he knew of any nice, single men that I might ask out. He told me he had a friend who he would introduce me to. I hadn't been with a man for such a long time I was ready to jump someone's bones, and soon. (I didn't tell him that.) Merv set up a meeting to have coffee with his red-headed friend. I asked my friend to come along to see what she thought. The four of us sat in the restaurant. The redhead was okay, nothing to write home about. A few days later I called him and asked him out. He was busy with his kids. I asked if he wanted to do something with all the kids. He said no, not at that time. I called again, and again he said not at that time. Well, that was enough rejection for me. There would not be a third phone call.

Three weeks later I was on the day shift and back for a coffee in the first aid room. Merv came in and opened his brown briefcase on the counter.

"Hey Merv, thanks for the redhead's number, but he doesn't seem interested."

He shuffled through some pay stubs and handed one to the attendant.

"Yeah, nothing like breaking down one's self-esteem," I said.

"Maybe I'll keep you for myself," Merv said, looking straight at me.

I put my hand in the air. "No. No married men for me. Did that once and hurt a woman really badly. I will never do that again."

"My wife is leaving me." His voice cracked.

"Yeah, yeah, do you know how many times I've heard that line? You've been married for eighteen years; why would you get separated?" My lip was curled, showing him I didn't believe him.

"It's not me, it's her." His voice was strained and quivered a bit.

I threw my paper cup in the garbage. "Hey, boss man, call me when she's gone." I said my goodbyes and headed back to the anode.

Chapter 74

More Men Killed in the Mines
June 20, 1984

About 200 workers were on shift at Falconbridge Mine that morning. Four of them never got out.

At 10:12 a.m., a seismic event that registered a 3.5 on the Richter scale struck the mine, causing a major rock fall and trapping many of the miners underground between the 3800-foot level and the 4200-foot level. Despite rescue attempts over the next several days, Sulo Korpela, Richard Chenier, Daniel Lavallee, and Wayne St. Michel each lost their lives.

Chapter 75

Be Careful Whom You Ask for Help
August 1984

If you ever thought it was hot outside in the heat of summer, try working in the anode.

My blue jeans stuck to me like duct tape. It had to be 45° to 50°C this day. My long dark-brown hair was jammed under my hard hat. It was so snug I could bend over and my hat wouldn't move. I was on the water that day, keeping it regulated to keep the furnace cool, and emptying the hot cars. The furnace was running hot, so I had to climb up and down the ladder to the top of the furnace many times. I checked the pipes that ran the length of the furnace, using my gloves to wipe away the dirt and grime that was stuck to the gauges and aluminum tags. Ray had told me the skim bay was running hot as well, so I was to try to cool it down. This was the part of the furnace that the furnace crew worked on, skimming and poling. It was hard to breathe up there. The thick copper dust was everywhere; piles of it looked like little mountains sitting on the pipes and cables. A hot car was coming in and I didn't want to be up there when it did. I didn't want to breathe in the heavy thick sulphur gas that spewed out from the large opening in the top of the hot car.

I went down the stairs and then climbed up onto the hot car. I pulled my shield down and poured the magnificent molten metal into the furnace. I loved this part of the job.

The foreman was sitting at his desk when I entered his office.

"Why don't we have a warning alarm when a hot car comes in so whoever is on top of the furnace can come down?" I asked.

The foreman rolled his eyes and told me that they had been doing it the same way for years and no one had ever complained. If it got too bad up there, common sense would tell you to come down.

"Just because nobody's complained doesn't mean there isn't a problem, and sometimes you don't know a hot car is in until you breathe all that sulphur in," I said.

He shrugged his shoulders and continued doing whatever he was doing.

I decided to put in another suggestion, even though the last suggestion was stolen from me. Back to the foreman's office I went to retrieve a suggestion form.

I began to fill it out and was having trouble with the spelling. The foreman came out and said the furnace was running hot, so up the ladder I went. I turned up the valves and played with the others until the gauges, which were hard to see, said the temperature was coming down. I wasn't the only one up on the furnace. A general foreman from maintenance was there too. I nodded—there was no sense saying anything; it was so loud up there he wouldn't hear. As I was descending the ladder, I had the idea that he could help me fill out the form. He wasn't part of our department and it wouldn't make any difference to him. I waited in the charge aisle, approached him, and asked for help. We went over to his office and filled out the form together. He told me he thought it was a great idea. The suggestion read that an alarm with a flashing red light should be installed to warn people that the hot car was in. I thanked him for his help and went back to my department. Little did I know that I had entered a very dark place. I had opened up a cage that shouldn't have been opened.

Chapter 76

The Harassment Came into My House September 1984

My sitter was moving out of town. I placed an ad in the newspaper with my name, address, and phone number for a live-in babysitter because of the different shifts I was working.

The phone rang; a man on the other end said he was calling about the ad for a sitter. He began yelling at me: "I know who you are! You're that bitch that works for Inco. You're nothing but a slut. I know what kind of woman you are. I would never let my daughter work for you." His tone was full of rage as he barked out his dislike for me. He was not calling for the ad, he just wanted to tell me what he thought of me. It sent chills up and down my spine.

My anger surfaced and I yelled back. "You cowardly piece of shit, you think you're so brave calling me and talking to me like this? Tell me who you are." There was a pause. "Yeah, you haven't got the balls to say what you just said to my face." I slammed the phone down hard. My heart was pounding in my chest as I reached for a cigarette.

Another phone call, another man. I held my breath. This man said he had a daughter who could move in with me and she was good with kids. He said he could drive her over so we could meet; we arranged it and they arrived the next day. Her name was Laura. She was very shy and wouldn't look up from the table. She had brought her suitcase and all her belongings. I need a sitter and she needed somewhere to live.

You know, it is said that people come into your life for a reason. Over the next year I learned all about bulimia after a large jar of peanut butter and a bottle of ketchup disappeared in one week. She was emotionally upset and would vomit every time she ate. I learned that as a child she was sexually assaulted, raped over and over by her stepfather. This was just another thing I had to deal with. This is not my story to tell. She will tell it someday. She was a good worker and things were going to work out.

I had received obscene phone calls in the past and now they were starting up again. Sometimes they would be late at night and I would run naked in the dark into the kitchen to the only phone I had. My son had just turned thirteen and he answered one of these phone calls. The man told him I was a slut, that I fucked men at work or gave blow jobs on the cat walk, the bridge that connects to the crane. My poor son had to deal with this at such a tender time of his life. I called the police and reported it. I was told to get a tracer put on my phone. Bell Canada would do this, but only for a few days.

The person calling must have known the rules, because when the tracer was off the phone calls would start again. I knew it was the man who lived next door to us, but I couldn't prove it. He worked in the tank house at the copper refinery, just off the anode. He was very odd, creepy, like a stalker. When he looked at me at work or over the fence, I got an eerie feeling that sent chills all over my body. One day I caught him looking in my kitchen window from his own, so I put Mactac over my window. It was a glacier window film to prevent him and any other unwanted viewers from looking in. Another time he was in his front yard looking into my house with binoculars. When I called the police, they told me they couldn't do anything because he was in his own yard. There were more phone calls, but we couldn't catch him.

October is fire-prevention month. A friend and I decide to take the kids and the sitter out for pizza. I saw Merv, the first aid supervisor, drive by and then drive by again. Fear whelmed up inside me. Could he be the one who was making these calls? I stopped at the bank and waited, and sure enough he drove in. I jumped out of my car and cautiously walked to his window.

"Why are you following me?" I demanded. By the look on his face I could tell he was a little nervous too. He said he just wanted to talk to me. He was on his way to a meeting for the volunteer fire fighters.

I told him I was busy going for a pizza, so maybe some other time. My friend and I talked about him on the way. "He's nice, but he is a little older than me, by nine years, and those fucking geeky grey dress pants turn me off. I wonder what he looks like in jeans. He seems a little shy, and really square," I said. We both laughed. "He can't be all bad if he's a volunteer firefighter. I wonder what he looks like dressed as a fireman." I moved my eyebrows up and down. We laughed again. I wondered why his wife was leaving him. I told him we were going to the Kingsway Hotel for a while that night, and if he wanted to join us he was welcome. He did show up and we had a few dances before he headed back home.

The next day, Merv called and asked if he could come for coffee. We sat at the kitchen table and talked for a few hours, telling each other about our lives. I listened, trying to pick up on why his wife would be leaving him. I found out he was from Renfrew, cow-shit valley, the same area as my grandparents' camp was.

Finally, I just asked. "Why is your wife leaving you?"

He told me she didn't want to be married, that she didn't want to be a mother anymore. Her apartment wasn't ready yet, so she was still at their house. This sounded strange; I wasn't sure if I should believe him or not. I picked up the empty cups and headed for the sink. He could tell I was skeptical.

"What if I can prove to you that she is leaving, then would you go out with me? Can I use your phone?" I nodded, and he dialled and said, "Someone wants to talk to you." He handed me the phone. It was his wife. I asked if she was leaving and she told me as soon as the apartment was ready.

I called Val that night, my old boyfriend from Hamilton. He's such a great friend.

"He's management, Mulroy." I could hear the laughter in his voice. "Well, go with your heart; you will know if it's good or not. Management"—he laughed again—"now that's funny."

After I thanked him and told him to fuck off, I sat there thinking about what I should do. Merv and I began to date. The sex was wonderful. Merv made up a room for his wife in their basement, in the laundry room so they were not sleeping in the same room. It was a few weeks before she moved out, and to my surprise it turned out that she was moving in with that red-headed guy Merv tried to set me up with. She was not taking her three kids with her, but she did take the antiques. She wanted the microwave too, but Merv said he would need it for the kids.

Chapter 77

Stalkers ... Who Are They? October 1984

I went down to pick up my pay stub. Management had decided that everyone was to pick up their own stub instead of someone handing them out. The carpentry department made a shelving unit that had little pockets for the stubs to be placed in. All the pay stubs were in numerical order, with our name, employment number, and social security number in front for all to see.

I had to go through the tank house to get to it—that's the department the peeper from next door worked in. I scanned through the stubs, found mine, and pulled it out of its slot, opening it on its perforated edges. The top part of the stub had a carbon back. Someone had taken a finger nail or something and wrote the word CUNT in large black capital letters across my stub. I was sure it was the peeper. I looked around to see if I could see him. I was sure he wanted to see my reaction. Next week was the same thing ... CUNT. I reported it to my boss. He said he couldn't do anything about it.

"This is a threat; someone is threatening me." My yelling didn't help me. Frustrated, I went to security in the first aid. They said they would pull my stubs and I could pick it up in the first aid room.

Someone was out to get me. I could feel it. The phone calls kept coming in at home, but Bell Canada refused to cover me. The caller would call me vicious names like *slut* and *pig*. When I was outside in my backyard, the peeper would pretend to cough and say whore. I knew that the phone calls were coming from him, but how could I prove it? He was so creepy. How far was he going to take this?

I told some of the men on my shift. A man we called Snake who lived on the other side of the peeper said he was over at his place and he had fondled his daughter right in front of him. I told him he should report that to the police. All Snake said was that it was none of his business. I could never understand why men would stay quiet. Not many ever stood up for me, either.

Meanwhile, Merv and I were getting to know each other. His wife was moving out soon. We talked a lot on the phone because he lived an hour away. He's a really nice man.

One day while making supper, there was a knock on the door. It was a man from a flower shop holding a bouquet of flowers. He asked me if I was Cathy and to sign his clipboard. The note read: "To a special person." What a great thing: Merv had sent me flowers. I put them in a vase, sat back to admire them, and called Merv. There was a long pause after Merv told me he didn't send me any flowers. The hairs on the back of my neck stood at attention. A wave of fear went through my body. If not Merv, then who?

The card was not signed. I called the flower shop and asked who sent them. I was told the man paid by cash. Merv said I must have a secret admirer. A disturbing feeling swished through me. This was not a good thing, I knew it. Merv asked if he had any competition, trying to make light of the situation. This was affecting me in a negative way. I didn't sleep at all that night and was very tired the next day at work. Of course it was a full cast.

At break time, I headed for the lunchroom for a coffee and a cigarette. The general foreman, the one who had helped me fill out the suggestion forms, was standing just outside the lunchroom. "Have you heard anything about your suggestion?" he yelled in my ear.

"No, not yet," I yelled back. "Thanks again for helping me out." I went to walk around him, and he blocked me.

"How did you like the flowers?" The smile on his face petrified me. I thought the pounding in my chest was louder than number-two furnace's roar.

"You sent them. You can't send me flowers, it's not a good idea," I couldn't hear myself over the roar. He turned and walked away. I went after him.

He turned. "Come to my office." His office was small, just enough room for a desk and two chairs. He went around the desk and sat down, placing one foot over his knee and leaning back in the chair, his arms on the back of his head. He looked very superior. Again, I protested. "You can't send me flowers."

"I just did. Who is going to stop me?" He flashed a malicious grin. "Sit," he said, pointing to the empty chair.

"I don't want to sit. What the fuck is this?" My voice was loud—I wanted someone to hear me. "If you do this or bother me in any way, I will call your wife."

"She won't believe you." He unclasped his hands and leaned his elbows on the desk. "If you look at the card, you can see I didn't sign it."

I turned and walked out. When I got home, I grabbed the vase and emptied the whole thing into the sink, then grabbed the flowers and stuffed them into the garbage. Now there were two men I had to worry about.

Chapter 78

Brass Candlestick Holders November 1984

The stress was getting to me. Some days I wanted to hide under a blanket and never come out. I sat in the living room and puffed on a cigarette. I had a peeper for a neighbour who worked at the copper refinery. I knew he was the one making the phone calls. The cops couldn't do anything about it because he was in his own yard. Where was my protection? They could do something only after the fact, I was told.

I had met a nice man whose wife was living in his basement in the laundry room.

This was weird. Another man, a general foreman, was freaking me out at work. I was so glad I was off the next day and wouldn't be back on day shift for two more weeks.

I decided to do some yard work, and discovered that someone had cut my garden hose into pieces. I called the police again. "We can't help you out" was the message I got from them. The two weeks flew by and I was back on day shift. My neck was sore from all the stress, so I thought I would see the chiropractor after work.

Full cast, that's good, the time goes by so much faster. My wheel partner and I made two ladles and then the cast started. A wheel shack had been made to fit over the two wheel operators. I got comfortable in my chair and was ready to pour. About an hour into the cast my shack door opened and in walked the flower-sending general foreman and closed the door. I couldn't go anywhere because I was pouring molten metal from my ladle into molds. I couldn't take my eyes off of the ladle, it would be a mess. I had to watch the hoist operator too, to make sure the anode was picked up. When I was on the wheel I didn't want to be distracted. I asked the general foreman to leave. He unwrapped something bundled in soiled rags and displayed two beautiful solid-brass candlestick holders. Someone in his department had made them. They were about fifteen inches high and polished up so they shone like the sun.

"Wow ... those are beautiful," I said, trying to keep an eye on my work.

"These are for you. I know you are seeing someone. You can use them when you are having supper with him and think of me," he said, handing me one of the sticks.

Fear rushed in. "I don't want them," I said, pushing it out of my way so I could see my ladle. "Like fuck I will, get the fuck out of my shack. If I am having supper with a man, it's with that man alone, and I won't be thinking of you. If you don't get out of here, I will pour copper all over the floor. That should get my boss here in one minute."

"No, no, don't do that." His voice softened. "I will just leave them here." He placed them on my counter and gave me a creepy smile that made me shiver.

"You can leave them there if you want, but when I leave they will still be there. Someone else can have them. Besides, if I took them out of the plant it would be stealing and I could get fired. That would be a stupid thing to do." I let the molten copper spill out the back of the ladle. This got the attention of the tapper. It would only take seconds for him to get hold of the foreman. The general foreman wrapped the brass candlesticks in the soiled rags and left.

"Jesus, that man is sooo creepy." I put my attention back on the job and wondered if any man dealt with this kind of bullshit.

After work, I headed to the chiropractor's office. It was downtown right next to Nibbler's Restaurant. When I exited the office, there stood the general foreman holding the brass candlesticks. This was even creepier than at work. He was stalking me. I felt my animal instincts kick in, fight or flight. I had to think fast. I looked around—no one. He asked if I would go into the restaurant with him and motioned for me to walk in front of him. I was hoping he wasn't going to knock me over the head with the brass sticks like in the movies. I needed people around; the restaurant was a good idea. We sat at a booth and ordered two coffees, and he pulled out the candlesticks and sat them on the table. "They are so beautiful," I said, picking one up to admire it. The coffee arrived and that was my cue. I stood up and began to yell at him. The waitress and the other people in the restaurant watched. "Who do you think you are? You're a fucking nutcase. You are a boss at Inco, I'm an employee, you can't send me flowers and you can't give me gifts. You can't stalk me. This has to stop. I am sure there must be a law about this. If not, I will go to upper management. Stay the fuck away from me. Stay out of my life. Stop following me." Everyone in the restaurant was now listening to each word. The general foreman's face drained of all its colour. "If you follow me again, I am going to the police." I left as fast as I could. He still had to pay for the coffee. When I got into the car, the band the Police were playing on the radio:

Every breath you take
Every move you make
Every bond you break
Every step you take
I'll be watching you

I curled my lip as the hairs on the back of my neck tingled, and I turned the radio off.

Chapter 79

Sleeping with My Shotgun December 1984

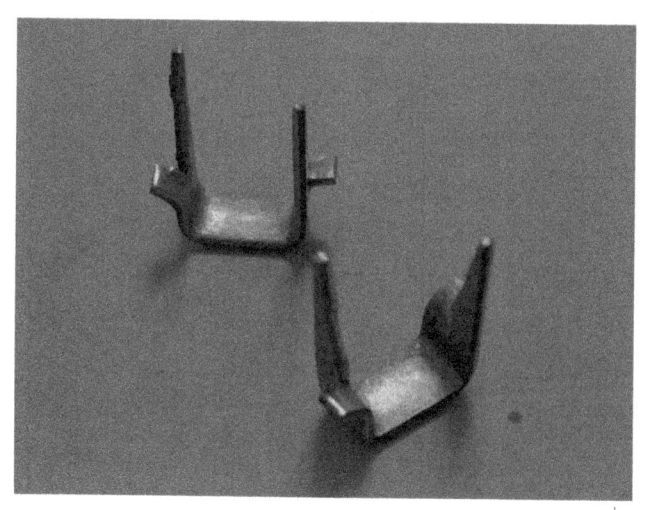

The electrical staples that were left in my driveway.

Christmas was on its way and the Boy Scouts were having a party. I was to drive Peppy and three of his friends, four excited boys, to the party. We all piled into my little Capri. After backing out of the driveway, the car began to wobble. I pulled over to check it out—all four tires were flat. After a closer examination, I saw strange-looking tacks stuck in my tires. The boys had to get a ride with another parent as I pulled the invaders out of the tires. They were industrial electrical staples. Someone had taken the time to twist each one so the prongs would be sticking up, then threw them in my driveway. A light snow had fallen so they were not visible. I gently shovelled the snow and found thirty staples.

I was mad, angry, and terrified. I had a feeling I knew who it was. This vicious sabotage had affected my children. The Sudbury Police took another statement asking me who

I thought would do this, and I said either the peeper next door or the general foreman of maintenance at work. I told them about the incident with the general foreman and the brass candlesticks and the flowers.

A week later, again the driveway was full of staples. I began to think that it was more likely the general foreman, as he would have access to these kinds of staples, but the police said anyone who is fixing up their home would use these. They advised me to call the insurance company and report the vandalism. My heart sank. Who would do this? I have to admit I was getting very nervous, and a bit scared for my kids. I told them about the staples and to watch out for strangers.

While I was in the car, the song by the Police came over the radio again:

> *Every breath you take, and every move you make*
>
> *Every bond you break, every step you take, I'll be watching you.*
>
> *Every single day, and every word you say*
>
> *Every game you play, every night you stay, I'll be watching you*
>
> *Oh, can't you see, you belong to me ...*

Okay, that was enough of that. I shut it off.

Wow, this was getting very terrifying. The thought of someone out there watching my every move and throwing staples in my driveway scared me. You would think there would be laws to protect women from these kinds of men, I said to myself as I lay in my bed.

Well, if they were not going to protect me and my kids, I would do it myself.

I dug to the back of the closet, pulled out a large green canvas case and placed it on the bed. I opened a zipper that went almost all the way around, displaying my beautiful 20-gauge Russian shotgun.

If I have to, I will, I thought to myself.

It was put away clean, so it was ready. I ran my hand over the cool metal barrel and the USSR stamped on its side, feeling a powerful sensation. This was the same power I felt when pouring the molten metal from the hot car. It demanded respect.

I put it back into its case but didn't zip it up, and placed it under my side of the bed for easy access. As for the shells, they were left in the closet. That's the safety rules: ammunition and firearms were not to be stored together. A calm came over me when I knew the shotgun was in reach. This wouldn't be the last time I'd find staples in my driveway.

Chapter 80

Christmas with Merv and the Gang 1984

On Christmas Eve 1984, my kids went with their father. Merv asked if I would go with him and his children to church. There were two separate services. Well, okay ... when in Rome. The first one was at 7 p.m. for the kids.

The next service was the 11 p.m. for the adults. All eyes were on me. I could feel the stares penetrating my back. Every time I turned to see where the feeling was coming from, I would catch a woman or two glaring at me. At that second, one would turn her eyes in another direction while another would force a smile.

Merv and his wife were a big part of this church. *Go ahead and stare*, I thought to myself. I will be someone to talk about at your Christmas dinner.

Very Christian of you, I thought. I could tell they were itching to get together with others and gossip. I had been having mixed feelings about what I believed in for a while now. I believe in God or a creator of some sort, but not in the Church. To me they are two different things. Merv's family was very much into the Church. I mean, *really* involved. They were on the board and volunteered. Their kids went to Sunday school and were in the choir. This was a whole lot different from my family—my kids know about strikes and unions and women's fights. These were our beliefs.

We went back to Merv's house and sang Christmas carols. It was fun, but I wished my kids were there. They would be coming home in the morning.

On Christmas Day I made the turkey. Merv and his children would join us for supper at my mom and dad's.

After supper we sat around the table and had coffee and apple or lemon-meringue pie. My parents seemed to really like Merv. They asked him questions about his ex-wife, and he explained that Gil, the redhead, the man he tried to set me up with, had secretly been seeing his wife. He also told them that he had somehow acquired Gil's cat.

My eyes widened and my mouth gaped open when Merv said, "Yes, Gil got one pussy and I got the other."

I froze in my seat. Nobody had ever talked like that in front of my parents, but they laughed. I couldn't believe it. He was in.

We went back to my place to open the gifts. Merv had bought a gift for my babysitter Laura. Her reaction was startling: she freaked when she saw a beautiful hat and scarf.

"I don't wear hats!" she said, slamming it back in the box.

"Well, he didn't have to buy you anything," I said. "You can at least say thank you."

Laura got up and ran to her bedroom. Little did I know, hats were triggers in her mental illness.

We watched our youngest girls play with the large basket I bought them for their Cabbage Patch dolls. It was one of the best Christmases I had had in a long time.

I checked my Christmas list of what I wanted in a man. He has kids, he has a job. Personal stuff. So far Merv fit—all I had asked for, plus more.

Chapter 81

The Stalker Gets Bolder
January 1985

Merv's father Charley had died in February 1983 of lung cancer, and he wanted me to meet his mother. I was apprehensive because we had just started dating. He said that since he had met my parents, it was only right that I meet his mom. That was a fair argument. We headed to Renfrew, a little town just outside Ottawa.

A tall grey-haired woman wearing a white dress with little blue flowers on it opened the door. Merv introduced me to Grace. We shook hands. She never took her eyes off of mine for even a minute. It made me a little uncomfortable; I thought it might be that she was used to Glenda. She invited us in, put the coffee on, and continuously stared at me. She asked if I played euchre as she dug the cards out of a drawer. I told her it was my favourite card game. She told me stories of Merv and Charley. Her eyes welled up when she talked about her lost love. She and Charley were very close. A sixteen-year-old girl entered the room. She too stared at me, like I was a ghost. Her eyes were wide and frightened as she walked to the far end of the table, then left.

"What's the matter with her?" I asked. Grace got up from the table and went into the living room. She came back with a framed photo and placed it on the kitchen table.

"This is Bev, my daughter who passed away eight years ago and Lisa's mother," she said.

My eyes widened when I saw the picture of Bev. You would have thought she was my twin sister. That explained all the staring.

On January 22, my driveway was full of industrial staples again. I got two flat tires and Merv got one. Again, the police were called. We were told there was not much they could do about this unless we saw the person do it.

In February, Merv's mom passed away. Merv felt she died of a broken heart over the loss of Charley. I wasn't sure Merv was ready for a relationship. First his dad died, then his wife left him for one of his friends, and now his mom passed. All I could do was be there for him. Merv's wife went back to the house to look after the kids while Merv went to Renfrew to help organize everything.

On February 25, the upset look on my thirteen-year-old son's face said it all. He had answered one of those phone calls asking him who his mother was fucking and saying that I was nothing but a slut. I knew that these calls were coming from the man next door, the one we called the peeper. I had to catch this guy. He was calling more, saying worse things; it was only a matter of time until the calls were not going to be enough for him.

On March 14, snow had hidden the malicious staples and two more flat tires for me and one for Merv. It's not like anyone can park on the side of the road up here in the north. The snow banks take up that space.

One day the caller called three times. He was getting desperate for something. This time he asked me who I was fucking.

The police said they would talk to both of the men I thought it might be. I must have missed a staple because I got another flat tire. I reminded the police that both men worked at the Copper Cliff copper refinery and they would both have access to my check stubs. I wanted to make sure they had all the information.

Merv and his kids were over at my house when Michael, Merv's fourteen-year-old son, came running in the house holding my black and white cat, Gismo. The cat was screaming in pain, spitting and coughing. His eyes were running pink. I could smell transmission fluid.

"Take him to the bathroom," I yelled. "Hold his back legs as tight as you can." I turned on the water, grabbed the cat's front paws and shoved his face under the tap. The cat screeched in protest. "Hold on tight or he will scratch the hell out of us. He is not liking this." We held him under the tap for about four minutes. I wiped him dry and put him in my room with the lights out. That was all I could do. I went outside and leaned over the fence. The peeper was working on his car. "I know you did that!" I yelled. He laughed.

"Just to let you know, I have a shotgun and I won't be aiming for your head." That wiped the smile from his face.

The next day, when my cat went out he didn't return. I called and called, feeling quite anxious. I went out to look for him, and lying on the ground just a few doors up was a black and white cat. I walked closer. It was my cat, Gismo. I went back in and grabbed a towel to wrap him up and ran back outside. My kids stood at the doorway crying. Blood trickled out of the cat's nose as I laid him on the kitchen counter. His body was still warm, but he wasn't breathing. The kids wanted to know how he died. The easiest answer was to say he was hit by a car. In my heart I knew the peeper had killed him.

The SPCA came and picked up the carcass. The kids and I had a good cry. When Merv called, I told him that the cat was dead. Forty minutes later he was at my door and gave me a hug. I was surprised that someone would be so nice as to come all the way from Levack to give me a hug because my cat had died. I felt something toward him I had never felt before. This man was kind.

I tried so hard to stay strong. The doctor was right: I was too stubborn to have a breakdown. My body was giving out. My bowel problem was, let's say, explosive.

Chapter 82

The Intruder
May 1985

I was constantly aware there was danger all around me and my children. When I meditated, I prayed and used these mantras: *I will not let fear be my choice. I will not hide. I will not back down. I will stand in front of a tiger for my children. My priorities are to protect my children at all costs. I can do this.*

It didn't stop me from worrying that something undesirable was about to happen. My health was deteriorating and I wasn't sleeping well. On top of that, my babysitter was stealing from me and from my mother's purse. She had to go. The new teenage babysitter didn't get along with my daughter. When I returned home, all I heard was "she does this, she does that" from the both of them. I wish their father would do his share and take them sometimes, but I didn't put any hope in wishes. All he did was complain that other people were looking after his kids. I didn't know how much more I could take of all this.

I was woken one night by a heavy pounding on my front door. I could see a silhouette of a man through the frosted glass on the door. He was yelling, "Open up this door, you fucking union bitch!" My heart pounded hard in my chest; my breathing intensified. I couldn't make out who he was. In the dark I went to the phone and called the police. He continued to batter my door along with his yelling. The door was hollow plywood with cardboard in between. It wouldn't take much strength for someone to kick it open. I went back to my bedroom and pulled the shotgun out from under the bed, then crawled through the closet to get the shells, but I couldn't find them in the dark and I wasn't going to turn on the lights. I leaned against the wall beside the door with my shotgun in-hand, feeling like a cowgirl in a movie. The pounding and yelling continued until the flashing red lights of a police car pulled into my driveway. I waited for a few seconds then opened the door. It was a man from my shift; he and his wife were up against the police cruiser with their hands on the roof and their legs spread. He was yelling at me to tell the police that I knew them.

The police officer saw the shotgun in my hand and asked if it was loaded. I told him no and opened the barrel to show him. He asked what I was going to do with an empty gun, and I told him I couldn't find the shells so I was hoping to scare this man away. I filled the police officer in on all that had happened over the last few months. The man was so drunk he could hardly stand, and he was driving. The police officer told the man that his wife had better drive. The police left, leaving the drunken man and his wife at my door.

"What are you doing here?" I asked, still standing at the door with my shotgun hanging at my waist.

"Let us in and we will tell you," he said. "We were at a party and thought we would drop in and say hello."

I let them stand at the door, keeping the shotgun in my hand. The memories of this man hitting me with a banana peel and leaving welts on my legs returned, along with the ones about the Indian rug burn on my wrists and screwing around with the weights of my anodes. And he had the gall to come to my house.

The man was angry that I called the police and that I had a shotgun. He said he just wanted to visit.

"You had no right coming to my home. You and your wife have got to leave." I raised the shotgun and cradled it in my arms. They left; she drove.

The next day I confronted him in the lunchroom. "Who do you think you are, coming to my home and pounding and yelling on my door at 1:30 in the morning? What gives you the right to do such a thing? I am not your friend. I'm a single mother with two children who were sleeping. You're lucky I couldn't find the shells for my gun or you would have left with holes in your body just like the shirt you have on with all those copper splash burns. Don't you ever come to my home again!" All the men in the lunchroom were quiet as I blasted the intruder. I knew he'd pay me back with the weights of my anodes, but I didn't care.

Chapter 83

Merv Sells His House July 1985

Merv decided to sell his house and move into Sudbury. We sat at my kitchen table and he told me of a house only two blocks away. That didn't impress me. I thought it was too close. He was able to store his furniture in the basement of the new place until the owners moved out at the end of July. While he was organizing that, I took the kids to the lake, leaving the kitchen window open. When we returned, the kitchen floor was drenched. The peeper had put one of those pulsating sprinklers on and faced it toward the window. The police were called, and he said he wouldn't do it again. Again, no protection for a woman.

In July, Merv took me to Montréal. It was so romantic. Things were going good in that department.

Then in August I had two more flat tires. These were different staples, but they did the same damage to the tires.

Merv turned forty years old and I bought him a blue sapphire ring. My birthday was a week later.

Meanwhile, getting two families to co-exist wasn't easy. Lots of drama. Over the next year our gang would spend weekends together. There was Barb, 17; Michael, 14; Peppy, 13; Marcy, 9; and Melanie, 8. I liked that I could go back to my house during the week, but I wasn't sure if I was ready for this big commitment. (Later on, when Barb moved out, Merv's niece Lisa, 16, moved in.)

I was glad that I had my own home to go back to. More tests for my health were needed.

My mom had a mini stroke, fell off the counter and broke her femur. She stayed with me for a while. Looking after her took away some of the fear I had about the stalkers.

On October 3, I went out my back door to find another garden hose cut into pieces. The police talked with the peeper again. When they came back to my place, they told me I should move. I was insulted. "Nobody is moving me off my land," I said in a cowgirl voice. The police gave me a funny look; he didn't like my joke. I rolled my eyes and curled my lip.

Merv and I decided to get the boys involved in hockey and the girls in ringette. This was our way of getting them to work together.

Chapter 84

Accident 1986

The phone calls were still happening. I kept telling myself we were going to catch him; we just had to be patient. Merv and I were doing our best with the kids and took them all to Wonderland in Vaughan, Ontario. The oldest daughter wanted to bring her boyfriend too, so we had to take two cars. We did a lot with the kids over the summer, and now they were all back to school.

In September, my boss asked if I would do him a favour and work in the electrowinning department doing sampling. It was only two shifts, afternoon and days. I jumped at the chance to get out of the anode. Chris, a good man I worked with in the anode, was going to be off for a few weeks. The job was to get samples of sludge or muck, then put them into an autoclave, or little oven. The samples were to be taken to the laboratory in plastic bottles. The lab was above the first aid room off the tank house. I was in a different building. The lab people took a half hour or so to check the samples, then I brought them back to the electrowinning. Eight bottles fit in a wooden carpenter's tool box. This was going to be fun.

One night it took much longer than a half hour for the lab people to do their work. When I got out of the building it was pouring rain and the night was black—no moon, and no lighting. Thoughts of the peeper or the general foreman filled my head and I got scared and began to run. I picked up speed, trying hard not to dump the bottles out of my carrier. It was so dark I didn't notice that there had been a run-out of iron cake: very greasy, slippery, reddish-yellow mud. Someone had taken a hose, put it out the door, and emptied the iron cake into the walkway. I slid through the greasy substance, and at the speed I was going I became airborne. My mind was on the bottles as I tried to hold them up so they wouldn't fall out. Down I came, landing hard on something large and metal. The first part of me to hit was my lower back on the left side, and then my right shoulder blade. Pain seared through my body and I passed out. It must have been for a while, because when I came to I was soaked from the rain. I was sitting on what looked like a big rim from a truck. I couldn't take a deep breath and it was hard to breathe. I rolled off the rim and struggled to get up. No one was around. I had to go back to the first aid room by myself. Dripping and crying, I entered the first aid room and the attendant rushed to help me. He examined me and was concerned about my breathing, so he called an ambulance. It was like I was in a dream state.

A nurse asked me questions at the hospital, but I didn't know what she was saying. I was more worried about the mess the iron cake was making as it dried and fell to the floor in a powdered form. All I remember was that the doctor took X-rays and said it looked like my upper spine was pushed in a bit. Reddish-yellow powdered footprints covered the area I had walked, and a cleaning person was busy mopping it up as I kept apologizing for my mess.

Off on WSIB (the Workplace Safety & Insurance Board of Ontario). The foreman was mad that I was a lost-time accident on his shift. He wasn't mad at the idiots who let the hose of iron cake fill up the walkway, though. The physiotherapist asked what kind of jobs I had done over the years and I told him about the hoist. He said that I had a lot of weakening and scar tissue in my shoulder from repetitive use on the hoist. The fall had pushed my spine in and now I had no "S" left in the upper part of my spine. It may never go back to the way it was. I had months of physio.

Meanwhile, I put my house up for sale. My brother wanted to buy it. Now all I had to do was figure out when I wanted to move. Merv and I had an objective to stop smoking when we moved in together. His son was a cancer survivor and one of his daughters had asthma, so it was a good idea.

Chapter 85

More Men are Killed at Inco 1986

The First Aid team.

I went back to work on light duty, the first aid team. This gave me time to heal. I was now the first captain and I loved it. I could still go to physio and doctor's appointments, and not worry about having to be shorthanded in the anode. Our team did great; we lost again but only by a few points.

Meanwhile, back home, Merv's oldest daughter moved out and his niece was looking for a place to move in. With a little persuasion on my part, I convinced Merv to let her live with us.

We wanted to keep the kids involved with different things to keep a close eye on them, so the two youngest girls and I joined St. John Ambulance.

Merv's job was supervisor for all the first aid departments throughout all plants and mines; it was a common occurrence to find out about the workers killed on the job. One day a man was killed at the Crean Hill mine, a forty-three-year-old with a wife and children. So many people died at Inco and Falconbridge. Dave Patterson always said there should be some kind of memorial for the people who gave their lives to the mining industries.

Meanwhile, the peeper's phone calls were still coming in and Merv bought me a telephone that taped phone calls. I felt we were going to catch him.

On April 14, 1987, four miners were killed at Levack Mine. A run of muck slid down the shaft they were working in. The aluminum top was not strong enough to hold the muck back. This mine had just won an award for being one of the safest mines around.

Merv was on the scene and had to identify the men. One of them was his fishing buddy. It was a hard job, but he was good at talking to the wives and consoling them. All I could do was write another poem.

Disaster at Levack Mine
April 14, 1987

There's been an accident in the mine,
The dreaded phone call read,
From what we know there's four of them;
We think that they are dead

Down the shaft a waterfall
Of rock that we call muck
Killed our brothers instantly
When tons of this stuff struck.

Rene J. Bedard
And Wilbrod (Curly) J. Gauvin
Germain (Butch) St. Amour
And Donald Knight
Were the men working there
At number-two shaft sight.
From 900 feet above them
Muck came down the shaft,

The aluminum barrier wasn't enough
Death was the aftermath.

Their buddies worked for hours
To get their bodies out,
Thoughts of them still alive
But there was little doubt.

The doctor at the scene
Pronounced that they were dead,
Now the families had to be told
Something that was dread.

Wives with no husbands,
Children with no dads,
Friends with no buddies;
This is oh so sad.

Remember these men in your prayers,
Remember them during the day,
Remember all who have died
In a similar way.

For an accident that shouldn't have happened
In the safest mine around,
That 5 star the mine was awarded
Should be buried underground.

– Cat Mulroy, thirty-two years old

Chapter 86

Modified Work Centre 1987

The company offered me a job at their rehabilitation centre making signs. They built me a drafting table that sat in the middle of a small room. Two other sign-makers had larger drafting desks that were against the window. The room was like a horse stall. Its door could open on the top or on the bottom, just like a horse-stable door.

I was getting the hang of making signs. And as we had stopped smoking, it kept my hands busy. The other man I worked with told me I had to slow down, that I was working my way out of a job. I wasn't sure why they wanted me to slow down. What do I do if I am not making signs?

The rules were very strict: a worker couldn't leave the room unless they had to go to the washroom, and lunch was right at 12:00. We had two fifteen-minute breaks. The foreman would come to work drunk and men covered for him; he was not very nice to me. I tried to stay quiet so I wouldn't get into any trouble. I didn't care that he was drunk. The days flew by; I didn't fit in. One day, one of the men had a heart attack and was taken to the hospital. I was asked to take his euchre spot at lunchtime. This was the opening, I thought: I could win some of the men over by playing cards. One of the men on the other team, the one who covered for the foreman, was a sly little man. I didn't trust him and for good reason. He was cheating at cards. He wanted his partner to play clubs, so he hit the table extra hard to relay the message. Well, no one in the anode would ever stand for someone cheating at cards and I was still an anode person. So, without thinking I confronted the man about his cheating. His face grew red with anger and he jumped up, swearing at me in French. I stood up and swore back at him in English. It wasn't long before I was transferred out of the rehab.

Chapter 87

Meanwhile ...

Well, we caught the peeper. It was the man next door. Yes, it was him making all those phone calls. The police told him not to do it again—that was it. This was all the protection a woman would get in the '80s. As for the staples in the driveway, there were no more after that general foreman was sent to Indonesia. So, was it the peeper who had just been caught who was leaving the staples, or was it the general foreman?

However, the peeper was still being creepy. He would stand at the corner of my house and stare in. The police said they couldn't help me because he was in his own yard. This didn't make any sense to me. How come this was not illegal? There were no charges laid against either of these predators. That's just how things were back then.

My ex was getting married; I felt sorry for his fiancée.

Merv's ex left the redhead for greener pastures.

In September, Merv reached twenty-five years of service at Inco. I went with him as his date to a huge party that was put on by Inco for employees with twenty-five years.

In June another man was killed at Inco.

In October another man was killed at Inco.

Chapter 88

More Men are Killed at Inco 1988

The dreaded phone call once more. Two men were killed in the transportation department. 37° below zero—so cold the smoke from the chimneys went straight up as frosted fog blanketed the area. I gathered Merv's long johns and sat them on the chair, telling him to dress warmly as he would be outside most of the day.

It was a common occurrence for Inco and Canadian Pacific to use the same railroad line. There was bad communication because the engineers from CP didn't know Inco was using that line. The engineers from CP parked their train and went for something to eat in a small greasy-spoon restaurant across from the railroad tracks. Our employees didn't know CP was parked on the line when they came around the bend at a good clip, and they slammed into the parked train. The impact was so great that the train cars now resembled flat cars.

Their bodies were mangled throughout the heavy steel. Merv knew these men, they were friends from Levack. He told the rescuers to try to keep the bodies as intact as possible. They were to use a cutting torch to cut around the heavy metal to free the crushed body parts, keeping them attached to the rest of the body.

The police held spectators back. One woman said she wanted to get in to talk with Merv. Her husband was one of the men in the accident. He held her and told her she didn't want to see it. She insisted. He let her.

It was a hard day for Merv. When he got home, he told me about the accident, then said we wouldn't talk about it again.

Meanwhile, back home we were trying our best to amalgamate our family and decided family counselling would be a good idea. What I got out of it was that my kids felt out of the picture, that they found it hard to share their mother with these other kids. This wasn't going to be easy.

Chapter 89

My Mom Passes 1988

Cathy and her Mom. *Rita Kennedy Mulroy*

    In March, Laurene Wiens won her twelve-year battle that would give Canadian women the right to access and choose whether or not to risk exposure to workplace environment hazards. Laurene began her struggle in 1976 when Inco refused to promote her, ruling that one section of the nickel refinery would be off limits to female employees of childbearing age. In a decision handed down by the Ontario Human Rights Commission, the company was found guilty of sexual discrimination and Wiens, at thirty-four years old, would be awarded the next available job at the nickel refinery. This was a groundbreaking decision, as the company previously had no problem putting her in other dirty parts of the plants, and it was a double standard.

    I was sent to the engineering building as a cleaning person. This was not how I wanted my career to be going. I gritted my teeth and promised to give it all I had. I was sitting in a large janitorial room with other modified workers from different plants and some from underground. Most were smokers. The room was always filled with stinky cigarette smoke. Many were taking painkillers, so discussions were pretty foggy. The room was also filled with cleaning chemicals, and there was a floor drain to empty the pails. I didn't want to breathe any of this in, so I wanted to be by myself. I thought it better to continue to clean because I didn't want to breathe in the smoke. It was a far cry from the copper refinery. I missed some of my friends. Some of the cleaners told me that I thought I was too good for them because I wouldn't stay with them in the storeroom. I told them they shouldn't imagine that they knew what I was thinking. That didn't go over well.

I went back to night school, taking Introduction to Psychology; I thought that if I could understand how and why people acted the way they did, it would help me. I recorded all the information onto a cassette tape and studied while I buffed the floor. It was funny, when I entered the classroom I discovered that my dad was taking the same course.

What I learned from working in that office setting was that men acted the same in suits and ties as they did in coveralls. One day a man brought in visitors to the engineer building where I was buffing the floor. He called out "hi sweetie" as they passed.

"My name is Cathy, and I would appreciate it if you called me by my name and not sweetie." The look on his face told me he was insulted. Oh, well.

Another time I entered an office to empty the garbage basket from under a boss's desk. He had a visitor in his room, and I asked permission to retrieve the basket. When I walked around the desk, he said, "This is the woman who makes love to my garbage." Without thinking, I pushed the back of his office chair, ramming its arms into the desk. I smiled and said, "Sorry, I slipped." I tried to fit in, but I was so unhappy. I missed the refinery.

Most office workers worked in little cubicles, surrounded by grey material dividers. When picking up the garbage, I noticed that one man had pictures of naked women dotting his walls. Memories of the anode came flooding back, along with the changes that were made. I asked the man if these were legal here at engineering and he said if he wanted to put these kinds of pictures up, he had the right to. I was to mind my own business. I told him that it was my business.

Summer holidays came and I was glad to get out of that strange building. Merv and I took the girls, now fourteen, to Nova Scotia. On our way back, we stopped in Montréal at Merv's relatives. This is where I found out my mother had passed away with a massive heart attack. I told Merv I would drive. I needed to take my mind off what had just happened.

Sad didn't begin to express how I felt and more anger grew inside, especially when I got back on that stupid job.

I wished I was back in the anode, among the men who knew me, and some friends. I grabbed my pail and mop, taking my frustration out on the hall. A few hours later, that hallway was so polished it shone. I felt proud. When I stood back to admire it, the man who had called me sweetie did it again, adding laughter as if to mock me. I leaned over and whispered in his ear, "Fuck you, you piece of shit." I am sure no other woman in this building would dare talk to him like this.

All I wanted was to do my work and be left alone. Sad and overwhelmed at my mom's death at the age of sixty-four, my anger brewed.

A few days later, the man with the naked women's pictures on his cubicle was surrounded by people looking over his daughter's portfolio. He was bragging about how beautiful she was. Sickened by his arrogance, I leaned in to get a better look.

"Where are the other ones?" I asked mockingly.

"What other ones?" he asked, surprised at my question.

"The ones of her with bare breasts and legs spread, like the ones you have up in your office." I smacked my gum.

"This is my fourteen-year-old daughter!" he yelled. The crowd stared at me.

"Yes, well, those naked pictures on your wall are someone's daughters too." I walked away. I could hear the office workers muttering to one another. I didn't care anymore. All the anger I felt inside of me from all the shit I had lived with was now in control of my actions. I didn't even know who I was anymore.

Sexual harassment training was now law, and everyone at Inco was going to be trained on what that meant. I was curious about how this would play out in an environment where men had the upper hand in all the jobs. My training was on Wednesday. I sat at the middle part of the table facing the door. Power seat. Men slowly piled in, complaining that there was no such thing as sexual harassment.

The foreman who always came to work drunk sat on one side of me and a Scottish man sat on the other. A shy woman stood in front, waiting for the men to take their seats. The Scottish man leaned over me to talk with the man who was always drunk. He said that this was a waste of time, and that he would love it if someone would sexually harass him. I turned my face inches from his, and with a flirtatious smile I said, "I'll keep that in mind," and gave him a wink. He smiled back, his ego lifted. The woman did a good job, then asked if there were any questions. I raised my hand. "These questions are for this man beside me," I said, pointing to the Scottish man. "Is it true what they say about Scottish men?" I gave him my best bedroom eyes. "Is it true you don't wear any underwear under the kilt?" The man's chest puffed out like a peacock flaunting his feathers.

"Yes, that's right," he smiled.

"But do you know why?" I was still smiling sweetly.

The question caught him off guard. "No, are you going to tell me?" Now he was flirting back.

Everyone in the room was listening. "It's because you have fuck all to put in it." I was still smiling.

He wasn't. His face grew red and he was ready to say something when I cut him off.

"There you go, you have just been sexually harassed. How do you feel?" I got up from the table, thanked the woman, told her she did a good job, and went back to my floor polisher.

It wasn't long before I got called into the office. A short round man stood up when I walked in, and he pointed to a chair.

"Cathy, you have burnt a lot of bridges in your time," he began.

The memories of the last eighteen years played like an old movie on fast forward. My marriage, the gun, the rape, the fights with bosses, the right to refuse, bosses swearing at me, me swearing at bosses, name-calling, graffiti, staples in my driveway, my dead cat, my mom's death, and the accident that brought me here. I didn't hear much more of what else he said. It didn't matter, he had his mind made up about me before I even walked in his room. He was okay with what he had heard. My reputation was my reputation and it was growing.

"You're right, I have burned a lot of bridges." I stood up and leaned over his desk. "And I would burn them all again if I had to. If you don't want me here, that's fine with me. I don't like it here anyway. There is no way to improve myself by being here. I don't want to clean floors and pick up after anyone." It wasn't long before I was asked to go into light maintenance at the general office in Copper Cliff. Now this was more my style, something I would like to do.

Chapter 90

The Flood

Back home, Merv and I were awakened by my son yelling for us to come to the rec room. There was a foot of water on the floor. The first thing we did was check how close the water was to the wall plugs. We put on rubber boots. Merv grabbed towels and began jamming them into the floor drain pipe, where the water was pouring in from. The towels expanded and the gushing water stopped. We carried the computer and the TV upstairs.

I watched through the living room window as Merv and our neighbors stood by the road, now a fast-moving river. Everyone looked scared.

We were lucky, we had bought back-up water insurance the year before for $12. Others were not so lucky. The next day, after the water had receded, everyone's personal belongings were piled outside. Couches, chairs, clothing—everything that got wet. There were drawings by our children from they were little. Everyone's keepsakes were destroyed. Nothing was salvageable because it was a backed-up sewer. Merv's trick of stuffing the towel stopped the water from rising in our basement. Some people down the road got five feet of water. The city was on strike and one of the pumps was down; no one was qualified to fix the problem. It had been raining really hard for days and all of the creeks had overflowed their banks. The city tried to say it was an act of God and that they would not be paying for the people who did not have sewer back-up insurance. It was a long fight for them, but in the end they won and the city did pay for their damages. It would take months for us to get the renovation in the basement done. More stress.

Chapter 91

Light Maintenance: Some Men are Just Mean 1989

The general office was a large brick building in Copper Cliff, the same building we had burned the effigy in front of. The president of Inco and all upper management worked there, along with purchasing, their own mailroom, and so much more. At first all I did was change the burnt-out fluorescent tubes in the offices.

During this time, I met a beautiful and tall red-headed woman named Wilma. Everyone called her Big Red. She asked if I would put a shelving unit together for her. I had never done anything like that, but I said I would give it a try. It took all day but there it was: my first wall unit. I felt very proud. She invited me for coffee in her office and I found out she was the first and only woman instructor. She taught communication, writing skills, and a whole lot more. Everyone loved this lady and we became friends.

I was partnered up with another modified worker, Big Al. We climbed into a truck and headed to the tailings area. The tailing was up on the hill in Copper Cliff where Inco dumped waste from their processing. It was becoming a great concern to all Sudburians. When exposed to air and water, tailings oxidize and produce sulphuric acid which liberates the great amounts of heavy metals already present. There were also high levels of contamination from heavy metals and other toxic substances related to mining exploitation. Nothing lived up there. We were to dump paint from five-gallon pails. I said I wouldn't do it. Big Al told me to stand back and that he would do the dumping. I scanned the area. I could see at least twenty miles if not more of brown-red sludge, black gooey rivers, and ponds with grey, crusty surfaces. Downhearted, I wondered if it was safe to breathe. I kicked the red mud and watched it flake—no bugs. I kicked it some more. It was like a horror movie and I was in a trance.

"What the fuck are you doing?" Big Al yelled.

"Looking for bugs," I said, kicking some more.

"What do you want with bugs?" he said, his hands up in the air.

"Just wanted to see if anything can survive up here," I said.

"Nothing will live up in this toxic waste. I did hear of a beaver that was found up here. He was bald, like one of those hairless cats. The company is working on a re-greening project. They have planted 80,000 trees."

We climbed back into his truck. Tears rolled down my face. The devastation was hard to comprehend. I didn't say too much on the way back to the general office.

Big Al and I got along great. We worked together through the summer while the boss was on holidays. I was in charge of the office cleaning staff. They would come to me if they needed anything. These jobs were contracted out to a group of Italian women who lived in Copper Cliff's Italian district.

Two elderly women came to see me one day because they were told that the rugs had to be shampooed during the summer, and there were a lot of rugs. They asked if they could rent a better machine because the ones they were using didn't work well and they were hard on the wrists and hands. She showed me her gnarled fingers and the scars on her wrist from a carpel tunnel operation. They gave me a demonstration of the machine and it was horrible. It jumped and turned on its own and was very heavy.

I told them I would look into it. I went through the files and found their contract. After reading it over, I found out the company could contract out other cleaners who could bring in their own equipment and do the rugs at a really good price. The women were happy; all I had to do was get permission to do it. *Who do I go to?* Well, I should go to the top, so I went to the top floor to ask the vice president. I told him my dilemma. He said it was a good idea and that I should go for it. Everyone was happy.

Well, not everyone. My boss didn't feel that way. He told me I had no right going to the vice president, and I had no right reading the cleaner's contract. He said that I was on probation, and if I stepped out of line again I would be gone. I was devastated and depressed because I thought I had done a good job. I asked if we could sit down and discuss it with his boss so we could clear it up. Didn't happen.

Day after day, people would come into this building asking where so-and-so was. This was Inco's main office; you would think there would be numbers on the doors. How were people supposed to find someone if there was no numbering? I put in a suggestion to have all the doors in the building numbered. The rehab centre was to make them and I would put them up. I was awarded two hundred dollars.

One day I read on the board there was a course being offered on communication. It was mainly for people who wanted to be supervisors, but it was open to everyone.

I didn't want to be a supervisor but I wanted to take the course, so I applied. Big Red was the instructor for this course, and she was fantastic. The men in the room had so much respect for her. Her smile and her humour won them over. I also had a lot of respect for her. My boss, on the other hand, got his nose out of joint and told me that this maintenance job was no longer available. He must have thought I was after his job, but all I wanted was to take the course. Back to the cleaning crew.

Training was becoming a big deal at Inco. I was asked to put together a training course for cleaners. With the help of a cleaning company that supplied Inco, we worked hard to put a course together. It had everything from polishing floors to how to get gum out of a rug. I delivered the course once. Then I was told to bring everything to the boss's office. He told me that a man was going to deliver the course from now on.

Devastated and depressed, I put away the beautiful briefcase Merv had bought me for Christmas. Now I was going to drive a school bus to bring workers to different parts of the plant. It was hard on my shoulder opening and closing the doors, but I liked driving the bus. My son had an appointment in Toronto so I asked the boss if I could work Saturday and take Wednesday off to take him there. A few of the other bus drivers complained I was getting special treatment. One of my so-called union brothers threatened to put in a grievance so he would get the overtime. I would work, and because I had less seniority he could get paid too. To me, this was a misuse of what the union rights were all about. I never heard if the grievance was put in or not. There was backlash. I believed he riled up the other bus drivers, triggering what happened next.

We brought my son to the Toronto Hospital. I told them that ever since my son was five, he had been making strange noises and facial tics. My doctor in Sudbury told me I was just a nervous and worried mother and that there was nothing wrong with my kid. After a few hours he was diagnosed with Tourette Syndrome.

My anger was once again out of control. I stormed into the Sudbury doctor's office and threw the pamphlets on his desk. All this did was get him mad and I was told I would have to get another doctor.

Saturday's shift didn't go as well as I thought it would go. I did my circle check of the bus, lifted the hood, and checked the rad cap and the air in the tires. It was a ghost town at the smelter, as there were not too many workers on the weekends. It was on the second run up to the divisional shops when I heard clicking noises, and smoke bellowed from the hood. I pulled over and noticed that all the water in the rad had drained out from the bottom. Someone had loosened the nut. I tightened it with my fingers, drove the bus back to the parking area and retrieved another bus. Someone had done this on purpose.

The men at div shops were angry with me because it took so long for me to pick them up. I could only apologize.

I reported the incident to my boss. A meeting was set up with the general foreman of the cleaners and bus drivers. He cringed and made a face every time he saw me. That's okay, I am sure I made a face when I saw him too. Nothing was done about this sabotage to the bus, there was not even an investigation. He was so arrogant when he told me I was nothing but a troublemaker. I don't like to be called names.

"I am not a troublemaker. When I go to places and there is trouble it's because trouble is already there. I bring the trouble to your attention. Other people's actions, like what was done to the bus, are not my fault!" I was yelling.

He was not impressed with me.

Chapter 92

Proposal, and We Lose One of Our Sues 1990/1991

Suzanne Dignard

Down on one knee, Merv asked me to marry him, handing me my mother's ring. He had gotten it repaired because the diamond had been lost for years. How romantic was that? I said yes, but didn't want to get married right away. I was nervous about getting married again. We decided we would get married after all the kids had moved out. Then it would feel like we were always on a honeymoon.

The Women of Steel (Inco LU 6500 Women Steelworkers) brought a number of women together for a Christmas party. I had never met most of these women. The company separated the women, placing us in different parts of the Inco operation. I wondered what kind of life they had at Inco; I wondered if they were as hard as the one I was having. We planned to get together during the year to keep in touch.

On New Year's Eve, I picked up Laurene to celebrate. She worked at the nickel refinery. We watched as the blue moon shone in the sky and grey clouds passed in front of it. We began to sing "Blue Moon" and laughed. We were becoming good friends.

The next morning, we were hit with terrible news. One of the women who was at our Christmas party had committed suicide on New Year's Eve. I had just met her; her name was Sue. She looked so happy at the party, so beautiful. What had happened to her to drive her to such an unhappy ending? It was so sad for her children and family. I cried.

Many of the Women of Steel showed up at the funeral home. We sat with her mother for a few hours and listened to her story. She told us how hard Sue's life was. (This is not my story to tell.) I did understand how Sue got to that point. We were asked to be pallbearers. I was proud to do it, but my shoulder was still sore. There would be eight of us. Another woman who also had an injury would be across from me. The other Sue from the anode said not to worry, that the other women would take up the slack. Besides, the Sue who had passed was very tiny, so she didn't weigh much.

I cried that night, knowing that someone died because they were so sad, because of a man, because of her life at Inco, etc. I wondered if this might not have happened if the Women of Steel had met earlier and shared our stories with each other. I knew how sad and lonely it was to work in an environment of men. I felt it was a good idea for me to get involved with other women, so I began to attend meetings of the Women of Steel.

Chapter 93

International Women's Day 1991

The Women of Steel decided we would put on a big bash for International Women's Day, wanting Inco to hire more female miners. Betty and Susan (another Sue) were in charge of putting it together.

Betty, our spokesperson and head of the committee, said that with employment equity coming soon, Inco had better get prepared to hire more women. We were going to help the new women break into the industry, get involved with the union and know what their rights were.

The women's committee put on a celebration for International Women's Day. The guest speaker was Jennifer Keck, a professor in the schools of social work at Laurentian University, a gifted teacher who had mentored hundreds of social workers in the practice of community-based social work. She was a writer, academic, and activist organizer for anti-poverty initiatives and breast cancer survivors and a researcher in women's issues, labour, and health care.

She and I hit it off and became great friends. She was interested in the stories of the women who worked at Inco. The money raised that day was donated to the women's centre and the sexual crisis centre. Some of the money went to the LU 6500 Christmas party.

This group started meeting on a regular basis. Cameras were discussed so we could have video surveillance system for the Elgin Street underpass, which was located in a seedy part of town. Bushes were cut down at the far end of the underpass, bright lights were installed, and the underpass was painted. Donation boxes were set up throughout the city to help pay for the four cameras and the cost of maintaining them.

We organized the Take Back the Night march. Over four hundred people joined in. Getting to know women opened up a new life for me. Both of our now-sixteen-year-old girls participated.

Meanwhile, our girls had jobs. Peppy was moving to Ottawa to go to school. Mike was at collage taking a chef's course. Barb got married and Lisa was in nursing. We were doing okay as parents.

Chapter 94

Turmoil for the Women in the Offices 1991

Bad news: fifty-eight women office workers at Inco were told to become miners or face being laid off. What was this? Hourly-rate women had been fighting for years to go underground. That's where the money was. The company up until 1990 had said it was unsafe for women to work underground. They claimed it was—are you ready for this—*unlucky* to have women underground. Most of these women were scared, and I don't blame them. Working underground was scary and hard work. They had three weeks to decide. Inco said they had too many white-collar workers and had to cut back to keep costs down. The Inco spokesperson said, "Most women will be able to do this work." It was 1990 that they finally allowed women underground. Now Inco wanted to get rid of some women in the office, and this was how they were going to treat them. Some were over fifty years old and wore dresses, high heels, and makeup every day.

Sue Vallier, my good friend from the copper refinery, told the women not to panic, to try it out because they might like it. The difference in pay would be fifty thousand a year, up from the thirty-five thousand they were making, not counting the bonus mining. It was sad to see these women being forced into this kind of work. It wasn't what they had signed up for.

The staff had only unionized the year before. Many of us thought that was why Inco did this, to pay them back. Some women were worried about the men's bad language and crude jokes. I told them that some of the office men were no different.

Some women said their rights had been violated. The company said it wasn't because they unionized, it was because eighty-five office workers had to be reduced. Some women with less seniority were staying in the office, while some with twenty-seven years were going underground. In my mind the company was out for revenge.

One day when I was at Lola's, I met a woman who was to go underground. She was crying. I didn't mean to be insensitive, but I told her she should stop crying and go underground, and later bid out. Her anger for her predicament came my way as if it was my fault. She yelled that I might want to work on a job like this, but she didn't. I raised my hands in the air as if to say *I'm out of here* and left. This was not my fight.

Meanwhile, Leslie Mahaffy and Kristen French had been murdered. I was back on the cleaning crew, cleaning trailers. Everyone who used the trailers were staff people. Newspapers were always lying around the lunchroom. I began to read them and cut out all the stories about the two slain women. My boss told me there was a complaint. One man said he didn't think a cleaning lady should be reading in their lunchroom. Jesus Louise, who did they think they were? They were working in a trailer. It's not like I was in there when they were having their lunch. The newspapers were already a day old, so I wasn't taking anyone's paper. What is with some men and their attitude toward women? He wanted me to stay in the storeroom with the mops and cleaners. Not going to happen.

Chapter 95

First Aid Instructor 1991

The general foreman of Cleaning Services didn't try to cover up how much he despised me. I applied for a few jobs, but he was adamant I wouldn't get them.

He called a meeting and told me it was to discuss training for the cleaners and bus drivers. It wasn't about that, however, it was so he could tell me what a horrible person he thought I was. All he did was bash me. His goal was to get me fired. *A lot of tough men have tried*, I thought to myself. *You want a fight, let's go.* I had no idea why I rubbed this man the wrong way. I told him we would discuss his feelings about me in front of a steward.

He began by saying that there were some people who were not happy with me or my performance, which he felt had not been satisfactory. He would not give any names, nor did he have any details of my unsatisfactory work. Bruce sat beside me like always. He got really angry when the general foreman said he was concerned that he saw a worrisome pattern developing wherever I was involved. He went on to say that I disturbed the workplace harmony. I thought I should break out in song.

He went on to say that I displayed conduct unbecoming an Inco employee. Again, no details, just more insults. Bruce asked to meet with upper management, because he said this was nothing but a witch hunt. I knew he meant that as a compliment. On the way out the door I stopped, wanting as usual to get the last word in. "By the way, that letter you sent out on the cleaners and custodians—it should read 'cleaners and bus drivers.' Cleaners and custodians are the same group." I smiled and curled my lip.

Bruce was not allowed to attend the next meeting. Instead, it was Kevin from the union hall. Nervous, my gut churned and growled. I wished I was able to throw up, but the last operation had made this impossible. Never again will I be able to throw up. Then there was the two large fibroids and one cyst that now sat in my uterus that the last X-ray had found. My nerves were shot.

The meeting was in a small room with an oval table and eight chairs. Everyone was seated when I arrived, leaving one chair at the head of the table facing the door. I liked that. The general foreman of cleaners sat to my right. I had never met these bosses before. I knew Merv knew them because many of them were his bosses. I spoke on my own behalf, going through all the things I had written down.

The general foreman squirmed in his chair. I could tell he was agitated with me. Maybe he thought I was sounding too good. Then he opened up his stupid mouth.

"You know what your problem is?" he interrupted.

"No, I don't, but I'm sure you're going to tell me." My lip curled as I made eye contact.

"You can't face reality. You have to accept the facts," he said, shaking his finger in my face.

I hate it when someone shakes their finger at me. I rolled my eyes, made a smacking noise, tilted my head just enough to show him how cute I was. I knew this would set him off.

His nostrils flared. "The sooner you realize you're the problem, the better. Not only are you a woman, but you are an injured worker—you are no longer part of the team. You are part of the woodwork."

"Yes, I am a woman, not much I can do about that, but I am not part of the woodwork, I am part of the team. You just keep me on the bench and won't let me play."

I was shocked but happy—he had put both his feet in his mouth at the same time in front of upper management.

"This!" I said, pointing my finger at the general foreman and looking at the man in charge of the meeting, MacLean. He had the biggest, most beautiful blue eyes I had ever seen; they were hypnotic. I had to shake my head a little to stay on track. "This is the stupid attitude I have to put up with." I was still staring at those blue eyes.

The general foreman began to stutter, trying to backpedal. "You … you … you just piss people off," he said, puffing his chest.

"What is it that I do that pisses you off?" I asked.

He stammered again. He shuffled his papers.

The blue-eyed boss had a slight grin. "Go ahead and answer that, I would like to hear your answer. What does she do that pisses you off?" The general foreman didn't have an answer for Mr. Blue Eyes.

"All I want is for people to treat me with respect, and I will do the same back," I said.

The blue-eyed boss looked at me. "How would you like to be a first aid instructor?" It was as if someone had just told me I had won a million dollars.

"I'd love to," I said, my face beaming.

"You will have to do some training," he said.

"Yes, yes." I nodded like a bobblehead dog. "When can I start?" I was shaking with excitement.

"When do you want to start?"

"I am ready right now," I said with excitement in my voice.

He looked at his watch. "It's 11:00 now; how about after lunch?"

"Thank you," I said. "I will do my best."

For the first two months on this job I couldn't have been happier. I was working with two other instructors. One was from my neighbourhood when I was a child, who had even babysat me. Like all good things, it was short-lived when he retired in November and the company brought back another instructor who used to work there. Before he left, he wrote a great letter saying how good I was at this job.

On the way out of work, I picked up a copy of the *Inco Triangle*, a magazine that Inco published monthly. Thumbing through the magazine, I came across a picture of the United Steelworker's Christmas party. Why would the *Inco Triangle* publish a photo from my union party? Union and company business should be separated. I curled my lip.

Chapter 96

They Called Me ... Troublemaker

There was a new label for me: *Troublemaker.* No one had the balls to explain what that meant. Word spread that I was now a first aid instructor and I was a topic of interest. The gossip must be true, they had heard it in the dry. I smiled, thinking of a bunch of naked men talking about me.

When I taught some of the men, they had a preconceived belief about me. Some accepted me, some didn't. My reputation grew like any gossip does, the next gossiper adding on whatever they wanted. I worked hard and studied all the time. I added subjects to the training, like diabetes and prostate cancer. This did not sit well with the other instructors.

I thought I would like to get on the human rights committee with the union. The office of the head of the committee was downstairs of North Mine where I was working. A black man sat behind the desk talking on the phone when I walked in, and I couldn't take my eyes off of his baseball cap. It had the emblem of the Playboy Bunny on it. Maybe I was in the wrong office. When he got off the phone, I asked him how the head of the human rights committee could wear that emblem, as it was derogatory to women. His reaction was very angry. I tried to explain to him that it wasn't okay for him to wear this. He didn't get the message; instead, he stood up. He was very big—not fat, big. He began to yell at me that I had no business telling him what he could wear. I asked him if he would be upset if I wore a KKK outfit on Halloween. He called me a bigot and told me I was putting down black people. Never mind, this was not the committee I wanted to be on.

I was not in a great mood when my class started. I dragged the skeleton—a real one—over to the middle of the U-shaped tables and began to talk about the skeletal system. One man who kept talking out in class said that a woman had one more rib than a man. I told him that was not true. His voice got louder, and he told me that it was in his Bible so it was true, and I shouldn't say it wasn't. I walked over to him and said that if men had one less rib they would be walking on a tilt, and for his information, there were *no* talking snakes. He didn't say much the rest of the day.

Meanwhile, back at home, we worked on the amalgamation of the two families. We decided to go for counselling again. Two of the girls were home sick with mono, one was able to go back to school in a few days, the other was sick in bed, so I took some of my holidays to look after her. Her mother wouldn't take her; she didn't want to catch it.

On New Year's Eve my dad fell off the roof of his garage trying to remove snow. He suffered mostly bruising. I went to the hospital and spent it with him bringing in the new year.

Chapter 97

Fighting the Harassment and More 1992

Tension was high in the first aid training office. One of the instructors had a doctor's appointment. He would not be docked because he was staff. While he was gone, I asked the other instructor if I could sit in on the advanced teaching for the plant protection officers and first aid employees. Inco covered all the first aid rooms in all plants and mines. He said no, the company only needed him and the other instructor, not me. When PPO's came for their instructing, I would be scheduled to work underground with the other instructor. This way I could not get my advanced training instructor's papers so I wouldn't be able to teach it.

They told me I was not part of their team, that I didn't hold the job, and that I was only there because I was an injured worker. As the weeks went on, I was still not allowed to sit in the course so I could get my advanced training. The boss didn't believe that these two fine men would do such a thing. One day when they were out, I found the schedule hidden under the desk mat and copied it. Evidence.

Things were changing at Inco. Staff had unionized the previous year. This was very surprising—after 100 years they needed help to save their jobs. My problems were put on the back burner. Jobs were going to be lost and there were talks of layoffs for staff. In my opinion, staff had it good with all the little quirks. They were always going to some kind of training. They would get full salary if they were off sick. They could go to the doctor and not get docked.

Inco staff always had new buzzwords. Their new training buzzwords were: "Getting to yes," "how to negotiate without giving in," or "let's talk turkey." The newest was "paradigm shift." Important changes were about to happen at Inco. They were going to do something new, something different than they had in the past. Many meetings were held about where the training was going, but the two instructors never told me about these meetings or invited me to go. I went to the boss. We sat together using a flip chart to do the "problem-solving technique" (more buzzwords). Nothing good came out of the meeting. We sat around with a coffee and the three boys huddled on one side of the room, discussing the paradigm shift. The two instructors nodded at each word the boss said like those bobblehead dogs in the back window of a car. The boss asked me if I knew what a paradigm shift was. Their three faces stared at me.

"A pair o' dimes ... is that like twenty cents?" I bobbed my head, mirroring what they had done. The look on their faces were priceless, wide-eyed. I burst into laughter. "Got ya!" They didn't laugh. I thought it was very clever.

With all that was going on with staff people—the layoffs in the air, job force adjustments—the other instructors didn't let up. Sometimes they were just downright mean. They didn't want to lose their job to me. Like the time one of them brought in a large salad for the advanced class and told me there was not enough for me, and not to come into the classroom. They even made comments on my weight gain. Just hateful people.

One day, Creighton Mine had asked the first aid centre to set up a mock accident with casualties. I found out from someone at Creighton, not from my coworkers. The two instructors left together in the same vehicle. You would think that after I knew about it that I could get a ride. So, I hopped in my car and went by myself. My coworkers told me to wait in another room. Time went by, and I went looking for them. They were already set up and one of them said I could hold the casualty's feet while they did the bandages. We finished around 12:30. When we got out to the parking lot, one of the instructors told me it was okay to go home instead of going back to the centre. They were surprised to see me in the centre when they arrived back at 2:00. I knew they were trying to set me up. They would have turned me in for going home early.

All departments were being shuffled around. I was told we had a new boss who wanted to see me down in the general office. Maybe, just maybe, this new boss would listen to me. My heart sank when I walked into his office. It was the general foreman who had stalked me, the one who tried to give me the brass candlestick holders, the flowers, and maybe the one who put the staples in my driveway. Really, with all the people at Inco, he was now my boss? I told him to stay away from me or I would go to the police.

What was I going to do? All this stress was doing a number on my intestines. I called Bruce and put in a discrimination grievance against the two trainers. At this time in history, a discrimination grievance was almost unheard of. The company representative told me I would have to use another steward, not Bruce. I called the District 6 Steelworkers office in Toronto and was told I could use Bruce as a steward.

The company said they did not need three instructors anymore and I would have to be moved.

In order to prepare, I asked Big Red for a character-witness letter. She wrote one, and it was glowing. At the time I was taking a night course called "Teachers of Adults," a four-year certificate program. My teachers also wrote letters on my behalf. The company said that I was going to lose my instructor position because they felt they didn't need three instructors anymore, using the cutbacks as an excuse.

Bruce did his research and wrote a great letter to the superintendent of the safety department. He stated that based on past experience, present figures, and future requirements, there was a proven need for three instructors. He told them that during first aid training from '90 to '92, the number of employees attending our first aid courses had more than doubled, and the number of CPR trainings had tripled. He said that 2200 employees had been trained by Mulroy in the five months she had been there. He went on to say that this meeting was not about whether three instructors were required, that the original problem involved conflict between the instructors that needed management involvement to resolve, and that there was no talk of getting rid of one instructor until Mulroy voiced her concerns. He mentioned Ralpha, the company's new contractor (who brought more buzz theories), who preached problem-solving techniques. He said it was easier to remove me than use this. He argued that there were still the same numbers of employees remaining in the department under their jurisdiction, just in different jobs, and that there was no force reduction.

There was another meeting scheduled. The general foreman from the training department cut me off as I was heading into the meeting room. The room was long and narrow, with an oval table and a few chairs just able to fit into it. He was headed to one of the power seats, the same seat I wanted. I put my books on the table and slid them down as if I was playing shuffleboard. The books stopped in front of the seat I wanted. He looked up at me, surprised. "That's my chair," I said as I squeezed between him and the wall. "I read the same book," I whispered. Bruce squeezed by him to sit beside me. I pulled out all the information I had pertaining to problem-solving techniques. Who was I kidding, they had their minds made up. I was not needed as an instructor anymore, so no job there for me. Blindsided. They went on to say there were no jobs available for me at all, because there wasn't a women's washroom in some of the plants. I was being penalized for putting in the discrimination grievance.

I wrote letters to Sopko, the chairman and chief executive officer of Inco in Toronto. I got an answer back from his representative:

Dr Sopko asked me to reply on his behalf. It is our understanding that the relevant parties have commenced the process of reviewing the matters you raised in your letter. It is our expectation that this process will continue until appropriate disposition of these matters is reached.

I wrote to Ashcroft, the president of Sudbury operations. I wrote to Vice President Blanco, asking them to help solve this problem. Ashcroft invited me to his office where he and Blanco met me at the door. There were two seats facing a horrible patterned couch. It didn't match the ghastly patterned rug. I noticed the couch was much lower than the two chairs. Ashcroft pointed for me to sit on the couch.

"If it's okay with you, I'll take one of the chairs," I said, and proceeded to sit before he answered. They listened but did they hear.

I was called back to the general office; another general foreman wanted to talk to me. (Inco was top-heavy with general foremen.)

He asked me to sit and then told me I should not be writing letters to upper management, and that I should respect the pecking order.

"Respect the pecking order?" I was confused. "What's a pecking order?" I had never heard this term.

His eyes narrowed, suspicious that I might be pulling his leg.

"You don't know what that saying means?" he asked.

"No, never heard it," I replied, shaking my head.

"Well, in a farmyard of chickens, there are strong chickens and weaker chickens. The stronger chickens eat first, and the weaker ones eat later. It's the same here: you have to wait your turn to eat."

I was confused—why was he talking about chickens? "I'm a city girl, I don't know anything about chickens."

He looked at me as if I was being a smartass. "You can't go to the top." His voice was louder, his eyebrows slanted inwards. He was definitely irritated with me. "At first you go to your first-line supervisor, then the GF and so on up the pecking line."

I clued in. "I tried that, and those chickens aren't doing a thing, so I thought I might as well go right to the food source." I shrugged my shoulders. He asked me to leave.

Under the law, the company needed to find me a job. I believe they wanted to fire me.

We went to the oxygen plant: no women's washroom, no job.

We went to many plants and every story was the same. No washrooms for women, no jobs. Why was it that washrooms were even an issue? It was a lame excuse.

They took me to this one particular place: black bubbling tar, smelling heavily of sludge in large tanks. At the very back was a men's washroom. It looked like it had never been cleaned. Steady afternoons too. They were trying to force me out the door. Tears rolled down my face. I knew I couldn't refuse a job, but I wanted to make sure they knew where I stood.

"It's obvious you are doing this so I will quit. Not going to happen. I have bettered myself as an instructor and will graduate a four-year program of the Teachers of Adults. You don't see the other instructors doing anything to improve themselves. This is discrimination," I said.

"You can talk to your union then," one of them said.

"No, I am going to the Human Rights Commission. You want a fight, I'm ready. I have more seniority than one of those instructors, and I am better qualified as an instructor. Let's see what the law says."

"Yes, but now that they are unionized, they just made this job a 6600 job and you are 6500."

What a slap in the face again. These people had never had anything to do with unions and now they were using the union to protect them.

All of this fighting and stress was taking its toll on my health, physically and mentally. Crying was not the answer for me. I remembered going to a women's conference. The instructor said women cry easily. So, she told us a trick to use when we didn't want to cry. We were to squeeze our bum muscles together as tightly as we could. You can't cry and squeeze your bum muscles at the same time. I squeezed and squeezed—there would be no crying for me. No job either.

Mine Mill was having a smelter workers centennial on May 13–15. Jennifer Keck and Mary Powell of Laurentian University were the moderators. My union said I couldn't go, that they would send another woman. The union was not going to let me represent them anytime soon. This was because I was a Dave Patterson supporter.

An appointment was set up with a Dr. Frances, an Inco doctor from Toronto. A union representative came with me. The doctor asked me to write down my goals and objectives and to have them ready for Monday. It was Thursday. I worked on it throughout the weekend, wrote twenty-one pages and waited for him to get back to me.

On May 27, I had a meeting with Dr. Frances, but he didn't show up. A pretty blond nurse from occupational medicine told me Dr. Frances wanted me to see a psychologist to do an aptitude test, to see if I was capable of learning.

"Oh yeah, get a woman to do your dirty work, Doctor," I said.

I was very insulted. Send me to a psychologist to see if I could learn, are you kidding me? I shuffled the twenty-one pages, unread information I had worked so hard on, and put it in my briefcase.

Later, I received a phone call asking me to go back to the office—Dr. Frances wanted to see me right away. There was no representation from the union. I sat across from him, twenty-one pages in hand waiting patiently to read them. The pretty blond nurse sat quietly beside him, taking notes.

"Well, Cathy, how would you like to take your pension?" he asked.

"Never thought about it. That would be my last resort." I eyed him cautiously.

"Let's talk about the problem you are having at work." His voice was cunning.

I was nervous and felt tears fill up in my eyes. I squeezed my bum muscles as hard as I could. I didn't cry.

He asked if I had ever taken antidepressant pills. I wasn't going to lie, it was in my file. He was definitely a wolf in sheep's clothing.

"Pills and I don't get along, so I stopped taking them. They upset my intestines," I said.

"Well," he said coldly, "people have to take insulin who don't want to."

I was surprised at what a stupid thing this was for a doctor to say. "That's life-threatening, it's not the same. Diabetes and depression are not the same."

"So, you agree that you are depressed. We think you may commit suicide." His dark-brown beady eyes stared into mine.

I gave out a sarcastic laugh. "I would never commit suicide."

"How can you be so sure?" he said, a smug look on his face.

I stood up and looked back into his eyes, grinding my teeth. "Because it would make too many people at Inco happy if I committed suicide. This meeting is over." I got up and left.

The union told me I had to go to see the psychologist or I would lose my job. This made me very suspicious. I asked how many men had to go through this. The union said there was some but couldn't tell me who because it was confidential.

Chapter 98

The Psychologist, and Sudbury Women Stand Behind Me 1993

My kids knew I was having a hard time. My son Peppy, now twenty-two, made me a cassette tape to give me strength. Songs like "I Won't Back Down," She Works Hard for the Money," and many more. I played it over and over in my car. On June 7, the day of the appointment, I turned up the volume and let the music fill my soul. I was feeling pumped, now to relax. I meditated for twenty minutes. I was as ready as I could be. The psychologist met me at the door of his office and shook my hand, motioning me to sit.

"So, why don't you tell me why you're here?" he asked.

"I was told to come," I replied.

"I understand you are having some difficulties at work." He waited for a response.

Oh, that's putting it mildly, I thought to myself.

"Yes," I said.

"Tell me all about it." He leaned back in his chair as if waiting to hear a long story.

The little voice in my head said, *You're kidding me, you want me to talk about it and then cry, and I would end up as an "emotional, distraught woman," no longer fit to work. Not going to happen.*

"I can't talk about it," I said. "It's going through the grievance procedures. It's like court, you understand … right?"

"I don't work for the company. I am a consultant."

"The company is paying you; the company hired you?" I raised my eyebrows, waiting for him to respond.

"Yes to both."

"Well then, you work for the company. I am here to do some tests. Can I start?" I stood up.

I followed him into a room, where he told me I could have a week to finish it. He handed me a large stack of papers. I worked eight hours a day, only taking half an hour for lunch and two fifteen-minute breaks. I was finished in two days. I never told him I was dyslexic.

The forms came in from the Human Rights Commission. I filled them out and sent them in, keeping a copy for myself.

On June 10, I went back to see the psychologist for his results. He said I had problems with numbers and letters. I told him that I knew that; it was because I was dyslexic. He wanted to know why I didn't tell him. "It's embarrassing. But put me in front of 10,000 people and I will give a great speech." He went on with the results. On the art scale I received an "above average," like I would need art at Inco. Social science: "very high," physical science: "very high," mechanically inclined: "very high," risk-taker: almost as high as the scores allowed, chosen skill levels: "very high," and my office work number read "average." I had leadership skills that were very high with special qualities. I couldn't have been happier when he gave me my copy.

It was hard taking on Inco, even with Bruce and Merv by my side. It was time to bring out the big guns, to go to the media. On June 27, I talked to another good friend: Mick Lowe, a writer for the *Northern Life* Sudbury newspapers. Let's tell Sudbury what was happening. I told him what the industrial relations man had said to me: "I can see by the way you handle yourself you're very sure of yourself. And I can understand how that can be taken as aggressive behavior."

He wrote great articles, a small bio of my life so far at Inco. We kept the pressure on. He tried to talk to Inco, but they declined to comment on Mulroy, and the union advised me not to talk to the press. When Mick talked to the vice president of my union, Gary, he said, "I don't want to piss these people (Inco management) off. They have been pretty good about our disabled people, and I don't think we should start hoofing them in the balls over it." When asked about sexual harassment, he said, "It hasn't been that significant, to my knowledge." Mick also wrote about Dr. Frances's opinion that I might be suicidal, and my response when I told him that it would make too many people happy if I committed suicide. Dr. Frances refused to see me anymore. I wonder if was because of the news articles or the positive results from the psychological tests.

Mick told the story about the staples in the driveway, the flowers and brass candlestick holders, the phone calls. He interviewed other women who were having similar problems.

He interviewed Laurene about her problems with the Human Rights Commission and how she was treated.

July. Once again I called on my old boyfriend Val Patrick in Hamilton, and asked him if he had any ideas on how to fight this. He sent me documented cases and copies of the Human Rights Code. He had highlighted the pertinent details. This was great and would help in my fight.

Another so-called union brother wrote an article in the paper asking why Mick would write a negative story and not a positive one of the experiences of women at Inco—why choose to discuss issues like this when it's only a select few? He went on to say that women have climbed the corporate ladder both at Inco and in the union.

I shook my head. It's negative, Mr. Stupid, because it is a negative story, and there are only a handful of women so we are a "select few." Just because not every woman was being harassed—and if they were, they would not come forward—we should still talk about the ones who are. It was hard to get some men to understand. As far as any women climbing the corporate ladder in our local union—how many women sat on the executive board? None! Another union brother wrote that Mick should get the other side of the story. I agreed. I would have loved to hear what the other two instructors had to say. He also said he took personal offence because he knew these two men and thought they were okay. He went on to say that "at Inco we have been working hard at improving sexual harassment and discrimination. This is going to cause a backlash of all the good work we have accomplished so far."

"What accomplishments did we have on these subjects? None!" I said.

Included in this statement of what they had accomplished was an admittance there was a problem of sexual harassment and discrimination at Inco. This same man, years later, put in a sexual harassment claim against a woman with twenty-five years and she was fired, losing a big part of her pension, and she was innocent. (This is not my story to tell.)

After the letters from my union brothers, the women's groups of Sudbury got behind me in my fight.

Betty, the chair of the Women of Steel Committee LU 6500, the same woman who I met during the strike who brought me into the kitchen to make sandwiches and introduce me to Dave Patterson, talked about the damage Inco had done by hiring only a few women, and about Sudbury operation's VP Blanco's statement that "if Inco hadn't gone through the major force reduction we would have a much larger number of women."

She stated, "That doesn't hold much water; after the layoffs in 1982 more than 800 people were hired and only eleven were women. Then again in May 1992: 271 people were hired and not one woman."

The same man wrote another article that said he wanted to clarify that he was a responsible union leader and that this problem with Mulroy was close to being resolved. He said that Mick was sacrificing my job for the sake of a news story.

That was news to me. Just to clarify: the statement that this was close to being resolved was a lie.

Other women wrote in about harassment, offering their support to me. Other women wrote that these things were indeed happening. They stated that the union shouldn't be turning their heads away to one of their own. She felt that LU 6500 had abandoned me. The Sexual Assault Crisis Centre wrote that they wanted Inco to hold an inquiry into the allegations. The Sudbury Women's Centre wrote that it wasn't good enough to just have a written policy on harassment, they wanted the company and the union to do something about it.

The rolling stone was on the move, collecting no moss. I had to keep it going. I called Sophie Bissonnette, the director/producer of the *Wives' Tale* documentary. She was happy to hear from me but was sad to hear what was going on. She told me she had just finished a documentary called *The Glass Ceiling*, about women getting so far in a job only to be stopped by the gender barrier. You can see the job, but the glass ceiling keeps you away. She said she would get it put into English and we could show it in Sudbury. It's funny how the gods get people to cross our paths.

Jennifer Keck and the Sudbury Women's Centre arranged a panel discussion. Over 150 people attended an event at Science North. It was held in the—ready for this?—Inco Cavern. Sophie's movie was shown. The obstacle was brought out in the film and discussions on discrimination were held. I told my story, Susan Hare from the law firm Pharand Kuyek told hers as a native women, and Penny Reneau spoke on disabled women.

It was a great night. After the discussion I met with a woman from the *Shirley Show* and *The Fifth Estate*.

A few days later I was called back to work.

Meanwhile, back at home, one of our daughters was a key witness to a murder. This affected her as well as the rest of the family. More stress. This is not my story to tell. All I will say is this just added to my stress. It was a lot of stress!

Chapter 99

No Job Description, CBC Radio Station

I was placed in a small office, sharing it with another employee. I asked what my job description was; I was informed that I would be told later. Days went by and I sat in this office, isolated, no one to talk to. There was no women's washroom, but I was assured there would be one built in a few days. Construction began. They had built a training centre that held eight tables, sixteen beautiful grey office chairs, a fridge, a microwave, a TV, a VHS machine, overhead projector, copy machine, a sink, cabinets, and files. I thought I had died and gone to heaven. I wanted to get involved with this. In the back there were VHS movies on safety, but they were really outdated.

The union wanted me to drop my grievances, but this was not going to happen. Some of the union boys hung out in one of the offices in this centre. They were in and out all day; I'm not sure what their jobs were. The dust was heavy while the construction for my washroom was being built. I went for lunch by myself and took an hour instead of a half hour.

A good-looking young man came into the office and introduced himself as Michael McDonald, and he told me he was my new boss. He asked me how long I had taken for lunch and I told him an hour. He made it clear that I was only to take a half.

Can you believe that my own union brothers would turn me in for taking and extra half hour, when they are gone most of the day? I told the new boss I would stay the extra half hour at the end of the day, and I needed permission to come in a little late as I was going to be on CBC Radio in the morning. He said that would be okay.

The next morning, I headed for the CBC Radio station. I was introduced to Marcus the announcer. We talked about *The Wives' Tale* and what it was like to be discriminated against. We went over the questions he was going to give me, about the panel and a little bit about what was going on at work. Then the headphones were put on and we were live on the air. My heart was beating so fast and hard I could hear it in the earphones. We chatted and all was going great until he asked a question we had not gone over.

"Cathy, can you give me an example of sexual harassment that has happened to you at Inco?"

For a second, my mind went blank. Then ... out it came. "Well, I was walking through the wire bar. A group of men that had been force-adjusted came from the mines to the copper refinery. They were standing against the wall as I walked by. A man in the middle called me over with that curled finger, saying to come here. I walked over and asked what he wanted. He laughed and said, 'I knew I could make you come with one finger.'"

The look on Marcus's face was that of shock and surprise. His eyes widened and his mouth stayed open. He stammered.

It wasn't that shocking. I had heard stuff like this all the time at work. He thanked me, stuttering over the words "this was Cathy Mulroy." Then he hit a button and music began to play. He got up and left the room, so I left too. As I drove to work and thought about the look on Marcus's face I began to cry, then I laughed, then I cried all the way to work. I sat down. I was in shock.

The phone rang, it was Jennifer. "Holy moly, Mulroy, that was fantastic. What a great interview. I'll bet you surprised Marcus, and the city too."

"It just came out of my mouth." I cried some more.

"It's okay, Cat, this will be one interview the CBC won't forget," Jennifer said.

With all that was going on at work and with the murder trial at home, my gut was always in spasms. My immune system had been compromised. I was always feeling sick.

Chapter 100

Maintenance Department 1994

I was now in the maintenance department. The training centre was to be run by union brothers. Michael, my new boss, invited me to sit in on a meeting. He told the boys I was now part of the team. That didn't go over well. One man wearing cowboy boots placed his feet on the table. The boys wanted to know why I had to work with them. It was more of a whine. One guy wanted to place me in a cage in the warehouse, since there were a few empty cages over there.

"What are you going to do, put a sign on the cage saying, 'don't feed the woman'?" I asked.

Michael put his hand up and told us to stop. This is what was happening, and the guys would just have to get used to it.

Still without a job description, I decided to take some initiative and look over the VHS safety movies. I put information together that would match the movies and gave it to the foreman for their safety talks. They loved it; all they had to do was pick up the safety talks in my office. Over the next few months I learned how to use the computer to do research and I started a library.

I picked up another *Triangle*, Inco's monthly magazine. There were stories in it about the anode. I missed some of the men. Ray, Maxie, Bill, Frank, Joe, Roger, Fred, John the tapper, John the wheel man, Charlie, Fern, and Moe, and a few more. Men who were nice to me.

Chapter 101

Stress, A Place to Cry, My Brother is struck by a Drunk Driver 1994

The stress in my life was really causing a lot of problems. The doctor tried different kinds of antidepressants, but I just put on weight. This in turn made me more depressed.

Meanwhile, back home: Merv and our daughter had to meet with the crown attorneys about the murder.

I had to fight with the crown attorney to get the $2100 that was in arrears for child support. Can life get any more complicated? *Yes.*

There was a clinic in Lively where I met a wonderful man named Alex. I went there and cried a lot. No bum-tightening for me there. Every time I felt overwhelmed, I went to see Alex. He had the box of tissues ready for me and I would cry for an hour.

It was my safe place to cry without any guilt. It left me emotionally lighter, and I had more energy to fight the fight. Merv understood about the depression. He was my rock. I couldn't cry at home and it came out in anger. When the teens fought about who was wearing whose clothes or didn't clean their rooms, I would explode. They were not interested in what I was going through. They were teenagers.

Nightmares crept into my sleep. I was back in the anode, the rapist in the same lunchroom, the men laughing at me when I opened my lunch pail to find a dead rat.

In the morning I would be exhausted. The doctor again told me that my body was giving out from all this stress. I found comfort in my Teacher of Adults night school and the homework.

Then there was my boss, Michael, the first boss to really treat me with respect. He gave me free range to work on making the library a great success. The centre taught respirators, WHMIS (Workplace Hazardous Materials Information System), fall arrest, how to report an accident or near miss (form 079), legislation policy, personal protective equipment, and the right to refuse unsafe work.

I made up modules and training programs. I had permission to buy new videos on safety. I loved my job; this helped keep the stress down.

Meanwhile, another woman in a different plant was having a lot of trouble at work. I told her to go to the media, but she said she would rather get a lawyer. I told her the company would only get a bigger lawyer. She too was in a deep depression. This made me depressed. I needed to talk to Alex; I needed to cry in a safe place.

One night I was woken by the ring of the phone. Another accident, this time close to home. My younger brother Shane was hit by a drunk driver on the Kingsway. He may not make it.

We drove through a terrible thunderstorm to the hospital. I was shocked when I saw my baby brother in the emergency room. There was blood everywhere; his face looked like it had been hit by a bat. His pelvis was shattered, his leg was broken, and he had deep cuts on his arm. When we were little, I always protected my little brother.

Memories of when Shane and I were at the Ottawa Exhibition came back to me. I was nine and he was four. We were in a haunted house and my mom told me to watch my little brother. My brother was always a little shit, and when we were in the totally dark house, he shook his hand free of mine. I heard him say that a man had grabbed him and picked him up. I jumped on the man's back, piggybacking him. I sank my teeth into his trapezius muscle and wouldn't let go. The man cried out in pain as he went for the exit, carrying a screaming little boy and a crazy little girl attached to his neck by her teeth. We found out the man worked there and was only trying to help my little brother out.

I came out of my dream state when the doctor entered the emergency room, and the memories disappeared. The news wasn't good: my brother could die. He had to get to Toronto or Ottawa. The weather was so bad no helicopters were allowed in the air. We sat all night with him, hoping the weather would let up. In the morning he was airlifted to Toronto. The storm had cancelled the specialist's plane that was supposed to fly out of Toronto.

But the gods were on our side. After hours and hours in the operating room, the doctor pieced back the cornflake state my brother's pelvis was in.

Inco was in a summer shutdown, so I stayed with my brother for four weeks. When he got back to Sudbury, he stayed with our dad, who was eighty years old and said he wanted to look after my brother. I was under so much stress big chunks of my hair fell out, leaving large bald spots, a condition called *alopecia*.

I put in a compensation claim about all the stress I was under and it was denied. Same answer when I had put in a claim back in 1993. I had no more energy to fight.

Chapter 102

My Union Brothers Fight Me the Same Way the Company Did 1994

Cathy graduating as a Teacher of Adults.

The safety training started up again in September—good, it kept my mind occupied. The union guys didn't change their attitude about me being there. At one of the meetings, I asked if we should call the centre "Health, Safety and Environment," like other places in Ontario did. One guy was adamant and said I wanted to take over and change everything, that our union called it "Safety, Health and Environment" because safety came first. They had a sign made and hung it on the front of the building. This centre would be called "Safety, Health and Environment." The acronym was "SHE," so when I answered the phone, I would say, "SHE training centre." I loved it.

Good news: I graduated from the Teachers of Adults course. I went to a graduation party and got to wear the gown and the hat. I was very proud.

My union brothers were still not happy that I was there. They taught their stuff and I taught mine. A meeting had been set up with Michael and the other instructors. I was not invited. Later I was told there was a complaint through the union hall about me.

The union, like the company, would not give any specifics, like who put the complaints in or what they were about. If I were a man this would not have happened. Another meeting, and this time I was invited because it was about me. The union brothers told management that I was trying to take over. They never said how I was trying to take over, they just didn't want to work with me. They said I was checking their work, that I didn't hold this job, and I was unapproachable. Michael gave me a chance to answer to their accusations. I asked what work I checked, and they wouldn't answer. I told them that there may have been four days out of the month that I might have been unapproachable. I would let them know when those days were, and they could stay clear. They knew what I was talking about.

The guy with the cowboy boots who always put his feet on the table showed his arrogance once more. This time he slammed his fist down hard. "If you don't get rid of her, we will not teach here."

Michael said, "The company will not give in to your bullying tactics. If you want to quit, go right ahead. We will find other instructors, and by the way, Cathy does hold the job as a safety surface instructor," he said.

Cathy's business card.

I thought for sure I was a goner. But I was saved and now I held a job. I was so happy.

The next day, the superintendent of training came down to see me. We sat in my office and he asked me if I saw a parallel between what was happening with those men and the men up at the first aid training.

"Oh yes, I see a parallel," I said.

"What are you going to do to change?" he asked.

"I don't think we see the same parallel."

Michael told me that I could go to the Inco hospital to try to relive some of this stress. Meditation and some kind of bio-feedback might be helpful. I decided not to take any more pills and that too was a big help.

School or courses seemed to be a big stress release for me. I took some courses on AIDS/HIV and prostate cancer.

One day, one of the union boys was teaching in the morning. I was at a meeting. When I got back at 11:00, he had done my training too. He must have whizzed through it. In front of the class he told the men I should let them go home because they had taken all the course materials that were legislated. The first aid instructor had tried to set me up like this before. I told them I had no right to send them home. So, I taught them about AIDS/HIV and prostate cancer.

Someone turned me in to management. After I explained the importance of this training under health, Inco occupational medicine wanted to do the training. Every time I came up with a good idea someone had to steal it. I swallowed my pride once more and thought that as long as the training was taught about AIDS/HIV and prostate cancer, I would step aside.

Chapter 103

Men Should Keep the Lights on When They Are with a Woman 1995

Employment equity. Ha-ha. I have to laugh at that. Inco, Steelworkers, and the Canadian Guards Association were working jointly to implement employment equity legislation in the Ontario division of the union. The intent of this legislation was to identify and remove any discriminatory barriers that might exist that separate qualified people in Ontario from opportunities in hiring, retention, internal training, and promotions. Well, let's see how far this would go.

The Human Rights Commission did not want to handle my case about the first aid training. They felt the union and our collective bargaining agreement or Ontario's Labour Relations Act would be better to handle this. I wrote back, stating I wanted them to handle it under section 34 of the Human Rights Code. I told them I had exhausted the grievance procedures and it was still not resolved. One of the grievances was about the jobs that were offered. They told me I couldn't have them because of my gender, as there were no washrooms. Pure discrimination. The union was not helping me. It was filed under the sexual harassment clause and they said it wasn't sexual harassment.

On February 17, I received a call from the CBC's *The Fifth Estate* wanting to hear my story. I told them about the year-long fight and that I was on WSIB, and how all of this affected me and my family. I also told them that the Human Rights Commission did not want to help to deal with this problem. They told me they could not get an interview with Inco.

I spoke at Laurentian University in Jennifer's class. These were fourth-year social workers. This gave me the strength to carry on.

Another man was killed at Frood-Stobie Mine, buried under muck. Clifford Bastine was fifty-nine years old with twenty-nine years of service. Merv and his supervisor had to talk to Clifford's wife and children on Valentine's Day. How shitty was that?

I was doing most of the teaching, as the union boys were slowly leaving the SHE training centre.

In March, the Ontario Federation of Labour asked the union if I would speak at the Community Unionism Conference in Toronto. I flew down and Merv drove down to spend the weekend with me.

OFL wanted the woman who was the liaison between the Wives and the union during the strike. My time on the stage was 10:15, right after coffee break. Not knowing anyone, I grabbed a coffee and sat on the sofa in the lobby. I watched as people mingled around a book sale that was going on, wishing I could read better.

A man in a dark blazer sat beside me and put his arm around my shoulders. A little stunned, I looked at his arm and then at him. I had no idea who this man was.

"Don't you recognize me, Linda?" The woman who he thought I was had many, many male friends.

Totally pissed off, my anger hit the roof.

"Why don't you guys keep the fucking lights on? My name is Cathy Mulroy, not Linda Black."

His arm slid off my shoulders. He sheepishly apologized, got up, and left. That was so disgusting. I didn't see him the rest of the weekend.

May 26, 1995. I resolved my human rights complaint. It was now finalized that there was a problem. I was okay with that. All this was just making me sicker.

The company and union talked to the first aid instructors about the sexual harassment complaint. Not that it was going to do any good. At the Steel Hall I agreed to drop everything. I can't tell you what happened because I agreed to a gag order. I didn't leave without a final word or two. "Mark my words: those two men are not nice men. This will happen again." Sure enough, I heard of a young woman who was underground training as a plant protection officer for the summer. One of these men grabbed her by the ass and said, "You have buns of steel." She put in a sexual harassment complaint against him and he was sent underground, no longer an instructor.

It reminded me of the day when two paramedics came to the training office. One was a beautiful tall blond woman. The two instructors acted like dogs in heat; it was disgusting. She seemed to get a kick out of it.

I wondered what Ashcroft, the president of Inco, thought of this guy now.

Meanwhile, I was still fighting for the child support that was owed. Sometimes it's just so hard to be a woman.

Chapter 104

Other Women Stand Up, and The Inco Club 1995

Sue Vallier made the front cover of the *Financial Post* magazine. It was not a good picture. The article was written by Mick.

The other story was about a woman who lost her job after a sexual harassment complaint against her was filed. The article had a picture of her crying. Again, a terrible picture. I pulled my story because things were good at work and there was a gag order on the outcome. I'm not sure why the magazine would use these horrible pictures. I guess it sells magazines.

Joan Kuyek received an honorary doctorate degree at Laurentian University in recognition for a quarter century as a social activist in Sudbury. She was the woman who helped the Wives to organize during the strike. Also getting a doctorate was Mike Sopko, chief executive officer of Inco. He was met by protesters outside. Sopko received his degree first. His speech was about the great job Inco was doing in Voisey's Bay Mine in Labrador. Joan's speech was about how Inco raped the land and a lot more. There was a stunned silence followed by applause and a standing ovation. Merv was there; I am sure he felt a little uncomfortable. Joan was a friend of his too, and he and his security team were there for Sopko.

September 1995. Another woman stood up for herself. She had been sexually assaulted by a boss underground. He put his hands on her breasts and tried to kiss her. There was nowhere she could go. She screamed but no one heard her. She went to a steward, to the union hall, and to the police. The company tried to discredit her, belittling her because she said she felt some of the men were staring at her. During the grievance investigation, it was said that on her days off she wore her skirts too high. She looked like a prostitute. The other women at Inco never heard much of what had happened to other women unless it hit the newspapers. Thanks again to my friend Mick. We had made a great team.

Meanwhile, I was fighting Veterans Affairs trying to get my dad some help, some kind of pension. After all, he was on the front lines for two years.

The SHE training centre was rocking. I got speakers to come in from many different organizations, like the Canadian Hearing Society on the importance of protecting your hearing. A man who was deaf in one ear talked to the class. A police officer came in and talked about snowmobiling safety, and in the summer he came back and talked about boat safety. I had no idea how many accidents happened in these two recreational activities.

Michael said I was doing a great job and I could bring the police officer to the Inco Club for lunch. Every time I brought in a speaker, I went to the Inco Club. They had a great kitchen staff and gourmet chefs.

The day the police officer and I went to the club, we went early so I could give him a tour. It was exhilarating for both of us. It had been built in 1915 by International Nickel Company of Canada Limited. It had its own board of directors and served for decades as the social and dining facilities for Inco employees—the big bosses, not the hourly employees. I heard the Italians and the Irish were not welcome, so the Italians built their own club.

We stood outside, admiring this beautiful three-storey mansion. The walls were constructed of granite from a nearby quarry. We entered the building and gazed up to a crystal chandelier gracing the main stairwell. My hand ran over the rich oak panelling as we walked up the stairs. The same panelling was in the reading area known as the Oak Room.

The main floor of the club featured the elegant Rose Room with a gorgeous black grand piano, a sunroom, a ladies' sitting room, conference room, and dining room with cathedral ceilings. "If only these walls could talk," I said to the officer. He smiled and raised an eyebrow.

We stood at the large windows. Long pinkish drapes framed them from the top all the way to the floor. The view overlooked Nickel Park. This is where one of the roasting beds used to be. I pictured the black smoke lifting into the air, poisoning everything around. That was back in the early 1900s.

We went downstairs and saw a four-lane bowling alley, billiards room, and an indoor swimming pool. I read on the back of a postcard that it was the first indoor pool in Northern Ontario.

The stairs were of dark wood too. We took them to the second floor. Originally this was the living quarters for the club staff. I would think it was for maids, footmen, butlers—all that European way of life. Now it was an executive suite, private dining room, and offices. The people who were invited to the club over the years were high officials, like politicians, governors, presidents for other countries, etc. I fell in love with the place. "If only these walls could talk."

Chapter 105

Merv and I Get Married
1996

Big changes were happening at Inco. They were tearing down buildings at the Copper Cliff copper refinery. I was very emotional to see the warehouse, the mechanic shops, the blacksmith shops all turned to rubble in shops alley at the smelter. This was the beginning of the end.

My job was so fulfilling it was like a dream. Michael asked if I wanted another modified employee to work with me. I agreed and Tom became my co-worker. He was a sweet man, with white hair and a great sense of humour. Tom had a bad back, so one day when I was ordering supplies, I ordered two ice packs—one for him and one for me at five dollars each. A few days later, Michael's boss, a general foreman, came to see me and asked why I order the ice packs. I pulled them out of the freezer of our small fridge and showed him the ice packs with our names on them. "Do you really need them?" he asked. I told him they were a good idea. When we are sitting too long, standing, or cleaning the classroom we could put them on our injuries. I wondered why Michael didn't come down to ask. When the general foreman left, I busted out laughing telling Tom to come and see something. I opened the cabinet and showed him hundreds of those black paper clips, all different sizes.

"He didn't look too close at what I ordered. I made a mistake and ordered them by the box and should have been ordered them individually." We both laughed at the cabinet full of clips.

Merv and I were starting to plan our wedding. We decided to get married in our backyard and now we had to find a place for the reception.

Wouldn't it be great if we could rent the Inco Club? The club was no longer going to be a hall people could rent. The company decided that all the staff were to be laid off. Merv checked into it and the club was booked and closing in June. Then came a phone call telling Merv that the people who rented the club for June 8 had cancelled. Merv went right away and paid for the club for June 8, 1996. Our reception would be at the Inco Club. This made me laugh out loud.

This was the best wedding gift I could have asked for.

If we thought friends and family were going to show up in the backyard, we would have put down plywood so the women's high heels didn't sink into the grass. Our friend Erwin was the minister and our son Michael and daughter Melanie stood for us. As I was getting ready to exit the back door onto the deck, I could hear loud buzzing noises. It was our new shitty neighbour cutting brick with a very loud saw. My brother had bought my old house and I thought I was through with shitty neighbours. The minister asked him to stop for about twenty minutes and he flatly refused. One of my girlfriends had asked a friend to the wedding who used to be a guard at Monteith Correctional Complex. He walked over and had a few words with the neighbour, and all was quiet.

Then came the reception at the club. It was more like a roast, and all our kids said a few words. Some of my ex-boyfriends were invited, one of them being Harley Charley. Another one went to the microphone and said, "Better you than me, Merv." Everyone laughed. Karaoke was played, people sang. Each table had a disposable camera, so each table was in charge of their own pictures. Prime rib and all the trimmings were served. It was one of the happiest days of my life.

Chapter 106

Meeting the Women Who Worked at Inco During the War Years 1997

The women of Inco who worked there during the war years.

Some days I really felt sick. Good thing I had Michael as a boss, and Ronno as a safety foreman in the other office. He and I became friends. They both made working at Inco so much easier.

Michael involved me in meetings with the maintenance department. He let me chair meetings. He was never short on telling me what a good job I was doing.

Meanwhile, Jennifer Keck, Mercedes Steedman, and Susan Kennedy gave us a copy of the draft they had put together about "Every Miner Had a Mother." That was going to go into a book about the celebration the women had back in 1983 to contribute to the city of Sudbury's centennial celebration.

Out of that, Jennifer Keck and Mary Powel were reaching out and studying the experience of women in production and maintenance jobs at Inco between '74 and '94. They believed the study would provide useful information relating to the experiences of women in non-traditional jobs. They would assess women's experience relating to hiring and promotions, work and working conditions, relations with coworkers and supervisors, and combining family responsibilities and work, in hope that this would improve an understanding of the situation that had traditionally been male-dominated. The researchers would also be providing an oral history of women in LU 6500 at Inco. We were so excited that anyone would want to hear our stories.

Meanwhile, Judith Finlayson was writing a book called *Against the Current*. Ha-ha, I thought to myself when I heard the title. Memories of those days in the anode—drinking the coffee that was for institutions only and how I would disappear into the current in my cup to feel safe. It was great that other women found our stories so interesting. My stories are in her book too.

International Women's Day was celebrated at Laurentian University honouring Judith Finlayson's book.

Mary and Jennifer from the Women of Steel organized a luncheon at the Steel Hall so we could meet some of the women from the war years. It was fantastic. Their stories were much different than ours. The main thing was that these women worked together in a group. Not like us. The company separated us—divide and conquer. The war women had female maîtres d's who managed them, looked after them, kept them safe. We had no one looking out for us. I sat with Cora Hyde and Violet Stevens-Wirta who told me how much they loved their jobs at Inco. They held their jobs for thirty months, but the law of the land would not let them work there for thirty years. When the men came back from war, all the women lost their jobs. Even if their husbands were killed, they could not have their jobs. Some of the women told stories of working at Garson Mine in the rock house from 1942 to 1945. 1400 women worked at Inco during the war years. We took a lot of pictures and felt this was a great experience for all of us. At a guess, their ages were from thirty-five to eighty-five.

We talked about how we felt that the law was unfair. That under federal law and the Provincial Mining Act it was illegal to hire women in production until the early 1970s. So, during the war the company talked to the federal government to invoke a clause in the War Measures Act allowing Inco to hire women to replace the men who left to go to war. My dad was one of these men. I felt a circle of life with these women. These stories they told were going to be a great addition to the book. Cora Hyde and I talked some more, and she told me how thrilled she was when she got the job. I could see her memories in her eyes. She said there were twenty-one women on each shift. There were three shifts at the rock house. She smiled as the memories came flooding back. She remembered cashing her first paycheck. She said it was hard work, but she loved it. "It was about forty-eight cents an hour," she said proudly. "I wish I could have stayed."

Cathy DeGagne (LU 6500), a mechanic at Creighton, said she was proud and admired the work these women did. All the women agreed it was an inspiring day.

Women of the war years together with the second generation of working women at Inco.

Cathy with two women from the war years.

Chapter 107

Big Changes at Inco, and Michael McDonald 1997

Michael McDonald

The company began to tear down shops alley. That was where the SHE training centre was. This is where all the skilled tradespeople and our apprentices worked. The locomotive repair shop to fix the trains was here, as well as the welding shop where they did arc welding—gas, flux, TIG (tungsten inert gas). The transportation department that looked after all the equipment and so much more.

Michael asked me to go into the shops and get the serial numbers off all the welding equipment.

"Is Inco selling all this equipment" I asked. He didn't say a word. "You know, Michael, silence is a strong reply."

He smiled. "When you're finished, give me the list," he said, and left.

All the tradespeople were being sent up the hill to divisional shops. The superintendent for the divisional shops was in one of my classes. His name was Yvan, another man with deep-blue eyes. He challenged me to make a film on personal protective equipment. I was up for a challenge, and so was Tom, and we worked hard over the next six weeks putting our own movie together. We went through the whole maintenance department. Tom filmed as the people worked. I did the editing on an old machine and added music and voiceover. What a lot of fun. Too bad there weren't more bosses like Michael and Yvan.

Yvan gave us an *atta boy* and *atta girl* on a job well done. He felt a forty-five-minute movie was a little too long. We laughed, because we knew it was long but we didn't want it to be cut any more, for history's sake.

I hadn't seen Michael in that time. I wondered what he was up to. I wanted to tell him about the movie. His boss, Brian, came down to see me. He told me Michael had been diagnosed with cancer. It felt like someone had hit me in the gut with a baseball bat. I told him I was sorry to hear that, trying hard to keep my tears from forming in my eyes, squeezing my bum muscles. He couldn't have left any sooner. Tears poured down my cheeks. I jumped up and closed and locked my office door.

Michael came back to work looking rundown. We took up from where we left off: getting all the machines ready to sell. Everyone at Inco had to take the legislated training once a year. Michael was no different. It was his turn to be in my class. A superintendent from another part of the plant sat beside him. I can't remember exactly what he said, but his remarks went something like *you are not going to be around here too much longer anyways*, and he laughed. Michael didn't react. A little while later, Michael's intestines gurgled loudly. The same superintendent made a nasty comment about the noise.

I leaned over his table. "You can shut up. Don't be so rude."

"It's okay, Cathy." Michael lifted his hand in the air, dismissing it.

"This is my classroom; I am the boss in here. If you don't shut up, I will throw you out of my class. Your name will not be entered into the computer and you will have to come back and take all of it again, because this is legislated and you must take it." I was leaning over the table right in his face. Michael smiled; the other guy didn't but he did shut up.

Tom was sent back to the shops and a new man, Sam, was coming in.

Sam and I hit it off and became friends fast. We talked about personal stuff, like two women would. He had a crazy girlfriend and a crazy ex-wife. He was so fed up with dating crazy women.

I would go home and tell Merv everything. Meanwhile, my hairdresser and good friend was having trouble with her boyfriend. Again, I filled Merv in. He suggested we get Sam and Lori together. I organized a meeting for them, and they were soon married.

I had to go for another operation to remove the two fibroids and a cyst. The cyst was the size of a baby's head. The other two were not much smaller. The doctor said I should feel better. While in there, they gave me a partial hysterectomy. I was back to work in six weeks.

Chapter 108

Day of Protest March 1997

Eight hundred people took to the streets in Sudbury on a Friday to march in opposition to the policies of the Ontario Progressive Conservative party. We marched and didn't disrupt the busses or close any buildings down. There were assemblies from social action and labour groups, but not our Steelworkers. I was disappointed in them. It was an education rally that brought us to Civic Square. It was a peaceful, non-confrontational protest, more like a festival. Music played and some speakers said their thoughts. Big snowflakes began to fall. It was beautiful. My union said they didn't think this was the way to go. We didn't need any more protests, we needed to have an educational campaign instead. We didn't agree with that and went ahead without them. Even Syd Ryan, labour leader and head of the OFL, was there. Also, the president of the Ontario division of the Canadian Union of Public Employees was in full support.

I was disappointed with the union for not standing with the people. I arrived a little late and had to meet up with the marchers. Another friend waved at me to join them in the front to hold a banner. That night I wrote a letter to the newspaper about how disappointed I was with LU 6500 for not standing up with the people. I reminded them of how the people stood with us through the big strike in '78–'79. I said that the members were not a reflection of the executive board. We were going into bargaining in June, and if we went out on strike again, who would support us?

This is not what a union is supposed to be. The thoughts about what I would like to see was a lot different than what was. I felt angry, sad, frustrated, and let down.

Chapter 109

Jennifer Has Another Lump, and I Run for Vice President LU 6500 1997

VOTE
FOR CHANGE

VOTEZ
POUR DU NOUVEAU

**CATHY MULROY
FOR
VICE PRESIDENT**

23 years service with INCO. Worked at the Copper Refinery Anode Department. Now a Surface Instructor for Central Maintenance. Past member of OSHE committee, member of the Women's committee. There is talk amongst our membership that we want change.

We want leadership that will serve the members.
Leadership that will keep the members informed.
Leadership that will keep us focused in the hard times ahead.
Leadership that is willing to work for it's members.
I am an independent candidate.
On April 3 1997 I am asking for your vote.

If I may use a popular cliche

"I HAVE A DREAM"

leaflet paid for by Cathy Mulroy

The phone rang. It was Jennifer Keck; she had found a lump in her right breast. Yes, it was cancer; she would be going for surgery, chemotherapy, and radiation, she would be off work for some time. Fuck! I cried. I love Jennifer like a sister, and we were just getting to really know each other. She always boosted me when I need to be boosted; I hoped I could do the same for her.

I remember sitting in my living room in a trance thinking of the union and about Jennifer, about how unfair the world was, and how the power was not even.

I turned to Merv, who was sitting in his chair beside mine.

"I am going to run for vice president of the United Steelworkers of America," I said.

"Okay," he said as if I had said I was going downstairs. I love him so much. In all the years we have been together he has never second-guessed me.

Bruce, my best friend next to Merv, sat with me over coffee when I told him my plans. He wanted me to run for a smaller position.

"No, I don't want a smaller position. I want to really stir things up down at the hall if I get in."

"They will crush you," he said. "You don't know anything about leading a union."

"Let them crush away, it will be fun," I smiled.

Merv got out his camera and took pictures of me in the living room. Then I put it all together and wrote my leaflet. "Let's get 500, that should make a splash. If I get in, then I will worry about what I am going to do. I just want to stand up to those pieces of shit."

I started passing out my leaflets at the smelter, then the copper refinery and the nickel refinery. Merv drove me to some of the mines—he didn't want me going there alone at night. He stayed in the car as I went to the gates by myself. The feedback was good. I thought there was a possibility I could get in. But I didn't want to think about that. I was there to make a statement.

The newspapers got hold of my story. The front page read: "Woman aims to break up old boys club." The following Thursday, 4700 production workers were going to the polls. I said our Locals need leaders who would mobilize the members and wider community to deal with what I thought were critical issues. With Inco in Voisey's Bay, how was this going to impact us in Sudbury? The union boys were not happy with me. So. What. I told them about the wall that these guys had created. Their attitude was that if you weren't on their side then you didn't belong. Most didn't like me because I supported Dave Patterson, a real leader. My platform was to see some of the benefits trickle down to the people who were on pension—the men of the deep, the miners who worked underground, who made Sudbury so prosperous; men like my dad, who was only receiving $500 a month after forty-three years of service. We should look after them too.

One day, a few of the union brothers came down to the SHE training centre. They didn't say anything, just looked around and left.

The next day, Michael called me to come to his office. I drove my car over to the general office and found a parking spot close to the building. That was luck. Michael was sitting behind his desk looking very businesslike. "Come in." He motioned me to sit. He was not wearing his usual smile. He looked uncomfortable. "Cathy ... we received a call from the union hall about you," he said.

"Okay. Who called?" I asked.

"I can't say, but the person said you have been making your leaflets on company property using company Xerox and paper."

"Oh really?" Anger rose in me. "Who called you?" I demanded.

"I can't tell you that," he said. "I just need to know if you are doing this."

"Michael, you know me. Do you think I would do such a thing?" I was yelling. Not at Michael; I just wanted to make sure others in the hall or others who were listening could hear. I knew others would be listening to this conversation.

"It doesn't matter what I think, I need to ask you this."

"Do you see 'stupid' written on my forehead?" I lifted my bangs up and pointed. "I would never use company property to do something personal." I was laughing. "You just sit right where you are. I can prove it." I got up and rushed out of his office.

"Cathy, we are not finished. Come back here." He was using his big boss voice again.

"You're right," I yelled back from down the hall. "We are not finished. Just wait right there, I will be back in a minute." I ran down the two flights of stairs and was huffing and puffing when I reached my car, grabbed a handful of my leaflets, and headed back to Michael's office, running back up the stairs. When I reached his office, I was out of breath. "Here!" I said, throwing my leaflets across his desk. They all fanned out, displaying a dozen Cathy faces.

Michael looked confused. "What am I looking at?" he asked, still with that big boss voice.

"You are looking at my leaflets. Take a good look at them." I needed to get my breath before I gave him the punchline. I waved my hand over top of the leaflets. "These leaflets were done on a Gestetner machine at the Mine Mill Hall. It's a duplication machine—it uses a stencil method with rotating drums and rollers. You have to stand beside it and turn the rollers. I paid for the ink and the paper. Does Inco even own a Gestetner machine?" I felt validated. Copies from a photocopier looked very different than those from a Gestetner.

A broad smile came across Michael's face—that was the Michael I knew. "You can leave now," he said. I gathered the fanned-out leaflets and handed him a few. "Here, have some, Michael, it's good reading. Now if you wouldn't mind calling those assholes back at the union hall and let them know your findings. I am not like them. I pay my own way."

"Wait, what if you do get in, what are you going to do?" he asked.

"First, I'll get rid of that bar in the basement," I said.

"Why would you do that?" he asked. I knew he wasn't asking for himself, upper management wanted to know.

"The strangest things happen at our union meetings. When there is a vote that the right wants passed, the drunks from the bar come up and vote. That's all I will say about that."

"What would you do with the basement?" he asked.

"I would turn it into a dental and eye clinic for our members, this way the money could go back into the cost of the hall," I said proudly.

"That's a good idea."

"Oh, that's not my idea. That was Dave Patterson's idea. I would do it for him." If I was a peacock at that moment, my feathers would have been fanned out like my leaflets were.

The night of the elections, Bruce and I got a few scrutineers to monitor the votes and check for any irregularities. Mine were my friend Laurene and my co-workers Tom, Sam, and Luther, all modified workers. Luther was badly crippled by five different kinds of arthritis; he couldn't even move his neck. They had been trained as scrutineers using the same rules the union did when it sent members to learn from the NDP elections. Bruce, Joel Dworski, the chief scrutineer, and I told our scrutineers where to stand and at what polls. We told them that under no circumstances were they to move to different polls, even if they were told to, and to only concentrate on the polls we asked them to. We said that they may be told to move, but that they didn't have to. We sent out our little soldiers to the union hall as we waited at Gus's Restaurant. I got comfortable and began to watch the hockey game, when one by one our scrutineers entered the restaurant. Then Bruce's scrutineers came in behind them. They all looked rather pale. Poor Luther was shaking.

"What happened, why are you here? Is it over already?" I asked.

"No," Sam said. "We stood at the polls like you said. They told us we had to move, and we said no, we would stand right there. You were doing really well, Cat, you had over one thousand, three hundred votes when they told us we had to leave the hall. They yelled at us to get out. They said we were intimidating them."

I turned to Bruce. "Can they do that?"

"No, they can't. This is against the law, but it looks like they did it. We'll put in an appeal."

"Yeah, like that is going to do anything." I was very disappointed. "Just goes to show us their true colours."

Bruce wrote his letter and I wrote mine, stating that the democracy's rights as per the local union elections manual had been violated. The manual reads that the tellers shall afford observers a reasonable opportunity to observe either side's conduct of the election day, including observers and scrutineers. We were denied that basic democratic right. We referred them to Page 58, Article V. They denied our members in good standing the fundamental democratic right and procedure for the local union elections. Each scrutineer wrote down what went on that night. The tellers said they were standing too close, and they were told to move back. Our scrutineers told them that if they moved back any further they wouldn't be able to see the ballots. They were also tallying up the votes, using their own pads. They were told to stop doing this or they would have to leave. The counters took a break, and when they returned our scrutineers were kicked out of the hall.

Mick wrote a great article he obtained from Joel Dworski about the irregularities for Mulroy and McKeigan. During the investigation, we wanted to know how many ballots were ordered. The union would not tell us. It was odd: I had 1300 votes, and after the scrutineers left the hall I only received seven more.

Well, in a nut shell, we had our hearing with the international and it went down like a kangaroo court. They said no rules had been broken, that our scrutineers were at fault, blah, blah, blah.

Someone sent a message to Bruce that there were more ballots printed then what was needed. At the next membership meeting, I got up to the mic and told them that we wanted to see the unused ballots. The president said I was just mad that I didn't win, but that he would have another ballot count. "I don't want another ballot count, I want to see the unused ballots." This was not fair. He told me that was not going to happen. Even with all the evidence we had, the union and the international would not hear our cries for justice. No surprise.

Well, we were out on strike again. So much was changing. The members said no to a tentative agreement, but the bargaining committee unanimously supported it. This strike was driven by the members, not the leadership. We wanted improvement to our wages, as well as to our pension. Most of the workers on the picket line talked about Voisey's Bay and the $500,000 USD bonuses given to Inco chief executives Mike Sopko and Scott Hand. There was no money across the board for us. I felt we were spiralling down as a union.

Chapter 110

Another Operation, Fights with Home Care, and Inco Layoffs 1998

My dad and I put in a claim for his white-finger syndrome, a direct result of the work he had done using a jackleg drill while working underground most of his forty-three years at Inco. This was an industrial injury triggered by the continuous vibration of the jackleg drill. These drills were commonly used to bore into the face of the rock in order to position dynamite deep within its surface. It was a powerful machine and its use damaged the blood vessels and nerves in his fingers, resulting in loss of feeling and white fingers. He was turned down and the union would not appeal. Sins of the daughter ...

In February, Inco was talking about more cuts in Sudbury. Their investments in Voisey's Bay, Indonesia, and Guatemala weren't as good as they thought they would be. Who would pay for their mismanagement? Sudbury, again and again. The money should have stayed here, fixing our city.

I went to the membership meeting. Gary, the Guy I ran against for the position of vice-president, was now president. When Campbell retired, Gary moved into that position. It's not like he was voted in, if you know what I mean.

I was waiting out in the foyer of the hall, as the doors to the main hall weren't open yet. Bruce always got there just on time. I am an early person. About forty men stood around waiting. One man was against the wall; he eyed me and mouthed *whore*. It was like someone turned on a light switch. My anger surfaced. I walked over to him and got in his space, inches from his face. "You want to say that out loud?" He flinched, his eyes staring. He didn't say a word. My lip curled in disgust. "Yeah, I didn't think so, you chicken shit."

Back at work, I scanned the training room. I knew this too was coming to an end. Safety training was going to be contracted out in the future.

A friend, also named Cathy, was told she would be losing her job. She had twenty-five years' service and was in 6600. She and her husband had sunk all their money into a hobby farm just outside Sudbury, thinking they had at least another five years to work at Inco. She did get called back on contract, but after a fight she got her job back.

The morale was low in 6600 as they went into negotiations; there were more talks of more layoffs. There were talks about more cutbacks for 6500 also.

One day, three men from divisional shops came into my office and asked me to run for president or vice president again. I told them I had lost my belief in what a union was. The back-stabbing, the corruption, the lies—I didn't want anything to do with it anymore. I was delighted that they thought I would be a good candidate, but my answer was still no.

Sitting in Michael's office, he told me his cancer had spread to his back and his hips, and that he was in a lot of pain. I asked if I could take him for lunch the following week and he agreed. We talked about cutbacks and the low morale in the plants.

He told me I worried too much, that there were so many things in life that were more important. He said that once he was gone, the smoke would still come out of the stack. I wasn't going to say anything to that. I thought of all those shitty people in the world, rapists, murderers, harassers, etc., and here is a man, a good family man who loves his kids and wife. He treated people with respect. It was so unfair that he was sick.

Michael didn't come back to work that next week. I should have brought him for lunch sooner.

I watched the rain through the SHE training window. Trucks pulled in to the warehouse, but not as many as there used to be. The grey day mirrored the sombre mood everyone was in, some more than others.

They had begun to empty all the equipment out of shops alley. We had a meeting and the workers were told they would be moving up the hill to divisional shops. It was a general foreman who was giving the axe report. He said the company was broke.

At a Q&A, I asked:

"Are there going to be more layoffs?"

"I don't know."

"The money they save, will it be for Sudbury or are they sending it to Voisey's Bay?"

"I don't know."

"Who would know the answers to these questions?"

"Upper management."

"Are they going to come down here to shops alley and answer them?"

"I don't know."

"I heard the company wants 800 more Local 6500 people gone, is that true?"

"I don't know."

"If all those people don't retire, employees with ten years seniority will be gone."

"There will be a movie this afternoon about the shareholders meeting. Cathy, you don't have to go."

"Are you saying I don't have to go, or are you saying Cathy you are not going?"

The men in the room went silent, waiting for an answer.

"No, no, you can go; it mostly concerns 6600 and your 6500."

"Okay, I'll go. It's good to know everything that is going on, and that I have friends in 6600," I said. I knew he didn't want me to go.

More stress. My friend from the nickel refinery lost her four-year battle with the company and was out of a job. The guys treated the women ten times worse and nothing was done about it. This was so sad. This is not my story to tell.

The company announced they wanted 800 employees from 6500 gone by the end of the year. Bruce said they wanted to force older workers to take their pensions so there would be a fight between young employees. This was bullshit, because they were contracting out a lot of the jobs. This way they would pay less, offer no benefits, and the employees would not be in our union.

Even after all those operations, I was still not feeling well. Too much stress.

Meanwhile, home care was giving me a hard time about my dad's breakfast. A care worker could make him eggs but not bacon. That was considered a large meal. The head woman told me at a meeting I was to cook the bacon the night before and the worker could put in in the microwave in the morning. I was ready to fly across the table and punch her in the face. Merv put his hand on mine and I calmed down. Who are these people who hold this power? This is a man who fought in the war on the front line and worked at Inco for forty-three years, never asking for anything. Now we were asking for help and this is the way he was treated. Life was not fair.

Michael McDonald died on August 10, 1998. Fuck! Fuck! Fuck! I closed the door to my office, locked it once more and cried until I couldn't cry anymore. The tears were not just for him, but for me. What was going to happen next?

Chapter 111

Thanksgiving and Christmas Party

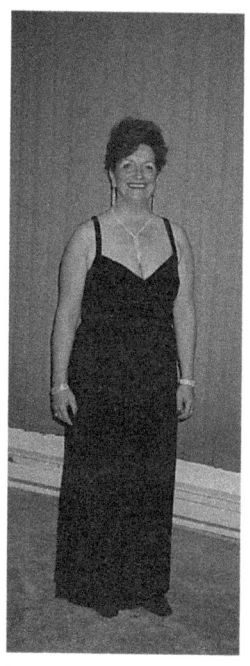

Cathy at the Christmas party.

The company hired a hack man, or cut man. By now I didn't care too much about anything. I was fed up with the world. I didn't want people around me, they just bugged me.

Boldly, I went up to divisional shops to meet the cut man. He was sitting in his office, not a very big man. I walked in and sat down. I was on my own time.

"Who are you?" he asked.

"I'm Cathy Mulroy. Who are you?" I asked.

"Randy Hiscock," he replied.

I thought he might be pulling my leg. "Is that your real name?"

"Yes."

"Your parents must have a weird sense of humour. With randy meaning horny and, well, your last name speaks for itself." I was very rude.

"What can I do for you, Cathy?" He brushed something off his desk.

"I wanted to meet the man who was hired to cut more jobs. Some of the men were talking to me about you and would like me to relay a message. They wanted to know how you can sleep at night, knowing you are cutting away people's livelihoods. Most will not be too thankful this Thanksgiving. I am sure you will be a conversation at a lot of tables this weekend. The message they want me to say is that they really dislike you. That they know you are here to do a job, but they really hate you. Have a good weekend. Nice meeting you." I left.

The fog was very thick on the way to work. It was hard to see the front of my car. I was just about to turn the radio down, as if that would help me see. The announcer said there was an accident at Inco. A thirty-one-year-old man had fallen to his death at South Mine. He was married with four children. He wasn't one of ours, he was a contractor. He fell 600 feet. He was wearing his safety harness but had forgotten to hook it back up after he came back from the washroom. "Fuck! Fuck! Fuck!" I yelled, slamming my hands on the steering wheel. And companies wanted to cut safety training. This should be second nature, just like getting in your car and hooking up your seatbelt. I yelled at the radio.

My mental state was extreme. I had so much anger. There would be no more tears. My depression increased and rage busted out a lot.

Merv bought me a black dress, saying it might make me feel better. It was very low in the front, showing off my big breasts, but looked good. He really liked it. That made me feel like a beautiful woman. He was invited to a boss's home for a party, and he brought me as his date. Many of these bosses were the ones who had been trying to fire me over the years. Merv gave me a drink and I stood against a wall, watching people. From where I stood, I could see a boss in one room kissing a woman who wasn't his wife, and I could see his wife in the other room working in the kitchen. These are the kind of people that made my lip curl.

Chapter 112

MIMS
1999

Inco had bought a new computer program for purchasing called MIMS (Maintenance Information Management System). The company who owned this program was MINCOM, a software and service company. They needed instructors to teach it, and I was one of them. One of our instructors, Ted, had to go through our department and input everything we used. That was a big job.

The group from MIMS came from the USA to teach us. We were doing great on learning it and were almost ready to teach the Inco employees.

One of the US instructors received a phone call from home. When he got back to the class, he was pale and shaking. He was in shock—I recognized that from my first aid training. He kept repeating that he had to go home. Another man gave him some water and told us there was a shooting at Columbine High School. That's where his daughter went to school. Twelve people were dead and many more were injured. We all recoiled in horror.

One of our instructors asked how his daughter was. The shaken father lifted his head and tears ran down his face. "She's okay." His hands trembled. "She forgot her makeup at home. She never goes home during the day, but she wanted her makeup. She was at home when the shooting started." There was relief in his voice.

We were all shocked that such a thing could happen. The distraught father was taken from the room and we turned on the TV. In addition to the shootings, the complex and highly planned attack involved a fire bomb to divert firefighters, propane tanks converted to bombs placed in the cafeteria, ninety-nine explosive devices, and car bombs. Twenty-one more students were injured, three more while attempting to escape. Then the shooters killed themselves. The rest of the day was a loss; we just sat around, letting this bad news sink in. What was happening in our world?

It was hard for me to understand how something like this could happen. The US instructors went back to the States. I began to teach MIMS the next week. I really liked it because we were teaching at the Inco Club.

Chapter 113

My Dad and My New Boss 1999

On April 25, I found a picture of my dad sitting on his lunch pail with an old oil lamp on his hard hat. It's one of my favourite pictures of him. It was in the newspaper, in the Anderson Museum and at Casey's Restaurant where there was a mining theme.

The shops were being demolished around my office. The Local shops needed me to move so they could move in. It was so sad to see. Over a hundred years of trades workers in this building, and it was now a pile of rubble. That's how I felt too, total destruction.

I met my new boss and I knew it was not going to be pleasant. He reminded me of a frat boy, a boy with money, a boy who thinks he is so much better than others. He talked down to me. I didn't like him and he didn't like me. Over the next few months, we fought as he tried to bury me in some shit holes. He wouldn't let me work with his men and all we did was butt heads. I missed Michael.

There was a spot up in divisional shops. That's where most maintenance workers were being dumped. I walked through with my new boss, past the machinist and the welders to the end where the heavy-duty mechanics worked. We climbed some stairs to a large room—it even had a washroom. The room was used for storage and the shop boss said they would clean it out and paint it. My new boss said it didn't need to be painted. *Power in the wrong hands*, I thought to myself. He was showing his arrogance. What difference did it make to him if they were nice enough to paint it? We were at it again. The room was cleaned and painted. There were glass windows all around the room. They must have been installed so that supervisors could keep an eye on the workers on the floor below. I met the two men who worked as heavy-duty mechanics. They were great and we hit it off right away. The other two who were there didn't like my presence. I found out later they were right-wing union supporters. No matter how hard I tried to be nice to them, they were as cold as ice. Later a woman came over and introduced herself. Lynn. She was an industrial mechanic. We too hit it off. I thought this was going to be great. I could work the next five years here and teach in the plant. I really wanted to keep teaching and be in touch with LU 6500 members.

Meanwhile, back home, Melanie, the last child, was moving out. She had her own apartment, not far from Mom. We were proud of our kids; they were giving life their best shot.

Chapter 114

Jennifer and Mercedes 1999

Sue, Mercedes and Jennifer.

On October 2 at Laurentian University, Jennifer and Mercedes held a Women's History Network conference. The theme that year would be "Women of Steel, Mining Their History."

We focused on the project we had been working on: the women of LU 6500 United Steelworkers of America. The women who were hired at Inco in non-traditional jobs in 1974 and after and the women who worked there during World War II were joined by some of the wives from '78–'79 to make up a panel.

There we were all at one table: women from 1940s, '50s, '74, '78,'79, and '90.

I was so excited about this project, it had fifty interviews so far. Information had been gathered from the company and the union. Our intent was to publish a book that would celebrate the experience of two generations of women at Inco, to hear the stories from the women, and to see the difference in their work environment. Life got in the way.

We were hoping to have the book done by the year 2000. That didn't happen. Maybe I can do it sometime in the future.

Chapter 115

Y2K: No Worries 2000

It seemed everyone at work was worried that the year 2000 would have devastating results on the computers. The programs didn't have the capability to make date changes into 2000. I went with Merv to a gathering at Inco to see what would happen. My superintendent saw me and wanted to know why I was there. I am sure he didn't ask anyone else. I just told him I was Merv's date. Nothing happened when the clock struck 12:01. All was good.

Chapter 116

Divisional Shops and Gassing, and the Frat Boys and My Balls 2000

Cathy's office with her 'balls' hanging on the corkboard.

Merv was ready to retire in February. The company wanted him to come back for two hundred hours to work on the annual emergency preparedness campaign.

It wasn't common for employees to put on a party when the boss retired. Merv's group threw him a grand party. They chipped in and bought him a beautiful statue of orca whales with a plaque inscription that read: *Good Luck to Our Friend Merv*. This said a lot about how his people liked and respected him. Many were sorry to see him go. He retired with thirty-six years seniority. He said his goal was to collect his pension for the same amount of years.

I came down the stairs from my office so I could have coffee with the two young heavy-duty mechanics. They told me that both of them had been sick for a long time and thought it was something in the plant, something they were exposed to while working. One man lifted his shirt to display a red rash with blisters. The other told me had a bowel problem and was always in pain. He had to stay close to a washroom. Both complained of their hearts racing at times. These were young men, what was happening to them? They put in a compensation claim stating it was from the environment they were working in. The company said there was no proof, and that these two were just lazy troublemakers.

"Troublemakers! Oh no, not you guys too." We laughed, but this was no laughing matter.

One day there was a terrible commotion coming from downstairs. I could smell a foul odour. A headache came on fast and my stomach was upset. When I looked down, the men were wearing gas masks. I didn't have one on. I ran to my locker, retrieved my mask, and slapped it on my face. My throat was already sore. When I went down to find out what happened, one of the young men apologized. They had forgotten I was upstairs. They told me a huge cloud of gas had escaped from a large motor they had been working on.

The cloud had gone, and we took off our masks.

"What's happened?" I asked.

"This is what we have been trying to tell management. We believe that someone underground mixed either transmission fluid or something else with the fuel that was in the machine." He lifted his shirt and it was clear the rash was worse. The other man did the same—they both had rashes. The men told me that they had talked to management about this bad practice. Men underground would top up low liquids with whatever was available. The three of us put in a 001, an accident report, the next day at the morning safety meeting. The gassing wasn't even brought up. I told the group what had happened, and the boss said if I didn't have any proof that I was not to talk about it anymore.

The two men and I needed proof. We put in a 079: request for an investigation. My job let me call anyone, anywhere in the world. I called the gas company that supplied Inco with different kinds of fuel and told them what happened. They told me that they do extensive tests to make sure all their products were safe. They also said that no one should ever mix gas with transmission fluid, as it would cause a toxic gas. Well, the shit hit the fan when we put in the 079 and 001. By now my throat was raw from the gas and my voice was croaky as if I had laryngitis. These two young men had been sick for a long time. This was not the first time they had gotten a machine in from underground that was topped up with something other than what was called for. We had to push the issue.

I was sitting at my desk when my boss came storming into my office. He was livid, there for a fight.

"You are moving out of here; you are no longer welcome in divisional shops," he yelled at me, his face turning red.

"The company wants me out of here because I've uncovered something no one wants to deal with." The words croaked out. I must have sounded like a wounded animal.

"You're nothing but a troublemaker!" he bellowed.

"Yes, I guess I am. There are two young men downstairs who have rashes on their bodies and are having trouble with their bowels. We know it's from the toxic soup because the workers are mixing the fluids underground. They have got to stop doing this." My voice was raspy; I could hardly yell.

"You can't prove anything."

"Yes, I can. Look at this." I waved the fact sheets I had received from the gas company. "You're a safety foreman now, and with that title comes responsibilities."

"You had better mind your own business."

"This *is* my business, I got gassed too. It's my responsibility to inform the company and the union that this practice has got to stop."

He told me he was sending me to Azilda to work, thirteen kilometres away.

"Go ahead. If I don't have a job out there for me, I will charge you under the Humans Rights Code for isolating me." He told me to start packing up my stuff and to get rid of the TV and VHS machines.

"Get the fuck out of my office." It came out as a screech. He marched over and placed his knuckles on my desk and leaned over it, trying to intimidate me. He had on one of those black snowmobile jackets on, making him look bigger than he was. He reminded me of a black Michelin tire man.

"I am the boss!" he yelled.

"So what? I am an employee, what's your point?" My crackly little voice wasn't too intimidating.

His face grew red with anger, and he leaned in closer.

"I don't like to be dictated to."

I stood up and placed my knuckles on the desk mirroring him and leaned forward. "Yeah, well, that makes two of us. I don't like to be dictated to either," I squeaked.

"You haven't seen the other side of me."

"And you haven't seen the other side of me either. Don't push me. How would the newspapers like this story of the gassing? That the company knew that the men underground were mixing up this toxic soup. The company has been covering this for years. The right stuff should be readily available underground. This practice is making workers sick. This would make for a great story."

"Oh, like you would put the miners at fault?" he said smugly.

"No, no! It's management that should make sure that all the stuff the miners need is down there and always available." My voice was so strained I could hardly talk.

We three gassed employees went through all the motions—doctors, company doctors, WSIB, union. The outcome was that all three of us were moved to different parts of Inco.

I was headed back to the general engineering offices. My anger was just below the surface, like Mount St. Helens ready to explode. That night I ended up in the clinic with a rash on my breast. The doctor diagnosed it as shingles. He said I was lucky to have caught it in time, as you only have seventy-two hours for the medicine to work. Oh my god, the pain that came with this rash was off the charts. I believed it was from the gassing, it had made my immune system low and I caught this virus. I couldn't wear a bra or a shirt, so I was off on sick pay for three weeks. It should have been WSIB.

I took all my training aids with me to the engineering offices and unpacked them. I didn't get rid of anything. I went for a walk through the building. There were many more cubicles than the last time I was there. I wanted to know where the exits were in case of a fire. It was one giant maze. When I passed one office there were two frat boys sitting inside: my boss and a new, good-looking one. I stopped at the door and leaned on the frame. They both stared at me. I didn't move.

"Yes?" the good-looking frat boy said. "Yes?" he said again. I didn't answer. I just stood there, thinking he might introduce himself, but that would have been too civilized.

"What do you want?" my old prat boss barked.

"Nothing," I said, and gave a smirk. This got under his skin. I didn't care about anything anymore. I had about four more years left, and I was just going to live them out.

"Well, you can leave," he growled.

"I know I can." I waited a few seconds, let out a puffed laugh, gave a shake of my hand in the air and left. I could imagine the conversation after I left. *She is nothing but a troublemaker, see if you can handle her.*

It wasn't long before my new boss, Eric—the other man who was in that room—met me in the hallway. No introduction again. Instead, he got really close to me. He was about six foot three and hovered over me. "I hear you have a lot of balls," he said. I shook my head, thinking, *You have got to be kidding me. This is how you greet a new woman employee, you ask her about her balls.* "You want to see my balls, you got it." I pushed past him to my new office, the one that was painted lilac. I loved the colour.

That night at home I dug through the toys and pulled out two tennis balls. I put them in a nylon sock, got out a pair of black stretch pants and situated the balls just right between my legs. Merv didn't think it was a good idea to wear them to work like that. I thought it was appropriate. I pulled them out and brought them to work, pinning them on my cork bulletin board with a sign that read "my balls."

It was obvious that the company did not want me to go back into the plants. There were no 6500 members where I was working.

Over the next few months, I showed up at the safety talks and rolled my eyes at anything the new boss said. I thought about his stupid comment about my balls. The men in this department were really nice.

Everyone in this department received a letter asking what their job description was. It had been over a year now. I held the instructor job, but I was not allowed to go into the plants to teach my brothers and sisters from 6500. I was told I didn't have a job description. The company had buried me and hoped that I would live out my time without stirring up the members.

Eric called me into his office and pointed to a round table with two chairs. "Why didn't you write a job description?" he asked.

"I don't know what my job is anymore, so the job description should be written by the company, not me. I want to go into the plants to teach but I was told no," I said.

"Just write down what you do," he said.

"No, you tell me what my job is." I shook my head.

He was getting upset with me. He got up and went back behind his desk. "What's the matter, Cathy, are you scared or just insecure?" By the look on his face he was proud of this comment.

"Well, I looked up your name on the company's system. You don't have a job description either. What's the matter, Eric, are you scared or are you just insecure?" I smiled.

"This meeting is over, go back to your office."

I did.

Chapter 117

My Twenty-Five-Year Service Party 2000

My twenty-five-year seniority party at Inco finally arrived. 385 people were to attend, with dates. The company had to split us up into three nights.

Merv had a surprise for me. A long black limousine was parked in front of our house. He had Sue, the woman who had started the same day as me, come over to our place and we were to go together. We also stopped and picked up a few more people. What a great thing for him to do.

It was a memorable night. I'd had too much to drink when a comedian came to our table and asked if we knew anything he could make into a joke. I told him the president of Inco was now Ron Aelick and the cutter's name was Hiscock and he could use his imagination. This became the joke of the evening.

Bruce asked me to run in the election for a smaller position. I really didn't want to; my heart was not in it. I had lost my belief in the union.

There was so much animosity at the hall it was hard to handle. Gary would call me out during meetings, telling everyone I was married to the enemy because Merv was on staff. He made fun of Mick, my reporter friend, calling him a draft dodger, which he was, but not in a negative way. I stood at the mic defending Mick and Merv, only to be drowned out by some ignorant drunken union brothers. I told them that Merv had gotten a letter from Leo Gerard, head of District 6, thanking him for his actions when the men were killed on the train accident on the CP Rail track. I told them that he was one of the men who went to talk to the widows and the children about their loved ones when employees were killed in work accidents. I told them that he was more of a man than any in that room. They sent out cat calls, calling me a slut and a whore, and Gary, now president, stood on the stage and laughed at this behaviour. This is where the union had gone.

Chapter 118

Women in Motion and 9/11 2001

I stayed mostly to myself in my lilac office. I did a lot of research on anything I thought might be interesting. I was still buying movies and making safety talks for the foreman.

My friend Ruby asked if I would join her and Sharon at a conference for young girls in grades 8–10. The company that went around doing these presentations was called Women in Motion. Ruby is a great friend of mine. She is also our financial advisor. She's always stood up for women and understands the importance of teaching girls to strive for their highest potential. Sharon was an English teacher, and one of Sudbury's MPPs, a Member of Provincial Parliament.

I was to talk to the young girls about working at Inco and suggest to them that the trades might be something they would be interested in. The talk was a success, so we decided to put a similar one on for the following year's conference. We organized it and came up with a name: Women of the Future.

Merv called and told me that two planes had just hit the twin towers. He said I should tell my boss and turn on the TV (the TV I was told to get rid of, but didn't). I ran to Eric's office and informed him of this horrible tragedy. He called and got the crew together. All day long people came to watch the TV. Some cried while other shook their heads in disbelief. We watched over and over as the towers fell, killing thousands of women, men, children, and firefighters. I watched the office people's reactions, covering their mouths when they saw the people running for their lives away from the toxic smoke that filled the air when the towers fell. It was a sad day.

Chapter 119

Could They Make It Any Clearer That They Hold the Power?
2001

Miniature wire bar.

Miniature anode.

Every year the pensioners put on a great maintenance party. It was held at the Caruso Club in Sudbury. It was owned by the Italians and opened in 1947/'48. It has two large halls, one upstairs and one downstairs. Around 1500 people were packed in. 100 prizes were donated by big businesses that dealt with Inco. I had never been to one and wanted to go. It used to be a stag with strippers. A few years ago, Merv told Ashcroft, then president at Inco, that he would not send any of his female security guards if there were strippers, and there would be grievances if they couldn't go. Women were now in the maintenance department too and they didn't want the strippers.

I asked to buy a ticket, and the frat-boy boss Eric said there were only a certain number and I couldn't have one. That didn't stop me; I called around until I got one. It was a great party.

The anode department at the Copper Cliff copper refinery produced its last cast in September. They had built a new casting wheel at the smelter. In celebration, they cast little anodes 6 × 6 inches that came with a stand. I wanted one so badly, so I called the woman in charge of passing them out. In her *I am the boss* voice she told me I would not be getting one. I told her I had worked in the anode for fourteen years, that I was one of the first women there. None of this meant anything to her. She said no and hung up. I had a few names for her in my head. To think a woman would do this to another woman when it meant so much.

I told Bruce, and he too was surprised the woman wouldn't give me one.

Meanwhile, a friend of mine who worked in the first aid department at the copper refinery got one.

She and her husband Frank were splitting up and she asked him if he wanted anything. He said he wanted the little anode. He also worked in the first aid department, but in another plant. She told him to take it. Frank worked for Merv and Merv had told him that I was shafted and didn't get a small anode. He arrived at our home with a box wrapped in Christmas paper. Frank stayed while I opened it. I began to cry when I pulled out the little anode. He had made me a very happy person. I proudly displayed it on the fireplace. He wasn't gone long when there was a knock on the door. It was Bruce holding a white box, similar to the one the little anode came in. He stayed while I took my second anode out of the box and displayed it beside the other one. This was the true meaning of Christmas. I gave the finger salute to the woman who wouldn't give me one.

Chapter 120

Different Kinds of Women, and Saying Goodbye to Jennifer Keck 2002

Ruby, Sharon, and I put on the Women of the Future conference as planned. It was a great success.

But sometimes I felt like I was at the bottom of a well with thousands of spiders, and I hate spiders. I spent most of my days in my office by myself working on safety talks.

Some of the office women had befriended me and invited me into their camp. They were nice but they belonged a different culture than me. They didn't watch the news, they didn't know much about politics, and most of them quilted and sewed. We didn't have much in common.

They invited me to lunch on Fridays. I would find it a little uncomfortable when a woman would leave to go to the washroom, because the rest would talk about her. One of the women who was having trouble with her daughter left one day and the things they said could have come from a soap opera. It was hard to get my head around why. I made a comment that they should wait until she got back to the table and say what they said to her face. Not a good move, Cat: the daggers came out. I never told her what they said.

Jennifer Keck and I met for lunch a few times. It was so much better talking to a woman like her. She was off to get her chemo treatment. I wish I knew that I could have sat with her during that time. She never asked and I just assumed it was a private thing. My belief was that she was going to pull through and all was going to be well. Soon the day came when she went into the hospital and she wasn't going to come out. I went every day to see her. Visitors were on a schedule, and I did just ten minutes at a time. I really loved this woman. I walked down the hall and saw her dad sitting at the window. There was someone in the room, her sister. I waited my turn. His eyes were filled with tears. He looked up and said, "Why can't that be me in there? I am old and I am ready to go."

I gave him a hug. "We have to play the cards we are given," I said.

Finally, it was my turn. "Hi Jen. It's Cat."

"Hi Cathy Mulroy," she said, her words muffled by an oxygen mask. "Can you do me a favour and remove my mask and wipe my nose, it feels like it's running."

With pride I did as I was asked.

"I am going to sing to you, my friend," I said, and she smiled. Using the melody from the song "Thanks for the Memories" by Bob Hope, I sang this special version just for her:

Thanks for the memories
Of dragon boat races
And women's celebrations
Of videos and conferences and marches in the street
We thank you, Ms. Jen

Thanks for the memories
Of smooth red wine
And sparkling times
Of women with their fight and Take Back the Night
We thank you, Ms. Jen

Thanks for the memories
Of women and our stories
Standing up for our rights
Let's not forget, Ms. Rogers, fight
We thank you, Ms. Jen.

We laughed and we cried. I knew I would never see her again. I leaned over.

"Jen, if I don't see you again, I will see you on the other side."

I kissed her goodbye. She died that day.

This was the last thing my body and mind could handle. My emotions spiralled down, down, down. Into that well I went. The song "Fields of Gold" by Eva Cassidy played at her funeral, which was held at Laurentian University, and the auditorium was packed. Every time I heard the song I broke down. My grief turned to more anger. My doctor explained my physical problems, my digestive problems, were connected with the depression and anxiety. I felt I was at the end. I couldn't take it anymore.

Chapter 121

Dad and the Nursing Home, and Bruce and Brenda Get Married

Bruce and Brenda

My dad had to go to a nursing home, and that whole thing was a nightmare. Merv and I knew his time on this earth was coming to an end. He wanted to see his family one more time out in Saskatchewan.

Three weeks before the trip, I noticed he was slurring his words. He had a hard time walking. He wasn't his usual clear-headed self. He kept saying they were giving him drugs in goop (apple sauce). I thought he might be losing it. When I asked to see his records, the nurse was reluctant to show me, but had to. I had power of attorney.

I found out that he was being given a drug, Percocet, a few times a day in his goop. I went into a rage. How could they be drugging him? I was never informed of this. I demanded to see this doctor. A meeting was held, and I asked Bruce to come and scribe the meeting. We all sat in a room; they thought Bruce was a lawyer. I didn't say he was a lawyer, but I certainly didn't say he wasn't. Now I had a reputation at the home as—you guessed it: a troublemaker.

I got him off the pills, which took three weeks, and we were off to Saskatchewan. He wouldn't have remembered going if he was still on those pills.

I went to see my dad every day, sometimes twice a day. Once he had bruises on his face and a few broken ribs but wouldn't tell me how it happened. The home said he fell. I wished I was retired so he could live with us. I became active in the home with a few other women whose parents were in there. We started a family council to keep an eye on what was going on. That Christmas, we decided all 250 residents were going to get a gift. We went to stores and got donations: candy, chocolate bars, pens, pad, and calendars for everyone. Even the plastic bags were donated. We bagged them and handed them out, every resident received a gift. We were very proud.

Bruce retired at the end of the year. I was all alone now. He and Brenda were married around New Year's at the Steelworkers Hall. She was a wonderful woman and didn't have a jealous bone about my friendship with Bruce. All four of us became great friends.

Chapter 122

Cancer
2002

I really tried not to get involved with anyone at work and just kept to myself. I received a letter from the hospital that said there was another growth on my ovary that had the same makeup as ovarian cancer. With Jen just dying I was scared; I didn't tell anyone at work, not even the women I had lunch with. One woman said she didn't want me going for lunch anymore because I was too depressed and I was bringing them down. When you're outside of a group, some women can be really mean. All of them together wouldn't have made one Jennifer.

Merv and I had our private cries waiting to hear what I should do next. Three months later I got a call saying there had been a mistake and the techie had read it wrong. "Sorry" that the growth had crystallized and was not cancer.

Those three months were a blur. The damage to my mental state had been done. Now I had to crawl out of that dark well. I had become a living pressure cooker. My response to everything was met with anger and I was very aggressive. It was best if I stayed in my office and didn't associate with anyone.

Chapter 123

Strike and Elections, and the Gang from '78/'79 get-together. 2003

Women of Steel picket line 2003. Inco 100 years wrong.

Contract time again, and of course, at the same time, the union executive elections. Who wants to change the executive board during negotiations? *I* did. My faith and trust in the union were gone, in the same way my belief in Christianity was lost or when I found out there was no Santa Claus. More stress, but I will not break. My doctor told me my body was starting to give up.

I sat at my desk reading over a flier. "Executive election cancelled; all positions acclaimed. April 1st." This was for our local union elections.

This was a real April Fool's joke. No one, absolutely no one ran against them. We were all fools.

June and we were out on strike again. The proposal was an insult. Inco wanted to cut drug benefits for active employees, retirees, and survivors (widowers). The bargaining committee recommended unanimously that we reject this offer. We were up against a wall. We had to strike or lose what we already had.

My description of this one was: "How not to organize a strike." Many of our members felt Inco had orchestrated a strike to save money and to allow maintenance work to be done. They wanted to take away pensioner's benefit packages. This was so wrong. Pensioners couldn't even vote. Inco had always cried broke. They wanted to take the rights away for employees to bid on other jobs in the Inco operation. Some workers didn't want to stay on the same job for thirty years. Some wanted to move around and learn new jobs. It's okay for management people to go all over the world and find out what the company does, but they wanted us to stay in one position, so we were easier to control.

The old boys' club was running the union. This strike was nothing like the strike in '78/'79, if you even wanted to call it a strike. There were no rallies. Most gates were not even manned. We didn't have enough vacation time to be off for three months. At the beginning, we wouldn't let anyone in the plants. Inco went to court and got an injunction preventing the stopping of vehicles at the lines. We watched as big machines went through to do the maintenance work. What we did get was a summary covering criminal law controls on picket lines, police power, injunctions, trespassing, the law on a picket line, and police presence on the picket line. It went on for thirteen pages. Even our little strike pay cheques went through Inco's payroll into our bank accounts. What the fuck!

The women of 6500 put a Women's Day picket line together. Remember that pin that Inco gave us? "Inco 100 years strong." I picked up a bright pink Bristol board and wrote in big black letters: "Inco 100 years wrong." We had a good laugh and the sign stayed up for the duration of the strike. The new buzz word was "collaboration." Both the union and company were using it. This was a dirty word as far as I was concerned.

I could never understand this company's attitude. They cried broke, yet you would look around the yards and see pieces of machinery left out in the rain to rust. So much waste, along with their bad investments in Indonesia, New Caledonia, and Guatemala—all of this on the back of the workers in Sudbury for 100 years. Yes, 100 years *wrong*.

There was so much negativity around I needed something to bring us up. I organized the old gang from the strike in '78/'79. About twenty-five spent a wonderful weekend at Yesterday's Resort on the beautiful French River. The theme song was "Yesterday"—*I believe in yesterday* ...

These were people who believed in the same things I did. Some brought T-shirts and buttons and posters from that time and shared stories of *do you remember when* ... This weekend lifted my spirit and we all went back to our lives.

Chapter 124

The Day the Lights Went Out

On August 14, 2003 at 4:10 p.m. there was a blackout. There were widespread power outages throughout parts of the northeastern and midwestern United States and Ontario.

The day started off like any other summer day. We were still on strike, so I had a lot of time to spend with my dad. At the age of eighty-nine, he sat in his wheelchair under a tree in the back of York Extendicare nursing home, his elbows resting on his thighs, his face buried in his hands, taking a nap. I watched the other residents who dotted the sidewalk in their wheelchairs. At 3:45 I reached over and gave my dad a gentle shake. We had to go in; we had an appointment for another kind of wheelchair. We got to his room and Matt, the man my dad shared the room with, was ready for me to take him downstairs for a cigarette like we did every day. I told my dad I would be back in a few minutes. The elevator was occupied with two passengers, an eighty-six-year-old woman who was visiting her husband and seventy-something Diane who was at the back with her oxygen tank. "Smoking floor," I said to the elderly woman. Matt repeated, "Smoking floor," and we laughed. The doors of the elevator closed. We began to descend, and it gave a jerk. Then everything went black.

The woman visitor began to panic. "Oh my God, oh my God. What happened? We are going to die!" she yelled.

Poor Matt cried out, "What do you mean we are going to die?"

"Shut up! Both of you. We are not going to die. The power has just gone out and the elevator has stopped." I tried to stay calm. "How do you know we are not going to die?" the visiting woman screeched.

"Aah, well," I stuttered, "because God, if there is a God, likes me. He or she is not going to let me leave this earth in an elevator."

"Well …" she said, a little calmer. "I believe in God."

"Well, that's great," I said. "Anyone else in the elevator believe in God?"

The other two grunted yes.

"Okay, that's great," I said in an upbeat voice. "Do some praying then."

I pulled out my cell phone; it said "no service." "Great, I buy a cell phone in case of emergency; here we are in an emergency and it says no service." But it did light up, so it wasn't totally dark; there was no emergency lighting in the elevator. As a safety instructor this made me angry, but I would deal with that later.

The elderly lady had become distraught and was crying that the elevator was going to drop. I told her that only happens in the movies.

I reached over to reassure her. I could feel the sweat on her arms. "Look, I told you that God likes me. He gave us light on my phone. Look …" I said, holding the light up to her face.

I yelled out, hoping someone would hear me. "Hello up there! Hello, there are people stuck in the elevator."

A gentle voice came back: "Hello, is everyone okay?"

"Yes, we are all okay," I said.

"Who is down there?" she asked.

"It's Cathy Mulroy and there are three others in here with me."

I heard her say in a lower voice, "Oh no, it's Cathy Mulroy."

I gave her the names of the other people.

"Cathy … how much oxygen does Diane have?"

"What! How much oxygen does Diane have in her tank?" Thoughts of Diane running out of oxygen and having a heart attack went through my mind, all of it happening in the blackness of the elevator.

"*I don't know!*" I said. "I can't see how much she has because you have *no emergency lighting* in this elevator; it's totally black in here. You are supposed to have back-up lights when power goes out." I used the light on the cell phone and read that Diane's tank was three-quarters full. That was a relief.

Matt began to fart.

"Who is farting?" the older women demanded.

"I am," Mat admitted in a mumbled voice.

"Well, stop it." She went over and began hitting him.

I could see the outline of Matt. He raised his arms to protect himself, yelling at her to stop.

She yelled back, "It's bad enough we are stuck in here, we don't have to smell you too."

"Stop it, both of you." I took control. "You guys are acting like kids. Lady, you get back over to where you were and leave Matt alone. If he has to fart, he has to fart." We just had to put up with whatever happened. It was getting really hot in that blackened elevator. The old woman was panting like a dog. Beads of sweat rolled off my forehead. We needed some water.

"Let's sing," I said. So we sang. The old lady began to panic again, banging her fist on the door. I told her the fire department was on its way. It just took a little time for them to get there.

"You said that an hour ago," she said tearfully.

It was another half hour before I heard the *honk honk* of the firetruck. A little rattle of the doors and they were opened. A swish of fresh air hit my face, and it was awesome. Fresh and cool air.

We looked like four drowned rats with our hair wet and stringy. We were perspiring profusely. The nurse brought over a wheelchair for the older lady, asking her if she was okay. She said it wasn't any trouble at all, that she wasn't even scared. I shook my head. I just wanted to get out and see my dad.

They gave us water and I pushed Matt back to his room. My dad wondered what had taken so long. He told me I missed the meeting about the wheelchair, something about the elevators not working. Matt and I smiled. I told him the story. When I was leaving, I took the stairs. There was a line of management people waiting for me by the door. "I will be back tomorrow at 9 a.m. Have the emergency lighting in that elevator or I am going to the newspapers." I said

"Oh, we do have emergency lighting, it's in a box in the storage area, along with a generator," the head manager said.

"A lot of good it's doing in the storage area." I shook my head, disgusted with them.

The next morning at nine, I took the elevator and saw that the emergency lighting had been installed. I was now a troublemaker here at the home. The way I saw it, the trouble was already there, they just never addressed it.

Chapter 124

The So-Called Strike Is Over

The summer was coming to an end. The maintenance strike shutdown was almost done. A tentative agreement had been reached. *Ha-ha-ha-ha* was all I could say. Health care benefits for retirees was protected and put in writing. No kidding, an agreement will be put in writing. Fuck! I had lost twelve thousand dollars. There was an increase in wages and COLA (cost of living adjustment). The best thing we got out of this after three months was—wait for it—the title "Health, Safety and Environment." SHE will now be HSE. They put this in writing too. What a joke.

A full-page thank-you note was in our contract book addressed to the general manager of Inco. It read: "Thank you for the dignified and professional manner you exhibited daily crossing the picket line."

If I could have thrown up, I would have.

I'm not sure why I bothered to go to the union meeting. As usual, I sat in my favourite chair, on the left beside the microphone.

On August 28, the vote was 62.3 percent (with an 80 percent turnout) to accept the new contract the bargaining committee unanimously agreed on. Many young members opposed the contract, saying there was nothing in it for them. They were right. I turned it down on principle.

Many of us felt the strike had been orchestrated by Inco to save money and allow maintenance work to get done. Many workers said they were not happy with the contract but felt they had no alternative but to vote for it, given the difficult financial circumstances they faced. I wanted to know why our strike pay was distributed through Inco's payroll. The union said it was just easier.

Cathy at the microphone during the Union meeting.

I went to the microphone and said, "This whole strike was a step backwards, given that the strike was convenient for Inco to save on the costs of wages, insurance, and compensation payments. I feel we were railroaded into this strike, and railroaded again into accepting this deal. The bargaining committee presented the tentative agreement information to the media as if it were a done deal before we even read about it. You said we didn't lose much money in three months. Well, I lost twelve thousand dollars. I think twelve thousand dollars is a lot of money." The young crowd cheered. It had been a long time since I got cheered at the union hall. It felt good, but a little too late for me to fight anymore.

Chapter 125

Raging Grannies Protest

Donna, Heather and Cathy in front of the smelter gate.

Cathy granny.

In October, I received a call from a lawyer. He said communities around the world were joining forces in the first-ever global day of action against the Canadian company Inco Limited for its poor environmental track record. Protests were taking place in Port Colborne; Nova Scotia; Vancouver; PEI; Indonesia; New Caledonia; Guatemala; New York; London, England; Australia; Japan; and Wales. Inco was still the worst mining polluter in Canada. I told the lawyer to call the union hall, LU 6500. They could organize something. He said they had, and after many calls the union would not get involved. My shoulders slumped down. I was not surprised.

He said, "Joan Kuyek asked me to call you. She said if anyone could pull something off it would be you. There are protests all over the world, and we need your help in Sudbury." I'm not sure if that was a compliment or if they were hitting the bottom of the barrel for help. He handed the phone to Joan.

"Hi Cat. We need you to organize a protest to bring the attention to the people on the pollution Inco has done around the world, especially in Sudbury. We have contacted the union and they don't want anything to do with the world day of protest. They will not call any of their members."

"Why am I not surprised. When do you need this protest for? I guess you want it to happen at the same time all over the world?"

"Yes, two days," she said.

"Two days? I'll get back to you." Later that night, lying in bed, it came to me. I knew the Raging Grannies.

The Raging Grannies began in British Columbia. A group of women were worried about the presence of US Navy nuclear-powered ships in the Victoria harbour. They felt they posed potential health and environmental risks to the city, so they dressed up in granny costumes and protested. The Raging Grannies became a popular way of a peaceful protest to get a message out.

We had our own group of grannies in Sudbury, a bunch of social activists. I could only get three together in such a short time. I called all the media I knew. I dressed in my granny outfit and was headed out the door when the phone rang. It was Cory, head of Inco's public affairs and their spokesperson. Cory and I had always got along.

"Cathy, what are you doing?" he asked.

I told him about the protests all over the world. Inco was the company they decided to educate people about, because of all the pollution it had made and was still making.

"Oh! Cathy, is it going to be big?" There was concern in his voice.

"No, Cory, not to worry. It is a demonstration, a vigil," I said.

"Cathy, you are going to turn my hair grey," he said.

I laughed. "Do what I do, Cory: dye it."

A poem/song came to me as I exited my car. I stopped and scribbled it down on my notepad: "On Top of Old Smokey," referring to the twelve-hundred-and-fifty-foot superstack that pours hundreds of tons of sulphuric acid along with other goodies out of its top. More media than protesters were at the vigil. Great newspeople.

The three grannies, Donna, Heather, and I, sang songs as the small group of protesters joined in. The media took pictures and the story was in the newspaper. I did my job.

Chapter 126

Dad's Death 2003

Creighton Mine.

Patrick G. Mulroy

The nurse asked if I wanted to sign my dad's DNR: "Do Not Resuscitate." "Well, don't ask me, ask him," I said, pointing to the little man lying in the fetal position on the hospital bed. She asked me to ask him.

I leaned in close to him. "Dad, the nurse wanted to know: if your heart stops, do you what them to take the paddles, shock your heart into starting again so you don't die?" He lifted his head up a little and said, "By all means."

"There's your answer."

That was two and a half years ago.

After my twelve-year battle with Veterans Affairs, my dad finally got a pension. He now suffered with post-traumatic stress disorder. He had become weaker in the last years and suffered emotionally when reliving stories of what happened during the war. The pension wasn't much, but enough to pay half the nursing home costs. This way my brother, the one who was hit by the drunk driver and crippled up, could stay in my dad's house. We didn't have to sell it to cover the cost of the nursing home.

The phone rang at 7:30 a.m. from the nursing home. I was told my dad was not well and we should get up there as soon as possible. I called the family: my sister in Ottawa, my son in Toronto.

Dad was in his bed; his breathing was very heavy. He was in a semi-conscious state. He could still communicate by a few grunts. His temperature was very high. I asked for ice packs. The staff told me it didn't matter much. He was going to die.

"I know, just get me the ice packs. I want his mind as clear as possible when he leaves this earth. This may happen if I can get the fever down." She got them. I placed the ice packs under his armpits and in the groin area. I kept telling him I loved him and that he could not die yet—Sandy and Peppy were not in Sudbury, and he wanted to go home to die. Every once in a while, I patted his chest and asked if he was still with us, and he grunted. *Hang in there.* My daughter Melanie and I slept beside his bed and he made it through the night. He was worse in the morning, but the fever was gone.

The director of care at York was working on getting an ambulance so we could take him home to die. At 2:00 I told the nurse that if there wasn't an ambulance there in half an hour, we were loading him into the car and taking him home. She was to get the paperwork ready. At 2:15 the ambulance arrived, and the elevator was locked out for us. His friends from the home waited and said their goodbyes as we pushed him into the elevator. The ambulance driver said he would follow me. Somehow, he went another way and got lost.

I waited outside my dad's home, wondering what the hell had happened to the ambulance with my dying father in it. Minutes seemed like hours, but finally there they were. I was hoping he didn't die en route. They placed him in a bed that was set up in his living room and put him on oxygen.

The October sun shone through the window on his face. He always loved the sun. I went over to him and whispered in his ear, "Dad, you are in your own home, in your own bed, in your living room. It's just what you wanted. Anytime you are ready, you can go. If you want to hold on another half hour, I am going to take a shower. While I was gone, he died. Melanie said the sun was on him. He took his last breath and a dark cloud passed in front of the sun. I called the coroner's office and they said they couldn't get hold of him. Well, we weren't going anywhere. Five minutes later, red flashing lights were coming from outside, and when I opened the door three paramedics ran towards me with a gurney.

"Slow down." I lifted my hand and smiled. "He's dead."

"Move aside," he ordered.

"He is in the living room." I pointed to where my dad's body was lying.

"Do you have the paperwork, his DNR?"

"Yes." I handed him the papers.

"These are not the right ones. These are for the nursing home," he said, handing them back to me.

"Well, that's where I got them, they gave me these," I said, shaking the papers. It turns out there needed to be different sets of DNR papers, but I wasn't sure which ones I needed.

Someone else was at the door, two police officers. They entered the house and began asking us questions, the same ones over and over. The police asked what happened, how he had gotten home.

I felt good that my dad had died in his own bed. Something he had asked me to do for him many times over the last year. Giggling over a few spots in my story, I told them about the ambulance getting lost. Two more police officers showed up. My brother brought out the beer and the family toasted my dad.

After the third time with the same questions, I said, "Why don't you four just sit together and I will answer your questions at the same time instead of individually."

"This is an interrogation," the policewoman said. "Why aren't you having a beer like everyone else?"

"I don't like that kind of beer. The mood I'm in, I don't think I should drink and drive. I have a low tolerance." She didn't ask much more. The hours passed as we waited for the coroner. Three paramedics and four police officers sat with us while my brother's pit bull cuddled up to them. Just after 8:00 all the paperwork was in order, the coroner pronounced that my dad had passed away, and his body was removed in a black body bag. I turned to Merv and thanked him for everything he had done to help me with my dad. I thanked him for getting him to the house so he could die in his own home, his last wish. I could never have done it on my own. I can't find the words to describe what I felt like giving my dad this gift. I was happy I kept my promise.

Cathy's dad was a World War II paratrooper.

Chapter 127

My Last Stand
2004

Cathy's office door.

    With thirty years seniority I can leave with a full pension no matter my age, thanks to Dave Patterson and his team, the Wives, and all who fought against Inco in the '78/'79 strike. I would be forty-nine years old when I was eligible, but because of the strike I owed the company six months. I would turn fifty when I was eligible. Did I want to go? That was the question. The song "Did You Ever Have the Feeling That You Wanted to Stay?" by Jimmy Durante played in my head:

Did you ever get the feeling that you wanted to go
But still had the feeling that you wanted to stay
You knew it was right. Wasn't wrong
Still you knew you wouldn't be long.
Go or stay, stay or go.

I stood in the storage area and looked over the years of work I had researched, created, and presented. I had made my own job description. There were hundreds of safety talks combined with many safety videos. I was proud of my library. There were also many memories of all the good times with my boss Michael, and my co-workers Sam and Tom.

After moving from a large training facility to a small office, and with the whole library in a storage area, it needed a good clean-up. I was not going to let anyone say I left all this stuff for someone else to deal with.

Setting up large garbage bins, I began to work. No one bothered me; I was happy. My New Year's resolution was to stay out of trouble. No more protests, no more marches. No more fighting with management. Just live out my days, then decide to go or to stay. There was little assumption a good job would come my way in the future.

One day I was stopped at a red light at the bottom of a hill near the Sudbury Costco. The Kingsway ran the other way. In my rear-view mirror I could see a black truck sliding towards me—his brakes were locked and he was still coming. I braced myself and let my foot off the brake, waiting for the impact. It was just a little bump. Both the truck driver and I exited our vehicles. Neither one had any damage.

That night I could hardly move my right arm. I knew that the vertebrae in my upper spine had popped out once again, flaring up my old injury. I needed physiotherapy, chiropractic care, and acupuncture. I stayed at work for a few days, but I needed an everyday workout and rest. There was no first aid room in the engineering building and I was told I could get a doctor's revisit slip from Inco's WSIB, which was in my building. The woman sitting behind the desk told me there were no revisit slips there. I remembered her from the 1970s. She used to go to the Village Steps dances, and I heard she had had a crush on Lloyd. She didn't like me, maybe she held that against me. As far as I was concerned, she could have had him. I drove over to the smelter and was told by the first aid attendant that there were revisit slips in the WSIB office. After seeing the doctor, she agreed I should go off work and put the time into healing the injury.

At the end of January, I was off on WSIB so I called them and told them I would be going onto vacation pay because we were going to Cuba and I didn't want to double dip. The vacation had been booked for months.

When I got back to work, I was told that I was being investigated by the board. They had received a letter saying that they were informed that I was in a motor vehicle accident. The call came from Inco's claims administrator office, the same woman who told me there were no revisit slips. I would not receive any money until they had done an investigation.

An investigator showed up in my office. He did everything but call me a liar to my face. I told him the truth about the truck and the bump, and told him to check my car to see if there was any damage. I told him all of it: the ovarian cancer scare, my dad dying, the loss of my friend, my gut hurting, and my depression. I showed him copies of the doctor and physiotherapist reports and all the rest. It proved I was doing my best to get back to normal. He said that this injury was because of the car accident. My argument was that if I wasn't already injured, a bump like that would not have caused a problem.

His proof was that the WSIB woman had overheard another woman talking about my car accident in the lunchroom. She felt it was her job to turn me in, suggesting I was lying to the compensation board. I was beyond angry. So much for staying out of trouble, so much for no more fights. The gloves were back on. Not only was I again in a depression, my fucking back and arm hurt.

She sat with a smug smile on her face when I entered her office.

"Why would you do such a thing? Calling the board and telling them I am a liar."

"I was just doing my job." She pushed a few papers around on her desk.

"You could have called me in and asked for my side of the story. It's obvious what your intentions were. This was personal. There has got to be a law you have broken. Whatever it is, breaking confidentiality, a denial of my rights, I am going to find out, and you have not heard the last from me."

Back in my office, I calmed down and asked another woman to go to lunch with me. We met in the hallway. The woman I had just had words with was approaching from the opposite direction and crossed over in front of me. She stood about five-foot-nine or -ten; I was five-one. She stood in front of me, hands on her hips in a threating posture.

I didn't move. "This is plain harassment, you don't scare me," I said.

She rolled her eyes, made a huffing noise and walked around me. I complained to my boss. He shrugged his shoulders and dismissed it. Okay, let's get out the law books. I submitted a 079 incident report on harassment. By now I knew this law well. I requested a meeting with her and her boss. I asked for a copy of the Code of Ethical and Professional

Standards in Human Resource Management so I could read it. I did. In short, it read "acquire and disseminate information through ethical and responsible means (not done here), ensure only appropriated information is used (again, didn't happen here), investigate the accuracy of the information (didn't happen here), safeguard restricted of confidential information (again, not here). There was a lot more.

While I worked on my presentation for this new battle, my boss came to my office and stood in the frame of the door. He was a big man, so he filled a good portion of it. He leaned his elbows on the frame and held his hands up. I had only been working for this guy for a while, as the other one had retired.

"You are not to socialize with anyone in this building." He barked out his order. "You are to stay in here unless you have to use the washroom; you can no longer leave your office. I went by here ten times and you were not in your office."

"Well, if you can go out of your office ten times, why can't I get out of my office ten times? This is what is called discrimination. One person can and the other can't."

His face grew red with anger. "You'll do as you're told."

I laughed as I got up from my desk and walked toward him.

"You should read the Human Rights Code. The law is very clear that it is against the law to isolate a worker. I am going out of my office right now," I said, being as defiant as I could be.

He puffed his chest out and wouldn't move, blocking the door, using his size as intimidation.

"I am going to tell you one more time. I want you to move so I can leave my office."

"No," he said.

I raised my voice so other people in the nearby cubicles could hear.

"I feel you are harassing me. I want your behavior to stop." I went through the procedure of harassment.

He didn't move.

"This is becoming more than just harassment," I continued, "but an assault, and I will go to the police; yes, outside Inco, and maybe the newspaper needs another story from me." He moved and let me by, and I smiled at him.

"I mean it," he snarled. "You are no longer allowed to socialize with anyone or go to the other side of the building. Is that clear?"

With a wave of my hand I answered, "Put it in writing," as I walked past him. When I got back to my office, I saw the email. "Holy shit, what an idiot, he put everything he said in writing. Love to have evidence." I sent it home.

After a short time, I decided to go out of my office again. I waited in the storage area where I could peek out to see my office. Sure enough, there he was. He went into my office and was out in a short minute, leaving like a thief in the night. I checked my computer: he had deleted the email.

I went to his office and stood in the same stance in his doorframe as he had done in mine. Being a little smaller it was a stretch.

"I saw you come out of my office. I checked and you deleted the email you sent me," I said.

"Did I?" He posed it as a question, so high and mighty.

"Yes, you did, but I already sent it home." I began to leave then, but acting like Colombo I turned to say one last thing. "You told me I couldn't leave my room unless I had to use the washroom. That back-to-work slip I gave you from the doctor and physiotherapist, you should have read it better before you made those comments. It stated that I am to get up and walk around every fifteen to twenty minutes. You are denying me the recommendation from my doctor. This again is discrimination and harassment. I will be filing both charges against you. I'm still contemplating the assault charges. There will be no white flag above my door," I said, taking that line from a song on the radio. He didn't say another word.

The big guns were out, and I didn't have Bruce to help me. I was on my own.

A letter came in from WSIB saying that I was denied because of lack of medical information. I had pages of medical information. There it was in writing after all these years of fighting for a job description. WSIB felt I could do my job based on the job description that they obtained from that woman and her boss. In the letter, the inspector stated that this job description had not changed since 1991.

"This is the job I hold, but it's not the job I do. So how can you say I was fit for the job because of the job description? Your evidence is weak; this is not my job. If this is my job, I can go into the plants. So, let's see what the company will say about this."

The company had pulled my rate of pay off of the computer and that's how they determined what my job was. I asked for a copy. At a meeting I told the company that if this was my job description then I should be going into the plants and instructing 6500 members on safety. Why was I not able to do this? I wanted to start going into the plants right away. I knew quite well the company and the union did not want me talking to our members. After the last four years of being buried and asking for my job description,

I was excited. A few days later, another letter came with more information. It stated that my job had been negotiated with upper management, and they had created a job just for me as a modified worker. I called for another meeting and asked if they had proof of this. They showed me the letter.

"Just to inform you, the information you used had a gag order on it. I have proof that the company and I signed that gag order. You just broke another law," I said.

I added the information to my binder. I told them that they were not complying with the laws under the Code of Ethical and Professional Standards on Human Resource Management.

So many lies and so much deceit, the stress was getting the better of me. I informed the company that I was going to the media, the only move I had left. After that, a member of our local union called and asked if he could talk to me. He told me a joint committee was being set up called the Conflict Resolution Committee. Art represented the union and Jody represented the company. The vice president of Inco had sent out a memo to some people and I asked for a copy.

Conflict of interest and business conduct surveys are intended to ensure that every employee of Inco conducts him or herself ethically, in accordance with applicable law and in accordance with Inco policies. In many instances, the codes of conduct applied to off-the-job activities as well as on-the-job. Each of us encounters business situations that call for the fundamental behaviour of good judgment, honesty, integrity, and respect. If something were to happen, all information is to be disclosed and the review board is left to determine if an actual conflict exists.

On April 12, 2004, I submitted a 001 and 079 against the WSIB woman. We were to sit down with the committee to resolve this. She booked off sick: stress. There wouldn't be any investigation on her booking off by any insurance company or board. *No!* She will get her full wages while she's off, because she's staff. What a cowardly thing to do. I took all the information I had and was ready to present it to the Conflict Resolution Committee.

There was never an investigation into what it was I did.

The bosses and the woman did not ensure the information was appropriate and current.

What was my job? I didn't have a job description, yet I was denied WSIB because they felt I could do the job based on the job description. My boss also said I could do the job, yet I wasn't doing that job.

If this was my job, then I should be allowed into the plants to instruct my brothers and sisters. If this was my job description, then I should have been able to do all of the job.

At a meeting, one boss said it was my job as described, and that the meeting was over.

Something must have happened, and I was told the woman would be back on her job in two weeks. I asked her boss how she knew her stress would be better in two weeks. Was it because I would be off on holidays? How convenient. Now WSIB won't pay me and the sickness insurance was denied me because of that job description. After many phone calls, I finally got paid from the sick insurance. So much for enjoying my job in my lilac room. My health was very bad over all this stress, but I would fight until the end. I needed more information to fight this.

The Conflict of Interest and Business states that every employee of Inco conducts him or herself ethically, in accordance with applicable laws and in accordance with Inco policies.

On April 26, 2004, I had talked to an Inco lawyer in charge of informing people about Sarbanes-Oxley, the legislation that was passed in the USA in 2002/'03. Inco had adopted this legislation and it was now Inco law. It covered a variety of concerns, including improper conduct, theft, conflict of interest, and the act of using a position of power or corporate resources for personal gain, thus creating new problems.

I made sure I was up on the new law before the next meeting.

On July 6, 2004, the conclusions of facts were finalized by Art and Jody of the conflict resolution committee. It was determined that everything I said was true, but it couldn't be finalized until the WSIB woman came back. She was still off on stress leave. There didn't seem to be an end in sight. The answer was going back to the media. I felt trapped; I wanted this over with. Inco was talking about this code of ethics. Well, let's see if they were going to talk the talk and walk the walk.

I wrote to the vice president. Fuck the chickens in the yard. I asked for a meeting to find out if Inco was really on board with these new buzz words. He complied.

At Inco on September 2, 2004, I filled him in on everything that had gone down. This was an end for me, the next thing was the media and charging Inco with not complying with their own new code of ethics. I told him I had already talked with the company lawyer. A letter came for the union that I was to sign a gag order, and I refused. What good is a gag order when the company used the information on the last gag order?

Something happened in the vice president's office. There was an agreement made and I signed a gag order on that, but not on the story. Before I knew it, I was told I could take my full pension. I left work right away and went home in a daze. I was pissed off that I was coerced into taking my pension. I hired Keith Lovely to represent me. Keith was one of the Dave Patterson gang on the bargaining committee back in '78/'79. It was like my life was coming full circle. Keith was a licensed paralegal by the Law Society of Upper Canada. This man had integrity. We fought WSIB and the company under section 147 (4), "supplementary benefits." The company and I had co-operated to find me suitable work for fifteen years. As you have read, my health, both physically and mentally, had deteriorated. So it was determined that the job that I held was no longer suitable for me. The company did not have any other work. The deterioration is reflected in compensable conditions and a restricted work history. It was found that I was entitled to section 147 (4) benefits. It made up the monies I lost if I would have continued to work.

The company should have found me another job before they sent me off on my pension. We won. Again, there was a gag order so I can't tell you what we won. What I can say is that I was satisfied with the outcome.

Now it was time to get all the information in order. I kept over thirty years of notebooks, diaries, emails, newspaper articles, etc. I kept everything, even stuff I wrote on paper towels. Three large plastic bins were filled. A young woman named Makenzie came to my place and organized every scrap of paper into files. Then I began to write my book about what it was like to be one of the first women to work at Inco in a non-traditional job in 1974 since the war years.

Sudbury Business and Professional Women honour The Women for their 30 years at Inco. Sue, Cathy and Sonja.

In 2013 Cathy was awarded the YWCA Women of Distinction in Sudbury.

Cathy speaking at the Women of Distinction Awards.

Chapter 128

Still Fighting, This Time for My Life

From years of stress, my body was giving out on me. I endured operation after operation, all done in Sudbury. Once a large hernia tore open my skin and hung out of my body. A doctor in Sudbury repaired it by using a mesh. While repairing it, I had a bleed that the doctor didn't stop before sewing me up. Because the doctor missed this, it continued to bleed into my abdominal cavity. It accumulated in the space between the inner lining of the abdominal wall and the internal abdominal organs. The nurse called it mining tunnels—how ironic is that? She said the blood had to go somewhere.

For the next nine months, I had to have packing done and more hernia operations. I was getting sicker and the pain intensified. A large stitch that was also left began to make its way out, but not before wrapping itself around the small intestines. I began to lose weight, and I had no appetite. After sitting for twelve hours in the emergency department, I refused to leave until I was set up for an MRI, a CT scan, and an ultrasound. After a month, I was given what I asked for and sent to a general surgeon. When he opened me up, he said my gut was a mess, with rips and many hernias. The mesh had wrapped itself into a ball and pushed its way into the small intestines. This was way over his expertise. He could not perform the surgery.

A few years before all of this, Dr. Nancy Baxter in Toronto operated on the very large hemorrhoids that were outside my body, which I had suffered with for three years. These were caused from my intestinal problems. I made an appointment with her and she talked to a Dr. Joao Rezende-Neto.

We made an appointment and went back to Toronto to meet him. Dr. Rezende-Neto said, "I just went over your records and your case is a challenge." My heart felt heavy; I thought that was it. No one was going to help me, and I was going to be sent home to die. He turned to me with a big smile and said, "But I am up to this challenge."

All the fear that I had been carrying with me for the last two years melted away like snow on a grill. I felt safe. I knew he was going to save my life.

It would take a few weeks to get into the hospital. In those two weeks I spiralled. I was full of infection. Nurses were coming in twice a day. Merv had set up a hospital bed in the living room. I was down to 127 pounds. The hardest thing to handle was the handful of hair that was left on my pillow every morning.

Merv kept my spirits up, telling me to keep holding on, that all would work out. The day we flew to Toronto I was very sick. The next day I went under the knife. The doctor said that most of my small intestine had to be removed, the rest of it was ripped by the mesh, causing so many hernias that he had lost count.

It was a hard recovery. I stayed in St. Michael's Hospital for sixteen days. The staff at this hospital were fantastic. This was in July 2016; by January I was on the mend. Merv and I went to Victoria, BC. I could walk and heal.

I can't explain how happy and thankful I am to Dr. Rezende-Neto, who saved my life.

Chapter 129

Anger and Magma

1978 was the year of the strike, the year that changed my life for the good. Sudbury began a regreening program. The land and the lakes had been destroyed by the continuous mining and pollution, the soil so full of acid and metal toxicity that nothing would grow. The soil had to be treated with limestone to allow the recovery and reforestation to occur. Almost four thousand hectares of land were limed. Then ten million trees were planted. It took many years, but the land has come back, along with the lakes. Regreening has improved the environmental conditions in the area, air quality has significantly improved, and landscapes are returning to their natural state.

This is how I felt.

I was blackened by my life choices and the things that happened to me while I was employed at Inco.

The only way for me to fight back was through anger; it was like the molten rock called magma that comes from the belly of the earth. My anger brewed in my belly. The molten metal and my anger mirrored each other. The treatment and behaviour of what happened in my life caused pressure to build up, like the gas bubbles in magma—when there is too much pressure there would be an eruption, a spewing of a large amount or lava and gases into the air; for me it was roaring, yelling, name-calling and swearing. It was the devil's calling card. There's no control over either eruption, not for me or for the magma. Our toxic fumes manifested, blackened everything around us. After cooling, sharp, jagged cutting edges would be left, causing intense mental and physical distress. My health had deteriorated. I spiralled down toward death like the land around me. My body was toxic and full of acid and nothing could grow.

Like the blackened rocks, I too needed to be treated. Treated with love and respect that I received from my best friend and lover, Mervin McLaughlin. It took many years, but my trust began to return.

I was able to finish this book that I have been working on for thirty years of gathering information. I'm letting my healing begin.

No longer am I that little girl who played up in the blackened, burnt, mountains. Now I sit on the green hillside, surrounded by trees and lush vegetation. My view is that of seven-and-a-half-mile-long Ramsey Lake that sits in the centre of our city, stocked with fish. The air is no longer blue, but clean and breathable. The sky is clear, no longer blocked by pollution. The Superstack that has dominated our sky since 1970 still bellows out some sulphur, but not too much. Two up-to-date smaller stacks have been built. The Superstack has come to the end of its existence. The plan is to tear it down in 2020. Some people are sad to see it go, looking at the stack as a Sudbury icon. I, on the other hand, will be cheering when I see it fall. We have always had a love–hate relationship.

I am re-greening, returning to my natural state, leaving behind the hurt and anger I once lived.

The first thing I'm going to do is forgive myself.

Before

After

Glossary

20-Gauge Shotgun – Suitable for hunting game birds such as quail, grouse, turkey, and other small game when using shot shells.

.30-06 – A hunting rifle, to take down a wide variety of game, moose, deer, black bear, elk, or wife.

Anode – A 508–620 lb slab of copper with two lugs, one on each side. This enables the anode to hang in the tanks.

Anode Casting Wheel – A large carousel made of copper weighing 220 tons. It carried twenty-two molds.

Anode Department – A large department that held three furnaces filled with molten metal. Five casting wheels produced copper.

Bill 70-139: The Right to Refuse Work – The Occupational Health and Safety Act (OHSA) gives a worker the right to refuse work that he or she believes is unsafe to himself/herself or another worker. A worker who believes that he or she is endangered by workplace violence may also refuse work.

Billet – Copper was poured into vertical moulds, eight inches around and six feet long.

Broad – Gauge railway with a track gauge broader than a 1425 mm, 94 ft 8½ in standard gauge railway.

Cage/Platform – A structure of bars to make a square surface on which people or things can stand.

Casting – A manufacturing process in which a liquid material is usually poured into a mold which contains a hollow cavity of the desired shape, and then allowed to solidify. The solidified part is also known as a *casting* (anode), which is ejected up by a hydraulic pin.

Cathodes – After the process in the tank house. Pure copper stuck to copper starter sheets, primary raw material to produce the wire bar.

Charge Aisle – A long, narrow gap behind the furnaces. The furnace was charged with cold charge, the hot car was dumped.

Charge Crane – Looked like a gigantic forklift truck that hung from the ceiling. It had three large forks in front and a hydraulic push arm.

Cost-of-Living Adjustment (COLA) – A COLA results in a wage or benefit increase that is designed to help you keep pace with increased living costs that result from inflation. COLAs are usually pegged to increases in the consumer price index.

Cold Charge – Any cold copper that could be melted back down in the furnace.

Contract Agreement/Collective Bargaining Agreement – A labour union negotiation process for labour. A union contract involves two committees, one that represents the interests of union members and another that represents management's interests.

Doors – Found on the end of the vertical molds, one-foot-square copper slabs on hinges to be swung closed using your feet. Stops molten metal and fills the molds.

Draft Dodgers – The influx of young men into Canada, because they didn't want to go to the Vietnam War.

Electrowinning – Also called electroextraction, it is the electrodeposition of metals from their ores that have been put in solution via a process commonly referred to as leaching. Electrorefining uses a similar process to remove impurities from a metal.

Employee Suggestion Plan – An employee could summit a suggestion that would save money, be safer, work better, and so on. Employees might receive money for their suggestion plan (unless it's stolen).

Employment Equity – As defined in federal Canadian law by the Employment Equity Act, requires federal jurisdiction employers to engage in proactive employment practices to increase the representation of four designated groups: women, people with disabilities, Aboriginal peoples, and visible minorities.

Face Shield – A device used to protect the wearer's entire face from impact hazards such as flying objects, chemical splashes, and molten metal.

Fatality – In the context of occupational health and safety, a death caused by an accident at the workplace.

First Aid Competitions – At Inco, teams of five people. A mock accident set up with casualties. The teams have to deal with injures and load them onto a stretcher for transport. Surface plants compete against each other. The mines do the same. The winners from each complete against each other for the Parker Shield.

First Aid Room – A fully stocked medical room with a qualified first aid attendant in all mines and plants.

Force Adjustment – A situation that occurs when the services of one or more indeterminate employees will no longer be required beyond a specified date due to a lack of work.

Force Reduction – Occurs when an employer institutes a mass termination of employees in efforts to reduce costs. It is also known as downsizing.

Furnace – A metallurgical furnace having a curved roof that deflects heat onto the charge so that the fuel is not in direct contact with the ore reverberator furnace.

General Foreman – Looks over all the processes and safety. One step above the supervisor.

Heavy-Duty Equipment Mechanics – Diagnosed faults or malfunction, repaired and replaced defective parts, cleaned, lubricated and preformed maintenance tasks on bulldozers, cranes, scoop tramps, drill jumbo, and all the large machines we had at Inco.

Holding Furnace/Ajax – A small furnace for holding molten metal produced in a larger melting furnaces at a desired temperature for casting.

Hot Car or Torpedo – Used to transfer motel metal from the smelter, which is then poured into the spoon and transferred to the furnace. The hot car was lined with ceramic refactor bricks that could handle 15,000° Celsius, the temperature of molten metal. It was the shape of an egg so as not to lose heat. It was large enough to hold 150 tons of molten copper.

Iberville Cable Staples – Able to withstand both indoor and outdoor applications. Zinc-plated nails resist rust and corrosion and feature a sharp tip for easy starting and to reduce cracking and splintering of wood during installation. Also may be used to puncture car tires.

Inco Triangle – A monthly magazine that was produced by Inco.

Industrial Language – "Fuck."

Industrial mechanic – Installed, aligned, dismantled, and moved stationary industrial machinery and equipment , like pumps, fans, tanks, conveyor, and furnaces, using hand-held power tools.

Ingot – In the anode, the copper was poured into a brick mold to see how much oxygen was still in the copper. Ready to cast.

Joint Safety Committees – Made up of five company representatives and five union representatives.

Ladles – A vessel used to transport and pour out molten metal into molds. A shell that had to be bricked and cemented so the hot molten metal wouldn't burn the steel shell.

Launder or Trough – A long, shallow, often V-shaped receptacle for molten metal that runs from the furnace to the ladles. A system that carries molten alloys from one location to another through gravity. Helps maintain metal temperature and prevent oxide buildup. In the refinery they were used to transport the copper from the melting furnaces to holding furnaces or directly into ladles and into molds.

Layoffs – Suspension or termination of employment, with or without notice, by the employer or management. They are not caused by any fault of the employees but by reasons such as lack of work, cash, or material. Permanent *layoff* is called redundancy.

LU – Laurentian University in Sudbury Ontario. Not to be confused with LU 6500, the Steelworkers labour union.

Magna-Crete – This cured faster than concrete, and unlike concrete it bonded to new and old concrete as well as most construction materials, including wood and steel.

Matte – The phase in which the principal metal being extracted is recovered prior to a final reduction process (usually converting) to produce a crude metal. Mattes may also be used to collect impurities from a metal phase, such as in the case of antimony smelting.

Magna Fright Brick – Brick to withstand the heat of molten metal.

Miner – A person who extracts ore from the earth through mining.

Modified Work – Jobs that would be easier for injured workers.

Molds – A matrix for casting molten metal to make different shapes.

Mold to Make Anodes – A hollowed-out cavity 8 inches thick, 42 inches wide and 48 inches long with two places for lugs for hanging. This shape was called an anode and weighed 580–620 lbs each.

Molten Metal – Metals in their liquid form are called molten. When metal is heated, its temperature is raised. When its temperature reaches the metal's melting point, the metal changes from a solid to a liquid and is called its molten state.

Narrow Gauge Tracks – A railway with a track gauge narrower than the standard 1435 mm (4 ft, 8 1/2 in). Most narrow-gauge railways are between 600 mm (1 ft, 11 5/8 in) and 1067 (3 ft, 6 in).

Overhead Crane – A crane that runs the length of the anode, one on the charge aisle and two more on the casting side.

Paradigm Shift – An important change that happens when the usual way of thinking about or doing something is replaced by a new and different way. "This discovery will bring about a *paradigm shift* in our understanding of evolution."

Pecking Order – A hierarchy of status seen among members of a group of people or animals, originally as observed among hens.

Peeper – A person who peeps at someone or something, especially in a voyeuristic way.

PPO: Plant Protection Officers, and First Aid Attendants – Each plant and mine at Inco were a staffed with a first aid room.

Pry Bar/Steel Bar – 3–4 inches around, 4 feet long, tapered on the end like a flat-headed screwdriver.

Rape – A type of sexual assault carried out against a person without that person's consent.

Rehabilitation Centre – At Inco it was a place where injured workers did work other than production.

Reverberator Furnace – A process furnace that isolates the material being processed from contact with the fuel, but not from contact with combustion gasses. The term *reverberation* is used here in a generic sense of *rebounding* or reflecting, not of *echoing*.

Skull – Copper that had not all been drained out of the spoon, ladles, and skimming buckets. Hardened in a large chunk.

SHE Training – Safety, Health and Environment Training

Shut Down – Cease (or cause something to cease) business or operation.

Skim Bay – A window or opening at the end of the furnace allowing the furnace crew to skim off impurities floating to the top in the molten metal bath.

Skimming – A technique of metal refining through concentrating metal ore. It is the removal of any material or particles that are floating on the surface. Most of the items float to the top and are skimmed off or removed.

Spoon – A very large ladle-like piece of equipment with train wheels. The molten metal was dumped from the hot car into the spoon. The spoon had a lip so that the molten metal could be transferred into the furnace.

Stalker – A person who illegally follows and watches someone over a period of time; a person who harasses or persecutes someone with unwanted and obsessive attention.

Step 1 – A written warning about an employee's actions or behaviour. There was no verbal warning.

Step 2 – A written warning that included a description of the problem, along with the manager's expectation of the employee's behavior, description of the consequences, whether expectations were not met, and the timeframe for meeting expectations. This step would stay on the employee's record for two years and could be added to when the same kind of incident occurred again.

Step 3 – More severe. The employee was to look at how they could improve. It stayed on your record for two years and could be added on to.

Step 4 – The employee was sent home with pay for one day to think about their actions. They could be terminated if there was no improvement (bosses did not get steps).

Stress – A physical, mental, or emotional factor that causes bodily or mental tension.

Strike – A work stoppage caused by the mass refusal of employees to perform work.

Sulphuric Dioxide – A toxic gas released from the smelting and refining process.

Superstack – The tallest chimney in Canada with a height of 380 metres (1250 ft). The superstack was built to disperse sulphur dioxide gases and other by-products of the smelting process away from the city of Sudbury. It did this by placing the gases high in the air, where they normally blew right past the city on the prevailing winds. These gases can be detected in the atmosphere around Greater Sudbury in a 240-kilometre (150 mi) radius of the Inco plant. The sulphur dioxide plume formed a permanent, opaque, cloud-like formation running across the entire horizon when seen from a distance.

Tailings – A dumping field containing acidic minerals, arsenic, and many other toxic substances left over from Inco's processing operation. It's about 10 km long and 10 km wide.

Tank House – A department in the copper refinery that housed large tanks of acid. Anodes would be placed in for twenty-eight days. Precious metals would fall to the bottom of the tanks in a sludge form.

Tap Hole – A controlled vertical slit in the furnace that allows the copper to pour out.

Tapper – The controller of the molten copper. Punches or chips away at a clay plug in the tap hole using a steel rod to allow molten metal to flow into the launder, then ladle, then mold. A tapper molds clay plugs and inserts them into the tap hold to stop the flow of metal, using a steel bar to help push it in.

The Copper Pit – Located under the launder and behind the ladles. Copper that runs out the back of the ladle ends up on the floor pit in one large chunk.

The WSIB: Workplace Safety & Insurance Board – Provides workplace insurance for workers hurt on the job in Ontario.

Tits - When copper freezes on the lip of the ladle forming long icicles (wire bar casting).

Tourette Syndrome – A neurological disorder characterized by involuntary tics and vocalizations and often the compulsive utterance of obscenities.

Troublemaker – A maker of trouble is not one who "causes" trouble, but who achieves a level of trouble by being mischievous, stunning, sensational, and smart. (Never underestimate the power of a mischievous troublemaker …)

Training – The education, instruction of a person being trained.

Welding – A fabrication or sculptural process that joins materials, usually metals by using a high heat to melt the parts together and allowing them to cool, causing fusion.

MIG Welding – The easiest types of welding for beginners. Two different types: one uses bare wire to join thin pieces of metal together, the other uses flux core, which can be used outside. It does not require a flow meter or gas supply. Many hobbyists use MIG welding.

Stick Welding – Better known as arc welding. Stick welding uses electricity to melt a metal filler rod/electrode/stick (electrode is the proper term) that melts both the metal joint and electrode all at once to fuse two pieces of metal together and fill the joint with filler metal at the same time.

TIG Welding – Extremely versatile, harder to master, should be used by a skilled welder. Two hands are needed: one hand feeds the rod while the other hand holds the TIG torch. This torch creates the heat and arc, which are used to weld most conventional metals, including aluminum, steel nickel alloys, copper alloys, cobalt, and titanium.

Wheelman (Operator) – He/she poured the copper into the molds.

Whitewater Rafting – Outdoor activity that uses an inflatable raft to navigate a river or other body of water on whitewater or rough water. Dealing with risk and the need for teamwork is often a part of the experience.

Wire Bar – A pure copper shaped a like a sausage weighing 300 pounds each. Used to make copper wire.

Wire Bar Department – A work area where the wire bar was bundled, piled, strapped, and shipped to market.

Women's Rights – Rights that promote the legal and social equality of women with men and include the fundamental human rights that were enshrined by the United Nations for every human being on the planet nearly seventy years ago. These rights include the right to live free from violence, slavery, and discrimination; to be educated; to own property; to vote; and to earn a fair and equal wage.